UNIVERSITY OF NORTH CAROLINA AT CHAPEL HILL
DEPARTMENT OF ROMANCE LANGUAGES

NORTH CAROLINA STUDIES
IN THE ROMANCE LANGUAGES AND LITERATURES

Founder: URBAN TIGNER HOLMES

Editor: CAROL L. SHERMAN

Distributed by:

UNIVERSITY OF NORTH CAROLINA PRESS

CHAPEL HILL
North Carolina 27515-2288
U.S.A.

NORTH CAROLINA STUDIES IN THE
ROMANCE LANGUAGES AND LITERATURES
Number 271

FORGED GENEALOGIES:
SAINT-JOHN PERSE'S CONVERSATIONS
WITH CULTURE

FORGED GENEALOGIES:
SAINT-JOHN PERSE'S
CONVERSATIONS WITH
CULTURE

BY

CAROL RIGOLOT

CHAPEL HILL

NORTH CAROLINA STUDIES IN THE ROMANCE
LANGUAGES AND LITERATURES
U.N.C. DEPARTMENT OF ROMANCE LANGUAGES

2001

Library of Congress Cataloging-in-Publication Data

Rigolot, Carol
    Forged genealogies: Saint-John Perse's conversations with culture / by Carol Rigolot.
    p. – cm. – (North Carolina Studies in the Romance Languages & Literatures; no. 271).
    Includes bibliographical references and index.
    ISBN 0-8078-9275-0
    1. Saint-John Perse, 1887-1975–Themes, motives. I. Title. II. Series

PQ2623.E386 Z813   2001
848'.91209 – dc21

                                                                    2001037050

Some of the ideas in this book took shape in talks and articles before being revised or rewritten. Early versions of five studies appeared in the following publications:

"The Textual Seas of *Amers*," in *Pour Saint-John Perse*, Schoelcher, Martinique: Presses Universitaires Créoles/L'Harmattan, 1988, 133-142.

"*Neiges* d'antan, neiges d'antilles," in *Saint-John Perse: Antillais universel*. Paris: Minard, 1991, 93-108

"Ancestors, Mentors, and the 'grands Aînés': Saint-John Perse's *Chronique*," in *Literary Generations*, ed. Alain Toumayan. Lexington: French Forum, 1992, 196-204.

"Les Eloges paradoxaux d'*Eloges*," in *Saint-John Perse: Les années de formation*, éd. Jack Corsani, Paris: L'Harmattan, 1996, 111-126.

"Saint-John Perse's *Oiseaux*: from Audubon to Braque and Beyond," in *Resonant Themes: Literature, History and the Arts in Nineteenth and Twentieth-Century Europe*, ed. Stirling Haig. Chapel Hill: University of North Carolina Press, 1999, 199-213.

Cover: Manuscript of *Nocturne*
Reproduced with permission of the Fondation Saint-John Perse
Aix-en-Provence, France

Cover design: Heidi Perov

ISBN 0-8078-9275-0

IMPRESO EN ESPAÑA

PRINTED IN SPAIN

DEPÓSITO LEGAL: V. 3.817 - 2001

ARTES GRÁFICAS SOLER, S. L. - LA OLIVERETA, 28 - 46018 VALENCIA

CONTENTS

ACKNOWLEDGEMENTS

I N his wonderful account of *How the Irish Saved Civilization,* Thomas Cahill observed that "some of the most deeply held things are sourceless–or, rather, one can no longer remember where one first learned them. They are like the radiation left over from the Big Bang–general, constant, and unplaceable." This book contains residues of various Big Bangs, ideas inspired by encounters, sometimes in person, often across written pages.

In a book about predecessors, it is essential to acknowledge my own. The first generation of *saintjohnpersiens* was a pioneering one. Roger Caillois, Alain Bosquet and Jacques Charpier brought Saint-John Perse to the attention of a French public that had lost track of him during his exile. At about the same time, Arthur Knodel introduced him to English-speaking readers in a pathbreaking book that the poet himself admired. Knodel later translated the Pléiade version of Leger's correspondence and expanded the annotations to make the letters more readily comprehensible. I have benefited from many exchanges with Arthur Knodel, especially while he read these chapters. René Galand's volume in the Twayne series provided another opening for Anglo-American publics. The interpretive skills of these early critics provided maps for subsequent travelers to Perse's world. Roger Little, author of many perceptive studies, compiled the first concordance to Perse's works–a contribution that deserves special thanks. When the Pléiade volume became the edition of reference, Eveline Caduc generously prepared a new, indispensable index (Champion, 1993). All references to word occurrence in Perse's works come from her invaluable concordance.

Jean-Pierre Richard and Georges Poulet traced early avenues, as did Pierre Oster-Soussouev and Antoine Raybaud. Albert Henry provided critical editions, while Daniel Racine and Jack Corzani organized forums for Perse scholars. Jean-Louis Cluse, Sylvia Desazars de Montgailhard and Mauricette Berne all illuminated the mysterious *Poème à l'Etrangère*. More recently, after the poet's library and manuscripts became available, a whole generation asked new questions. Régis Antoine, Colette Camelin, May Chehab, Mary Gallagher, Edouard Glissant, Henriette Levillain, Catherine Mayaux, Marie-Noëlle Little, Mireille Sacotte, Claude Thiébaut, Pierre van Rutten, Renée Ventresque, Steven Winspur and many others have enlarged the inquiry. Throughout this time, Jean-Louis Lalanne has played a vital role as the editor of the *Cahiers Saint-John Perse*. Most of all, the Fondation Saint-John Perse has enabled and inspired readers to know more and understand better. We owe a collective debt to successive directors and editors of the *Souffle de Perse,* notably to Joëlle Gardes Tamine. My own conversations with her have shaped this book. She and her team, Corinne Cleac'h, Arlette Ventre and Marie Josiane Duffès, in collaboration with their advisers, benefactors and the poet's descendants, make everything possible.

Jacques Hardré at the University of North Carolina and Roy Jay Nelson at Michigan were early catalysts in my admiration for Saint-John Perse. Many kinds of material and intellectual support have been offered by Princeton University deans and colleagues, including Martine Benjamin, Victor Brombert, Robert Connor, Shane Gasbarra, Lionel Gossman, Suzanne Nash, Alexander Nehamas, Albert Sonnenfeld, Edward D. Sullivan, David Thurn, and Karl D. Uitti. William McGuire knows all the reasons why he deserves special thanks. Gloria Emerson and Richard Eder have offered sustained friendship. My parents and brother have been hearing about Saint-John Perse forever, it seems; they have mattered very much in this project, as have the three people to whom it is dedicated: François, Sophie and Stephanie.

INTRODUCTION

S AINT-JOHN Perse (1887-1975) experienced in his lifetime the extremes of fame and fortune. As Alexis Leger, rising through the ranks of French diplomacy to the position of secretary general at the Quai d'Orsay, he knew the honor and glitter (as well as the weight and drudgery) of diplomatic life. Then, in 1940, deprived of his citizenship by a collaborationist French government, he endured the pain of banishment. Living in exile in Washington, D.C., he took up his pen and returned to the poetry that would be crowned in 1960 by the Nobel Prize for Literature.

From his earliest verses, dated 1904, to the last ones, in 1974, his poetry covers the widest expanse of time and space: from childhood through old age, and on toward eternity; from the intimacy of an island and a lovers' chamber to the vastness of deserts, sea and sky; from the Guadeloupe of his childhood to China where he served as a diplomat. After criss-crossing America during his exile, he ultimately settled on the Mediterranean coast. Yet, across seventy years and an entire globe, the poems constitute a coherent, evolving whole.

Perse's protagonists have many names—Prince, Queen, Conqueror, Stranger, Foreign Lady, Lover, Bird, Artist, Poet—but they are kindred spirits on multiple journeys of exploration and self-discovery. Their adventures are not the only ones, however, or even the most compelling ones to be played out in the poems. Behind them are the poet's own wrestling matches with a varied cast of angels and demons who inform the works. Through these encounters, Saint-John Perse shapes his poetic identity in relation—and resistance—to a long line of literary and mythological figures. Homer,

Plato, Virgil and the Biblical writers are among them, as are various inhabitants of Mount Olympus. Dante is also present and Marco Polo, along with more recent authors, from François Villon and William Shakespeare to Victor Hugo, Charles Baudelaire, Stéphane Mallarmé, Arthur Rimbaud, and even Jules Verne. Pierre Loti, Paul Valéry and Paul Claudel are significant, as are painters, Paul Gauguin and Georges Braque. Some notable Americans also participate in the conversations, notably John-James Audubon, Edgar Allan Poe, Ralph Waldo Emerson, Walt Whitman, and T.S. Eliot. Many of these figures belong to what Marc Fumaroli has called the "Republic of Letters." [1] Some are associated with canonical high culture while others, at least in their time, emerged from popular culture. But all of them participate in one way or another in the evolving legacy of intellectual and imaginative accomplishments–texts, artifacts, beliefs and practices–which we commonly call culture. [2]

Perse alludes to many different cultural traditions, from the Caribbean to the Orient, but his most sustained dialogues are with predecessors in the west, as it evolved from Athens and Jerusalem across Europe to the New World. They are the most prominent interlocutors in this book, but not the only voices to whisper through Perse's poetry. In 1958, when invited to participate in an exhibit at the Doucet Museum, Perse claimed that he never kept notes, drafts, letters or documents of any sort. [3] We have since learned that he was, on the contrary, an avid collector of books, travel brochures, postcards, newspaper and magazine articles, thousands of which are now in the archives at the Fondation Saint-John Perse in Aix-en-Provence. In recycled manila envelopes from the French Cultural Services or brown wrappers from *L'Express*, he filed prodigious amounts of information about all subjects, with a special liking for bizarre events, curious or noteworthy individuals, and advertisements for everyday products. As early as 1921, he told André Gide that his principal reading in China was pamphlets from travel agen-

---

[1] Marc Fumaroli, *L'Age de l'éloquence* (Geneva: Droz, 1980), 18.

[2] For a discussion of the evolution of the word culture in the twentieth century, see Susan Hegeman, *Patterns for America: Modernism and the Concept of Culture* (Princeton: Princeton UP, 1999).

[3] Saint-John Perse, *Œuvres complètes* (Paris: Gallimard, Bibliothèque de la Pléiade, 1982), 569. Henceforth, all quotations from this volume will be indicated in parentheses in the text.

cies and cruiseship lines, adding that such reading was hardly neg-
ligeable: "Ce n'est d'ailleurs pas littérature à dédaigner et je ne
souhaite pas meilleur compagnonnage aux œuvres que j'admire et
que j'aime" (894).

These diverse readings, along with Perse's real-life encounters
and experiences, supply his poems with an abundance of allusions.
Some may never be deciphered; other elusive references, like the
identity of Lilita Abreu as the Spanish Lady of the *Poème à
l'Etrangère,* gradually give up their secrets to patient, skillful, sym-
pathetic and serendipitous decoders.[4] Perse's poems resemble the
palimpsests Gérard Genette has evoked, referring to parchments
on which one text is superimposed upon another without totally
hiding it.[5] As palimpsests, they are privileged sites for observing the
relationships between one text and an earlier one and the dynamic
process by which prior texts are brought into a new circuit of
meaning. They invite the kind of reading that Julia Kristeva called
intertextual, referring to the interactions that occur within a single
text.[6]

Many other critics have elaborated on the notion of intertextu-
ality as a strategy both of reading and of writing. But readers of
Saint-John Perse were already hearing dialogue inside his poems
before Kristeva coined the word in the late 1960s. For the most
part, the echoes were from Perse's earlier poems. Critics have long
been accustomed to retracing his steps from later works back to his
own previous ones. The intertextual readings in this book retrace
different steps, along the camouflaged paths that lead from Perse's
poems to antecedents as near as Claudel and as far as Homer.

Reading Perse's poems is not unlike eavesdropping on a tele-
phone conversation where only one side is audible. In this antiphonal and even polyphonic poetry, many of the voices are si-

---

[4] The most recalcitrant allusions are undoubtedly the ones Lilita Abreu claims
Perse assembled "de façon mystérieuse, parfois mystifiante, dans le but de dépayser
son lecteur, de l'envoûter, et de l'emporter avec lui à travers les espaces [. . .]."
Saint-John Perse, *Lettres à l'Etrangère,* ed. M. Berne (Paris: Gallimard, 1987), 149.

[5] Gérard Genette, *Palimpsestes* (Paris: Seuil, 1982), 451. Genette's concept invites the kind of reading that Philippe Lejeune calls palimpsestic, p. 452.

[6] Julia Kristeva offered the following description of her concept of intertextuali-
ty: "tout texte se construit comme mosaïque de citations, tout texte est absorption
et transformation d'un autre texte. A la place de la notion d'intersubjectivité s'ins-
talle celle d'*intertextualité,* et le langage poétique se lit, au moins, comme *double.*"
"Bakhtine, le mot, le dialogue et le roman," *Critique* (avril 1967), 440-441.

lenced or muffled, and we must divine the words of interlocutors who are almost always reduced to anonymity. The poems are conversations, but removed from the unpredictable realm of real dialogue into a safer exchange.[7] This book is an attempt to capture some of the unspoken voices behind the poems and to analyze the poet's multiple strategies of dialogue with illustrious forebears. Perse's conversations pay homage, of a sort, to his invisible interlocutors, but they are rarely simple tributes. More often they are paradoxical praises of ancestors whom he alternately echoes, debates, edits and erases. Through these conversations with cultural figures, he nurtures a family tree of literary ancestors and seeks his place in their illustrious lineage.

The title, *Forged Genealogies,* calls upon multiple meanings of both words. Beginning in the earliest poems with the royal lineage of King Light and "Queen Heavy," whom the narrator addresses as "ô Lourde!" (59), Alexis Leger/Saint-John Perse creates various genealogies for his protagonists and for himself, both through his poetry and in the poetic (auto)biography he composed in the 1970s for the Pléiade edition of his works. All these genealogies are *forged,* in one or more of the senses conveyed by the French equivalents *forger, frayer, fabriquer, inventer, faire* and *contrefaire.*

Perse's poems are ateliers where a master blacksmith shapes his stories and his identity. In fact, when the Spanish statesman Salvador de Madariaga first met his French counterpart, Perse's appearance and penetrating gaze reminded him of Vulcan, from Velasquez' famous painting, *The Forge* (1154). In the forge of language, Perse, like every poet, sought to create "iron words" (202), as he called them, capable of resisting the vagaries of time. In his imagination, the forge occupied a special place at the intersection of fire and air, rebirth and inspiration. The narrator of *Chronique* undoubtedly speaks for the poet when he includes among his favorite childhood sites "l'enclume du forgeron d'étable" (396). Smiths recur frequently in the poems, and letters to Perse's friend Mina Curtiss are signed with the borrowed name of a medieval blacksmith, Pierre Fenestre.[8]

---

[7] Caryl Emerson discusses dialogism in *The First Hundred Years of Mikhail Bakhtin* (Princeton: Princeton UP, 1997), 127-161.

[8] Blacksmith imagery also appears on pp. 98, 172, 181, 195, 196, 200, 203, 204, 250.

Smithing is not unrelated to a second meaning of my title: to forge ahead. In Perse's world of energy and movement, heroes are those who forge special paths, whether to new forms of expression, as in *Neiges* (162), to renewed relationships, as in *Vents* (242), or to eternity, with the birds of *Oiseaux* (421). What matters is to move forward toward a new creation that is also a self-creation. A sense of self-fashioning is implicit in the wider meaning of forged genealogies.

Fashioning requires both art and artifice. At the extreme edges, it borders on forgery. Creative fabrication is, of course, as old as art itself. The poetic personae invented by Perse are surely not counterfeit. Nor are they plagiarized from earlier works. Rather, they are creative retellings of stories in which the past of Alexis Leger fuses with the present and future of Saint-John Perse. This book explores multiple genealogies–real and fictional–that Perse creates in and around his poetry.

For most of his life, Perse wrote little about his actual family tree. In an amusing letter of 1909, he asked his friend Gustave-Adolphe Monod to buy him a book, but warned that he could only spare twenty-five Francs, "à moins d'aller tuer à Paris un des ascendants que me traitent de 'fruit sec'" (659). Whatever the reality behind this jocular portrayal of his relatives, Alexis Leger in fact substituted one family tree for another, replacing the Leger-Dormoy genealogy with a literary lineage capable of producing Saint-John Perse. He devoted much of his life to creating a chosen family (506), composed of literary giants. To understand his poetry is to trace this inventive process.

These elected ancestors are not readily apparent. Critic Roger Caillois portrayed the poet as superbly solitary, with no evident ascendants and descendants (1263), an assessment the poet approved. But, while Perse's art may not be visibly connected to others, it is nevertheless sewn by myriad threads to the fabric of western culture. For the poet John Ashbery, "Our landscape / Is alive with filiations, shuttlings." [9] The landscape of Perse's poetry is also alive with filiations that are traced in this book.

In 1969 Perse was asked to update the French literature section of the *World Book Encyclopedia*. His revisions for Victor Hugo,

---

[9] John Ashbery, "Self-Portrait in a Convex Mirror," *Self-Portrait in a Convex Mirror* (New York: Viking, 1972), 75.

Paul Claudel, André Malraux and Jean-Paul Sartre are all instructive, but the most revealing changes involve himself. Perse expanded the existing entry by adding the following italicized words: "*In his great epic poems haunted by the universal and the cosmic (Anabasis, Winds, Seamarks), Saint-John Perse (1887-   ), whith* [sic] *all that he brings which is new and highly personal in modern creative poetry, shows a deep* awareness of the great tradition of French poetry." [10] Perse's poems may well be haunted, as he claims, by the universal and the cosmic, but they are also haunted by specific ghosts whose presence is crucial to our reading. His poems are a "family romance," fraught with ambiguities not unlike the ones that prompted Freud to coin that term in 1909. For Perse, the romance is not with his own family but with his literary elders, who inspire contradictory reactions of reverence and rebellion. Naturally, he aspired to belong to the *World Book Encyclopedia*'s "great tradition of French poetry." To judge from a 1911 review of *Eloges*, he succeeded at a young age. Valery Larbaud compared him to Homer, Virgil, Whitman and Hugo, at their best (1227). To enter the company of these notables (on their good days, no less!) was an achievement that must have pleased the poet, for he reprinted Larbaud's comment, sixty years later, in the Pléiade edition of his works.

Ancestors figure prominently in Perse's meditations. Reviewing the French political scene in 1957, he lamented to United Nations Secretary General Dag Hammarskjöld "l'absence d'Aînés, autant que de Cadets valables." [11] But if the absence of Elders is something regrettable, their presence, in art at least, can be equally worrisome. A "grand aîné" (79), as the poet once described Paul Claudel, can be a haunting predecessor. Much of Perse's poetry is an effort to overcome what he called, in *Amers*, the terrible majesty of the Ancestor (301)–all ancestors–and to situate himself as their equal, or ideally, their superior.

The practice seems to have begun early. In 1916, writer-diplomat Paul Morand remarked in his diary that the precocious Creole, as he called him, already had a completely formed intellect and talked of Claudel and André Gide as equals (1092). Whether or not Perse shared the fear, expressed in La Bruyère's famous phrase

---

[10] Fondation Saint-John Perse, Aix-en-Provence, ms. 78.
[11] *Alexis Leger - Dag Hammarskjöld Correspondance 1955-1961*, ed. M.-N. Little, *Cahiers Saint-John Perse* (Paris: Gallimard, 1993), 123.

"Tout est dit; l'on vient trop tard," he was obviously struck by Lautréamont's counter-proposal, which he underlined in red in an anthology of literary criticism: "Rien n'est dit. L'on vient trop tôt depuis plus de sept mille ans qu'il y a des hommes. [. . .] Nous avons l'avantage de travailler après les anciens, les habiles d'entre les modernes." [12] In the dialectic between ancients and moderns, early and late, tradition and newness, lies much of the tension of Perse's poetry. It is neither simple nor one-directional.

Writing about the Renaissance, Thomas M. Greene has observed that "The humanist poet is not a neurotic son crippled by a Freudian family romance, which is to say he is not in Harold Bloom's terms Romantic. He is rather like the son in a classical comedy who displaces his father at the moment of reconciliation." [13] The distinction is useful to keep in mind, even for a twentieth-century writer like Saint-John Perse. Relations with his literary ancestors were unquestionably ambivalent, but ultimately more creative than disabling. Far from being paralyzed, Perse wrestled with his predecessors in order to match their force. In these encounters, both ancestor and descendent were transformed. It is Jorge Luis Borges's insight that the word "precursor" needs to be purified of its connotations of polemic or rivalry: "The fact is that each writer *creates* his precursors. His work modifies our conception of the past, as it will modify the future." [14] Understood this way, Perse's conversations with individual ancestors affect both interlocutors. Their work shapes our understanding of Perse, while his poetry changes the way we read his elders.

Naturally, my project is fraught with perils. One danger is to see Perse's relationships as simple or even simplistic questions of influence. [15] Another is to deform the generational relationships through

[12] Jean de La Bruyère, *Œuvres complètes*, ed. J. Benda (Paris: Gallimard, Bibliothèque de la Pléiade, 1941), 85. Lautréamont's statement is in *L'art poétique,* ed. J. Charpier et P. Seghers (Paris: Seghers, 1956), 387. Perse's annotated copy is at the Fondation Saint-John Perse.

[13] Thomas M. Greene, *The Light of Troy* (New Haven: Yale UP, 1982), 41. Greene is referring to Harold Bloom's *The Anxiety of Influence* (New York: Oxford UP, 1975).

[14] Jorge Luis Borges, "Kafka and His Precursors," *Other Inquisitions 1937-1952*, trans. R. Simms, ed. J. Irby (Austin: U of Texas Press, 1964), 108.

[15] Like most writers, Perse thought about influence. Some of the most annotated pages in his library belong to André Gide's essay, "De l'influence en littérature," which he read as a young man, probably in 1909. Gide exhorts writers not to fear

the lenses of psychology. I have tried to navigate between these two shoals, listening without preconceptions to the muted conversations in this stereophonic poetry. I have not sought influences in the conventional sense, through what Arthur Knodel rightly named "the dreary game of source-and-influence hunting."[16] Nor have I knowingly engaged in what Roger Caillois called the futile play of erudition, based on pretended sources or influences."[17] Rather, this is a cartography of fault lines that seem to me to precede and inform individual poems.

Throughout my reading I have been mindful of two complementary truths about the ways artists relate to their predecessors. On the one hand is T.S. Eliot's observation that immature poets imitate, while mature poets steal: "The good poet welds his theft into a whole of feeling which is unique, utterly different from that from which it was torn."[18] On the other hand is the knowledge that borrowings are not always conscious; vestiges of prior reading may well be half-forgotten and still powerful. Most of the conversations in this book are so detailed and extended that I believe them to be deliberately woven into the fabric of the poems. But conversations that emerge from half-remembered or unconscious reminiscences are still worth discerning, since their power to shape the poetry can far surpass the poet's awareness of them.

---

the influence of other books but to see them, rather, as magic wands, opening up one's own riches. The role of reading, he wrote, in a passage Perse underlined, is to awaken the sleeping princesses within us. *Prétextes* (Paris: Mercure de France, 1903, 15). Annotated copy at the Fondation Saint-John Perse.

[16] Arthur Knodel, *Saint-John Perse: A Study of his Poetry* (Edinburgh: UP, 1966), 11.

[17] *Roger Caillois - Saint-John Perse Correspondance 1942-1975,* ed. J. Gardes Tamine, *Cahiers Saint-John Perse* 13, 1996, 148.

[18] T.S. Eliot, "Philip Massinger," *Selected Essays 1917-1932* (New York: Harcourt, Brace, 1932), 182.

CHAPTER 1

THE PARADOXICAL PRAISES OF *ELOGES*

W HEN, in Marcel Proust's *A la Recherche du temps perdu*, Céleste begins to read *Eloges*, her first reaction is surprise: "Mais êtes-vous bien sûr que ce sont des vers, est-ce que ce ne serait pas plutôt des devinettes?"[1] Certainly, the first four poems that constitute the *Eloges* collection must have seemed new and puzzling when they were published, individually in 1909 and 1910 and then all together in 1911. Their elliptical style leaves much for a reader to divine, and André Gide even feared they would lose subscriptions for the *Nouvelle Revue Française* (673). But if these poems seemed radically new, they also join two long and distinguished traditions. One consists of mythologies of paradise, from Genesis to Milton's *Paradise Lost* to Dante's *Paradiso.* The other is the tradition of *encomium* or literature of praise. In a twice-repeated refrain, the *Eloges* poems sing "la douceur d'une vieillesse de racines" (23, 29) and offer homage to roots, both in nature and in genealogy. In this collection, which Régis Antoine aptly calls a poetic biogeography of the poet's native island,[2] Saintleger Leger (as he signed his early poems) pays tribute to his elders, both biological and literary, and initiates a genealogical meditation that will continue across all his writ-

[1] Marcel Proust, *A la Recherche du temps perdu,* "Sodome et Gomorrhe" (Paris: Bibliothèque de la Pléiade, 1954), II, 849. Diplomat Paul Morand claims in his *Journal d'un attaché d'ambassade* that Céleste actually made that remark in his presence. See Arthur Knodel, "Marcel Proust et Saint-John Perse: le fossé infranchissable," *Revue de Paris* 76, Dec. 1976, 80-92. Wallace Fowlie describes a conversation in which Mina Curtiss cited Proust's phrase to Perse. "Comment traduire *Amers:* Un récit personnel," *Revue d'Esthétique* 12, 1986, 167.
[2] Régis Antoine, *Les Ecrivains français et les Antilles* (Paris: Maisonneuve et Larose, 1978), 331.

ing, even to the autobiographical chronology in the Pléiade edition of his works, published in 1972.

In *Eloges,* the most evident forebears are those in the narrator's own family: his father and mother, uncles, and the "aïeule jaunissante" (26) with the "paupières d'ivoire" (27), all of whom he honors. The protagonist pays homage to his biological ancestors, while, in a parallel tribute, the poet honors some of his most important poetic ancestors. These dual tributes, to family and predecessors, make up the substance of the poems. At the same time, the *Eloges* poems also contain hints of resistance and departure. Written by an exiled narrator, these are ambiguous homages and nostalgic tributes to a world that is already lost. As Claude Thiébaut has suggested, the opening poem, *Ecrit sur la porte,* while introducing us to the collection, also resembles a message left behind by an inhabitant who is no longer present to welcome visitors.[3]

In Leger's vision, childhood is a place as well as a time, and is frequently communicated through metaphors of space. The narrator remembers it as a white kingdom (23), as a cathedral beneath vaults and naves (23), and, above all, as the realm of light: "Et tout n'était que règnes et confins de lueurs" (25). He dreams of a secure place (23), but is already deprived of his childhood Eden. Like the sea of *Pour fêter une enfance*, which is portrayed as "une mer plus crédule et hantée d'invisibles départs" (28), these poems are haunted by imminent departures. Their stance toward ancestors betrays an early credulity from which a narrator has already taken some distance. In the space between reverence and revolt lie the power and poignancy of *Eloges*. By listening to the conversation that links Leger to the literary models of his early period, we can perceive some of the characteristics of the ancestral drama that permeates his work, both as a theme and as a creative impulse.

Well-known is the poet's explanation to André Gide about the title of the collection: "Vous me demandez un titre qui comprenne ces trois poèmes?–*Eloges*. Il est si beau que je n'en voudrais jamais d'autre, si je publiais un volume–ni plusieurs" (769). This choice of title, along with that of *Pour fêter une enfance*, places the poems in a distinguished lineage of works of praise. In the Biblical tradition,

---

[3] Claude Thiébaut, "'Ecrit sur la porte' de Saint-John Perse à l'épreuve de la traduction en créole," *Pour Saint-John Perse*, ed. P. Pinalie (Paris: L'Harmattan, 1988), 89-90.

their ancestors are the psalms; in classical antiquity, they belong to the genre Aristotle codified as epideictic works. Pindar, one of Leger's early literary heroes, was famous for his laudatory odes. Leger borrows from both the classical and biblical traditions, transforming each in special ways.

The spirit of the psalms is clearly evident in the first long poem, *Images à Crusoé*, where Robinson's island is the focus of cosmic praise: "Crusoé!–ce soir près de ton Ile, le ciel qui se rapproche louangera la mer, et le silence multipliera l'exclamation des astres solitaires" (13). In this poem, praises of creation are accompanied by similarly psalm-like plaints, where an aged Robinson, far from his island, prays in language reminiscent of the ancient Hebrews, also exiled from a dreamed-about land:

> ". . . D'un exil lumineux–et plus lointain déjà que l'orage qui roule–comment garder les voies, ô mon Seigneur! que vous m'aviez livrées?
> ". . . Ne me laisserez-vous que cette confusion du soir–après que vous m'ayez, un si long jour, nourri du sel de votre solitude [. . .]" (20)

Biblical echoes continue throughout *Eloges*, even as the prayer becomes progressively secular. In *Pour fêter une enfance* everything is praiseworthy:

> Appelant toute chose, je récitai qu'elle était grande, appelant toute bête, qu'elle était belle et bonne; (24)
> ô toiles que l'on plie, ô choses élogieuses! (25)
> O j'ai lieu de louer! (28)

Like a modern Book of Hours, *Eloges* takes us through the cycle of a day, sacralizing daily life. We begin before dawn, "Le pont lavé, avant le jour" (37), and go on to morning, afternoon and eventide, when "Ceux qui sont vieux dans le pays tirent une chaise sur la cour, boivent des punchs couleur de pus" (48). The circle then returns to its point of departure–dawn–in a verse that echoes the previous one: "Ceux qui sont vieux dans le pays le plus tôt sont levés à pousser le volet et regarder le ciel" (49). The cycle begins again, in a continuum of time: "Aussitôt c'est le jour!" (49).

Alongside this biblical spirit of praise lies another form of homage, inherited from Greek and Latin antiquity. In the classical tradition, praise was addressed to a wide range of subjects. Most often, encomiums honored noble deeds and individuals, but they did not have to be elevated. According to Aristotle's *Rhetoric:* "Praise, again, may be serious or frivolous; nor is it always of a human or divine being but often of inanimate things, or of the humblest of the lower animals."[4] The poems of *Eloges,* addressed to manifold things and beings, fit easily into this Aristotelian tradition. They explicitly praise the broadest range of objects, cosmic elements and curious personages, flora and fauna, down to the simplest rocks, "les pierres veinées-bleu" (52). But they are implicitly addressed to a series of noble individuals, and most specifically to the poet's late father, Amédée Leger.

Pour fêter une enfance, although first published in 1910, is dated 1907, the year the father died. These overlapping dates are not coincidental, as Perse suggests in his autobiography:

> 1907 Mort subite, à Pau, du père. Devenu chef de famille, Saint-Leger Leger interrompt ses études à Bordeaux pour se consacrer aux siens, parmi de graves soucis matériels. Villégiaturant avec sa mère et ses sœurs dans les Pyrénées (vallée d'Ossau), il y écrit les premiers poèmes d'*Eloges,* qui seront publiés en 1911 à *La Nouvelle Revue française.* (xiii)

Pour fêter une enfance honors a father "qui fut noble et décent" (29). It marks the definitive end of youth and a parallel need to revive the childhood milieu and relive a time before the son became a premature "chef de famille."

Novelist William Maxwell has observed that most serious writers have suffered some kind of major deprivation which they try, through imagination, to overcome or compensate or "or even make not have happened."[5] The narrator of *Eloges* would have it appear that the major disruption of his life is geographical–the departure from a tropical childhood setting. But for Leger this depiction is incomplete and inaccurate, since the geographical rupture hides an even more traumatic, though unsaid deprivation: the loss of his father and abrupt succession to a paternal role.

---

[4] Aristotle, *Rhetoric,* tr. W. Roberts (New York: Modern Library, 1954), 56.
[5] David Stanton, "Interview with William Maxwell," *Poets and Writers Magazine,* 22:3, May/June 1994, 44.

In narratives of childhood, dead, absent or failed fathers tend to serve as archetypes. According to Richard N. Coe, they "leave a void to be filled, an ideal somehow to be sought, a kind of quest which, consciously or subconsciously, provides one of the more powerful motivations for recreating the past." [6] In Leger's recreation of the past, he returns to a point in his life's story when the family was still intact and when he was innocent of the grief that lay ahead. Although it is well camouflaged, a longing for a lost parent underlies *Eloges*.

It may seem surprising that a poem of mourning, for a lost father and a lost childhood, should bear a title of celebration. Or that a poem of celebration might emerge from a period of sadness, which, as Leger later told writer and editor, Jacques Rivière, definitively ended "toute époque de fête, de complaisance et d'images" (665). One key to these enigmas, and to the fundamental ambiguity of *Eloges*, can be found in a letter to the poet's friend Gustave-Adolphe Monod, dated May 1908:

> Tu as de la musique à Paris. Je songe que tu entendais l'*Eroïca* le mois dernier. J'en suis heureux, pour toi, pour moi. Porter le deuil de quelque chose, ou de quelqu'un de grand! Grandir et s'émouvoir! (Deuil = capacité.) (Et je vois que, dans les vieilles éditions, la 3ᵉ Symphonie s'intitulait intégralement: "Symphonie héroïque pour *fêter* le souvenir d'un grand homme.") (650)

The great man commemorated in the symphony is, of course, Napoleon, who fascinated Beethoven as much as he captivated Alexis Leger. On his own copy of the score, Beethoven specifically wrote "Bonaparte," followed by the words "Geschrieben auf Bonaparte." [7] The name was later erased but Napoleon's presence remains in the work, and when the Emperor died, Beethoven is said to have announced that he had already composed his funeral march.

Through the intermediary of music, Leger perceived the links among mourning, commemoration and even celebration. Having

---

[6] Richard N. Coe, *When the Grass was Taller* (New Haven: Yale UP, 1984), 141.

[7] Maynard Solomon, *Beethoven* (New York: Schirmer Books, 1977), 133. I am indebted to Professor Kenneth Levy for commenting on the Beethoven manuscripts.

lost both his father and his childhood–*quelque chose* and *quelqu'un de grand*–he expanded his capacity to suffer, through the equation proposed in his 1908 letter by which depth of mourning equals the capacity to feel. Following Beethoven's example, he united celebration and mourning into his own song about what had been lost: "ce souffle d'un autre âge" (28). Borrowing Beethoven's celebratory verb *festeggiare/fêter*, Leger wrote his own version of the *Eroïca* symphony in a different genre and register to commemorate the memory of a great man from his own lineage, present in the poem as the noble father.[8] And by portraying his father as noble, the narrator-son transformed himself into a prince.

In this poem, not all forebears belong to Leger's family; other ancestors comprise his poetic genealogy. Despite the surprising newness of *Eloges*, it does not spring out of a void. Many writers influenced the young poet, including some he acknowledged, like the early 19th-century poet Maurice de Guérin, and others he tended not to, notably Lamartine and Bernardin de Saint-Pierre.[9] As André Rousseau has suggested: "Saint-John Perse n'est pas né de rien: si l'on ajoute Mallarmé, Rimbaud et Claudel, on obtient une bonne part de ses premiers poèmes."[10]

Predecessors are present in *Eloges*, but they are more audible in specific words and ideas than in the rhythms or structure of the poems. Leger engages with themes and personae, topoi and goals of earlier poets, but retains few traces of their versification or poetic texture. This may explain why his poems felt radically new, despite their continuities with earlier writers.

When Valery Larbaud first met Leger in 1911, he described for Léon-Paul Fargue the young writer's literary preferences:

> De la littérature moderne il ne connaît que *Fermina Márquez* et en admire la langue. Il aime Claudel, mais ne goûte que Baude-

---

[8] The first edition of the Symphony, published in October, 1806, has an Italian dedication, but uses the equivalent word: "composta per festeggiare il sovvenire di un grant Uomo." Georg Kinsky, *Das Werk Beethovens* (München-Duisburg: G. Henle Verlag, 1955), 129.

[9] In his later years, Perse spoke to Arthur Knodel about Maurice de Guérin, author of *Le Centaure*. He also mentions Guérin in his homage to Léon-Paul Fargue (519).

[10] André Rousseau, "Conversation à la Fondation Saint-John Perse," *Saint-John Perse: Eloges*, ed. N. Blandin (Grenoble: Fondation Hébert d'Uckermann, 1987), 67.

laire et Bossuet ("comme poète lyrique") en France [. . .] Rimbaud est trop sec et pas assez musicien, c'est "de l'écriture cur-
sive." (1091)

Despite this critique of Rimbaud, Leger was nevertheless drawn to
the poet of the "Saison en enfer." Indeed, Rimbaud was not only a
literary model, but also a personal one for a young poet who
dreamed of beginning his professional life as Rimbaud had finished
his: as a trader in Egypt or Chile or Guinea. [11]

As a precocious ancestor, Rimbaud presented a special challenge to his successors. By age seventeen, he had already written
two important poems, "Dormeur du val" and "Bateau ivre." It may
not be entirely coincidental that *Eloges*, although first published in
1909, was dated 1904, the year when Leger, too, was seventeen.
Rimbaud's poem, "Roman," begins with an accusatory verse: "On
n'est pas sérieux quand on a dix-sept ans," [12] which could only in-
cite the adolescent Leger to respond by creating, or at least dating,
a serious poem, *Images à Crusoé,* in the year of his seventeenth
birthday, 1904, even though it was probably written two years later.
In the same poem where Rimbaud questions the seriousness of sev-
enteen-year-olds, he also declares: "Le coeur fou Robinsonne à
travers les romans." [13] While Rimbaud transforms Crusoe into a
verb, Leger adopts him as the protagonist of a new version of the
Robinson story.

The links between Rimbaud and Leger were immediately apparent to readers. In 1911 Valery Larbaud seized upon the resemblance in his commentary of *Eloges*, noting both writers' gift for
translating into words the sensations and fleeting moments of childhood (1229). More recently Yves Bonnefoy depicted the affinity
between two poets whose portraits of the natural world make us
believe that some kind of "'vraie vie' soit possible, au-delà des
déchirements de nos morales tardives." [14] Rimbaud's talent for capturing the world in words and images is perhaps most evident in
the work Saint-John Perse later dubbed the "impérieuses *Illumina-*

---

[11] Régis Antoine, *Les Ecrivains français et les Antilles* (Paris: Maisonneuve et
Larose, 1978), 325.

[12] Arthur Rimbaud, "Roman," *Œuvres* (Paris: Garnier, 1960), 71.

[13] *Ibid.*, 72.

[14] Yves Bonnefoy, "L'Illumination et l'éloge," *Le Nuage rouge* (Paris: Mercure
de France, 1977), 221.

tions" (519). Here, and specifically in the first two sections, "Après le déluge" and "Enfance," the kinship between the two poets is most apparent. These two short prose poems occupy fewer than four pages of the Pléiade edition of Rimbaud's works, but they contain the germs of an unexpectedly large number of images and scenes that later figure in *Eloges*.[15]

Within a short space, Rimbaud evokes sensuous black servants; sorcerers and magic; the death of a young girl; the burial of old people; the sensations of a child observer; nostalgia for the past; and a hideous city, where sewers and slaughterhouses coexist with beautiful women. Each of these components of *Illuminations* finds its echo in characters and events of *Eloges*. Like Rimbaud's "Après le déluge," Leger's *Pour fêter une enfance* is placed under the sign of the biblical flood and Noah's ark. Evening unfolds "au parfum de Déluge" (29) and the boat carrying the narrator is "l'Arche" (41), with both words capitalized. The father's boat carries larger-than-life beings, of biblical stature: "de grandes figures blanches: peut-être bien, en somme, des Anges dépeignés" (29).

Rimbaud describes a "ville monstrueuse" (I-170), while Leger depicts a London as hideous as his adolescent impressions of Bordeaux: "La Ville par le fleuve coule à la mer comme un abcès" (13). Rimbaud locates sewers on the map of his childhood: "Moins haut, sont les égouts" (I-170). In Leger's Pointe-à-Pitre the sewer is clogged by a coconut: "le coco [. . .] détourne du dalot la splendeur des eaux pourpres" (45); in its waters ugliness and beauty merge.

In this world, women are especially enticing. Rimbaud evokes "la fille à lèvre d'orange" (I-168); Leger imagines "une fille vêtue comme un roi de Lydie" (45). Women of color are the most sensuous. Rimbaud's "superbes noires dans la mousse vert-de-gris" (I-168) resemble the black servants of *Eloges*: "Ma bonne était métisse et sentait le ricin; toujours j'ai vu qu'il y avait les perles d'une sueur brillante sur son front" (26).

Rites and idols fascinate both young narrators. Rimbaud evokes "Cette idole, yeux noirs et crin jaune" (I-168), while Leger's narrator participates in an even more elaborate initiation ceremony "devant l'idole à robe de gala" (29). Animals in both poems inhabit a

---

[15] Arthur Rimbaud, *Œuvres complètes* (Paris: Gallimard, Bibliothèque de la Pléiade, 1951), 167-170. All references to this poem are indicated by an I (*Illuminations*) and the page number to distinguish them from E (*Eloges*).

realm of myth or fable. "Des bêtes d'une élégance fabuleuse circu-
laient" in the town of *Illuminations* (I-168). In *Eloges* the animals
are almost divine: "Pour débarquer des bœufs et des mulets, on
donne à l'eau, par-dessus bord, ces dieux coulés en bronze et frot-
tés de résine" (42), even if they are destined, in both poems, for the
slaughterhouse: "Le sang coula, chez Barbe-Bleue,–aux abattoirs"
(I-167); "des nègres porteurs de bêtes écorchées s'agenouillent aux
faïences des Boucheries Modèles" (E-46).

Both poets evoke boats and a tiered sea, "la mer étagée là-haut"
(I-167) and "une mer [. . .] étagée comme un ciel au-dessus des
vergers" (E-28), but for Rimbaud, in landlocked Charleville, the
portrait is necessarily imagined rather than remembered, for, as
Arthur Knodel has observed, Alexis Leger lived the tropical boy-
hood Rimbaud could only dream about. [16]

Mortality darkens both worlds. Rimbaud's "enfants en deuil" (I-
167) become in *Eloges* "une enfance en noir" (44), as the narrator
grieves losses, including a young sister: "une très petite sœur était
morte" (E-24). For Rimbaud, "C'est elle, la petite morte, derrière
les rosiers" (I-168). An apocalyptic air pervades both poems. Rimbaud's child senses that "L'air est immobile. Que les oiseaux et les
sources sont loin! Ce ne peut être que la fin du monde, en
avançant." (I-170). In *Eloges,* the prediction of a new earthquake
engenders similar premonitions: "cependant que le ciel pommelé
annonce pour ce soir un autre tremblement de terre" (E-44).

A sense of precariousness renders all the more forceful the celebration of everyday events and sensations. One of the most memorable verses of Leger's poem is the simple chronicle of morning and
the aroma of coffee: "C'est alors que l'odeur du café remonte l'es-
calier" (50). Even this straightforward observation has a parallel in
Rimbaud's *Illuminations,* where "Les 'mazagrans' fumèrent dans les
estaminets" (I-167). These contrasting depictions of coffee reveal
fundamental differences between the two poets. Rimbaud's more
exotic word *mazagrans*, linked to Algeria and to coffee served in
glasses, conjures up a faraway reality that Leger domesticates in *Eloges.* Transporting the experience from cafés to home (and to an island where coffee is produced), he incorporates it into the simple

---

[16] Arthur Knodel, *Saint-John Perse: A Study of his Poetry* (Edinburgh: UP,
1966), 34.

routine of everyday life. He tames the hallucinatory dimension of Rimbaud's poetry while elevating common experience into a ritual.

The depiction of mothers is another example. Rimbaud's tableau of childhood includes a haunting scene where "La jeune maman trépassée descend le perron" (1-168). Leger replaces this spectral image with a friendly, domestic scene where children observe young mothers coming downstairs:

> Nos mères qui vont descendre, parfumées avec l'herbe-à-Madame-Lalie . . . Leurs cous sont beaux. Va devant et annonce: Ma mère est la plus belle! (E-48)

The eeriness of the *Illuminations* thus gives way to a celebratory vignette.

If *Eloges* echoes words and scenes from Rimbaud's work, Leger's stance toward the world, his attitude of praise and admiration, is fundamentally different from his prececessor's. Finding in the *Illuminations* a model for a prose poem about childhood, Leger borrows specific evocations of the sea and city landscapes, of parents, servants and rituals, but he transforms them in significant ways. Some of Rimbaud's images, like coffee, are domesticated; others are amplified and embellished with evocative details, like Rimbaud's "superbes noires" (I-168) who are more fully portrayed in the sensual black women of *Eloges*. Often Leger extricates Rimbaud's images from the realm of intoxication and hallucination to integrate them into a more quotidian reality. Characters in *Eloges* sometimes chew on the leaves of stimulants, like "les hommes et leurs filles, et qui mâchaient de telle feuille" (23), but the narrator himself keeps his distance from intoxication to describe an Antillean world that he finds superior to any kind of hallucination.[17] In place of Rimbaud's "Bateau ivre," Leger substitutes an attentive, lucid vessel that is capable of questioning the natural world, of knowing and not knowing: "Le monde est comme une pirogue, qui, tournant et tournant, ne sait plus si le vent voulait rire ou pleurer" (24).

Eloges closes with a narrator preparing to go off and contemplate the "gros œil à facettes" (E-52) of an insect. His project is a fitting end for a poem and a collection that examine varied facets of childhood. If Rimbaud had not scooped him, Leger could have

---

[17] Arthur Rimbaud, *op. cit.*, 327.

called his own poem *Illuminations*, since its different sections cast their light on specific scenes and sensations of a young narrator's life. They sweep across the horizon and focus on successive aspects of King Light's Settlements. The very name of the kingdom, which figures in English in the text, suggests a bilingual pun on the poet's own name, moving from one definition, lightness, to the other, brightness. With *Eloges* Alexis Leger/King Light founds a new poetic settlement, a "règne de tournantes clartés" (23). By rewriting Rimbaud, he pays a paradoxical tribute to his precocious elder. On the one hand, this poem bathes in the light of the *Illuminations,* but even as Leger incorporates Rimbaud into his text, he takes possession of the territory of childhood and becomes a sovereign in his own right: King Light.

A second ancestor, Charles Baudelaire, is present in similarly ambiguous ways. This chronicler of "l'immonde cité" and of "le vert paradis des amours enfantines" is never very far from the surface of *Eloges,* which often seems to echo the "paradis parfumé" of Baudelaire's "Mœsta et Errabunda" and its author's haunting question about whether it is possible to revive a lost paradise: "Est-il déjà plus loin que l'Inde et que la Chine? Peut-on le rappeler [. . .]?" [18] Leger's answer in *Eloges* is that this land is infinitely distant; the narrator's island, like Robinson Crusoe's, cannot be recovered by simple remembering, but the "éblouissement perdu" (20) of childhood can perhaps be relived by reading a prophetic text, as it is for Robinson:

> alors, ouvrant le Livre,
>   tu promenais un doigt usé entre les prophéties, puis le regard fixé au large, tu attendais l'instant du départ, le lever du grand vent qui te descellerait d'un coup, comme un typhon, divisant les nuées devant l'attente de tes yeux (20)

In an early version of the poem, this book was specifically the Bible. Later it became simply the Book, continuing to evoke the scriptures with its capital letter, but suggestively extending to other texts the potential for revelation. *Images à Crusoé* opens with a short section entitled "Les Cloches" that is imbued with spleen and reminiscent of Baudelaire's sonnet, "La Cloche Fêlée," which begins:

---

[18] Charles Baudelaire, "Mœsta et Errabunda," *Œuvres complètes* (Paris: Gallimard, Bibliothèque de la Pléiade, 1961), 60-61.

> Il est amer et doux, pendant les nuits d'hiver,
> D'écouter, près du feu qui palpite et qui fume,
> Les souvenirs lointains lentement s'élever
> Au bruit des carillons qui chantent dans la brume [19]

Bells and fire also open *Images à Crusoé,* but here the bells no longer sing, they sob; and the hissing fire destroys Crusoe's wooden bow. Like Baudelaire's protagonist, the hero of *Images* is an old man, remembering happier times, but his reminiscences bring more bitterness than consolation.

In the celebrated "Invitation au voyage," Baudelaire evokes the wonder of a mysterious, faraway place where everything is in harmony:

> Là, tout n'est qu'ordre et beauté,
> Luxe, calme et volupté.[20]

Given Baudelaire's well-known distaste for nature, we can rightly suspect that his dreamed-of place has less to do with the outdoors than with an exotic interior, but Leger borrows the same language to depict the atmosphere of a tropical island that he systematically endows with the same attributes: order and beauty, luxury, tranquility and voluptuousness. He begins with order:

> –Sinon l'enfance, qu'y avait-il alors qu'il n'y a plus?
> Plaines! Pentes! Il y avait plus d'ordre! (25)

Beauty also pervades Leger's island, whether in landscapes, women or animals:

> Appelant toute chose, je récitai qu'elle était grande,
> appelant toute bête, qu'elle était belle et bonne (24)

The childhood world also appears calm: "Il fait si calme et puis si tiède, il fait si continuel aussi" (37), but in fact it is highly eroticized; a Baudelairean *volupté* pervades the atmosphere and even the sea "est rose de luxure" (49).

---

[19] Charles Baudelaire, *Œuvres complètes* (Paris: Gallimard, Bibliothèque de la Pléiade, 1961), 68.

[20] *Ibid.,* 51-52.

Women dominate a childhood that evolves "entre les robes, au règne de tournantes clartés" (23). Of all the inhabitants of his world, the black women are the most exotic and erotic. One of the first evocations in *Pour fêter une enfance* is the period when the "servantes de ta mère, grandes filles luisantes, remuaient leurs jambes chaudes près de toi qui tremblais . . ." (23). This becomes a kind of refrain: "Et les servantes de ma mère, grandes filles luisantes . . ." (24). The native women are often associated with shining: "Ma bonne était métisse et sentait le ricin; toujours j'ai vu qu'il y avait les perles d'une sueur brillante sur son front, à l'entour de ses yeux" (26). What is most surprising, and even shocking, about these depictions is that the poet uses the same vocabulary of brilliance and shininess and the same words, *briller* and *luisant,* to describe both women and animals. Of his favorite horse the narrator says: "Quand il avait couru, il suait: c'est briller" (34), and when the cattle and mules are brought ashore, with their oiled skins, they are "un peuple dénué, vêtu de son luisant" (42). This association with animality and nudity heightens the stereotypical portrayal of sensual black women by contrast with the white daughters, mothers and grandmothers of the "haute condition" (23), chastely clothed in "toiles empesées" (48), "mousselines" (26) and "bas blancs" (26).

The dreams that punctuate *Eloges* are filled with sensuality and violence. Once the little boy is interrupted in "un rêve aux ombres dévoué" (26). Another time, he awakens from "un vieux songe tout rayé de violences, de ruses et d'éclats" and goes downstairs "comme une femme qui traîne: ses toiles, tout son linge et ses cheveux défaits" (33). Throughout the collection, whether in dreams, acts or landscape, the *luxe* and *calme* of childhood are intertwined with *volupté*.

One of Baudelaire's privileged strategies is to conflate multiple senses in the process known as synesthesia and famously illustrated in "Correspondances" where "Les parfums, les couleurs et les sons se répondent." Leger also mingles smells, sights and sounds to recapture an idyllic island where images call out (12), dawn tastes like unripe fruit (12), air is milky (12), breezes are tinted (14), odors are grey (17), light and shadows sing (18, 24), flowers cry out (24), voices are luminous (29), solitude is green (37), and noon is as noisy as a mosquito (28). Through all these images, a Baudelairean climate pervades Leger's collection, from the spleen of *Crusoé* to the

sensuality of *Eloges*. Nostalgic for another world, attuned to intimations of the spirit and to relationships between the visible and the
invisible, Baudelaire was also the poet of scandal and controversy.
The French professor at Leger's lycee in Pau forbade students
from reading the *poète maudit*, thus making him all the more intriguing.[21]

Yet despite Valery Larbaud's 1911 report that Leger "ne goûte
que Baudelaire" (1091), the young poet's borrowings have more to
do with ideas and ambiance, with the evocative possibilities of language, than with specific rhythms or rhymes. *Eloges* is less indebted
to the fabric of Baudelaire's verses than to their goal, particularly
that of the prose poems: a "prose poétique musicale sans rythme et
sans rime, assez souple et assez heurtée pour s'adapter aux mouve-
ments lyriques de l'âme, aux ondulations de la rêverie, aux soubre-
sauts de la conscience."[22] In Leger's eyes, the agenda was ideal but
unfulfilled; he saw Baudelaire's texts as more prosaic than poetic:
"[c]es 'poèmes en prose' de Baudelaire, qui n'ont rien du poème,
ne poursuivant, sur un mode analytique ou discursif, sans souci
proprement mélodique, qu'un intérêt psychologique" (519). Despite these failings, the prose poems offered programmatic models
for Leger's own efforts to create a truly poetic and melodic form,
liberated from fixed rhyme and woven from varied, sophisticated
structures of internal rhythms. The author of the *Fleurs du mal* bequeathed to younger poets an agenda and a poetic geography.

In the prose poem entitled "L'Invitation au voyage," Baudelaire
conjures up a magical land "où la vie est grasse et douce à respirer
[. . .]."[23] Leger accepts the invitation to travel, but in place of
Baudelaire's land of plenty he finds his own country. Rewriting the
"vert paradis" and distancing himself from all "paradis artificiels,"
he portrays his own idyll as real, despite the transformations
wrought by memory and art.

In Leger's recreation of a lost paradise, Baudelaire is an essential
and pervasive predecessor; he is also, like Rimbaud, an ambiguous
one. The one context where he is cited is an unhappy one. In the
Pléiade autobiography, which Perse composed many decades after
Eloges, the entry for 1899 features the well-known account of
Amédée Leger's library, transported from Guadeloupe to France:

---

[21] Mireille Sacotte, *Saint-John Perse* (Paris: Belfond, 1991), 104.
[22] Charles Baudelaire, *Œuvres complètes* I, 275-276.
[23] *Ibid.*, 301.

> Arrivée de la bibliothèque du père. Neuf grandes caisses dou-
> blées de zinc, chargées au port de Pointe-à-Pitre, avait d'abord
> coulé en rade [. . .]. A leur arrivée à Pau, dans la cour de la de-
> meure familiale, la puanteur était telle qu'il fallut recourir à
> l'aide de la police, et les déballeurs ne purent mettre au jour
> qu'une masse compacte et noire en pleine fermentation. La seule
> page encore lisible arrachée à cette pâte fut une feuille du titre
> des *Fleurs du mal* de Baudelaire, édition Poulet-Malassis. Le fils
> vit la tristesse muette du père et en garda, à jamais, une étrange
> aversion pour les livres. (xi)

In this episode, Perse rewrites the story of Baudelaire's forma-
tive influence. In retrospect, he links his predecessor, not with the
"vertes délices" (12) of childhood, but with the disgusting putrefac-
tion of a moldy library. The early literary model becomes, in this
anecdote, a source of Leger's supposed lifelong aversion for books.
Perse's many retellings of this story tend to render all of them suspect. Was a page of Baudelaire really found? Claude Thiébaut has
pointed out that the overlap of the tale with Baudelaire's own verse,
"La puanteur était si forte que sur l'herbe [. . .]," makes the story
almost too good to be true. [24] At the same time, Perse's insistence on
the episode highlights Baudelaire's importance in his mental landscape. This revision of the relationship is paradigmatic of Perse's
complicated relationships with his literary elders. The case of Mallarmé offers another striking example.

In the lineage of French letters, Mallarmé is an inescapable forebear. During the last two decades of the nineteenth century, his
Tuesday salon on the rue de Rome was a gathering place for André
Gide, Paul Claudel, Paul Valéry and other writers. Subsequent generations also felt his influence. Yves Bonnefoy claims that all French
poets are, to some extent, disciples of Mallarmé. [25]

Emilie Noulet was one of the first to write about Leger's debts
to Mallarmé; other critics have since elucidated them. [26] There was,

---

[24] Claude Thiébaut, "Alexis Leger / Saint-John Perse dans l'œil du cyclone,"
Trois poètes face à la crise de l'histoire, ed. P. Plouvier, R. Ventresque, J.-C. Blachère
(Paris: L'Harmattan, 1996), 87.

[25] Yves Bonnefoy, *Baudelaire parlant à Mallarmé: Entretiens sur la poésie*
(Neuchâtel: La Baconnière, 1981), 94.

[26] Alain Girard, "Le Mallarmé de Saint-John Perse," *Souffle de Perse* 5-6, 1997,
79-95; Mireille Sacotte, *Saint-John Perse* (Paris: Belfond, 1991), 105 and *Parcours de
Saint-John Perse* (Paris: Champion/Slatkine, 1987); Renée Ventresque, "Saint-John

of course, Mallarmé's independence from hexameters and his typographical freedom in arranging words on the page. There was his dislocated sentence structure, with multiple layers of meaning and rare, archaic words. The controlled and seemingly ascetic voice of his poems contrasted with the personal lyricism of the romantics, while his experiments with the musicality of words sought to merge sound and meaning. Mallarmé's enigmatic verses inspired others to look behind appearances and find symbolic meaning in everyday objects. But his most seductive power may have been the mystery of his ellipses. Although Leger rejected the hermeticism of Mallarmé's later poems, he admired the patient crafting of language and the nostalgic search for a lost paradise. Yet here again, as with Baudelaire, the legacy may have had less to do with poetic practices than with particular themes. [27] The memorable lament of Mallarmé's "Brise marine," for example, "La chair est triste, hélas! et j'ai lu tous les livres. / Fuir! là-bas fuir!" might be seen to anticipate the mood of Leger's Robinson Crusoe. [28]

Famously haunted by nothingness, despairing at the blank page and the inability to translate his vision into words, Mallarmé pushed language to the verge of silence and offered a model for Leger's future poems which are constructed around the impossibility of writing. [29] Metaphors of artistic creation, like "Le blanc souci de notre toile" of "Salut," echo in the sand and snow of *Exil* and *Neiges*. But these preoccupations are more apparent in Perse's later works. At the time of this first collection Mallarmé's most valuable contribution may have been his role as a liaison to Edgar Allan Poe.

For Leger and generations of French readers, Mallarmé's translations (which Leger owned in a 1897 edition) were the intermediaries to Poe's verse, just as Baudelaire's translations offered access

---

Perse, un grand poète du XIXème siècle: l'héritage symboliste de Mallarmé," *Souffle de Perse* 5-6, 1995, 96-105.

[27] It is revealing that when Mireille Sacotte seeks specific textual echoes of Mallarmé in Perse's poems, the most salient example is a parody, from *Vents*: "Tant de vers blancs d'onyx, et d'ongles forts, et de tambours de corne où vit la pieuvre du savoir" (203). The proximity of *onyx* and *ongles* recalls, with ironic distance, Mallarmé's famous sonnet which begins "Ses purs ongles très-haut dédiant leur onyx." But this unusual kind of citation comes decades after *Eloges*. Saint-John Perse (Paris: Belfond, 1991), 105.

[28] Stéphane Mallarmé, *Œuvres*, ed. Y.-A. Favre (Paris: Garnier, 1985), 40.

[29] Arthur Knodel, *op. cit.*, 108-109.

to Poe's prose.[30] The strongest affinity among Mallarmé, Baudelaire and Leger may have been their shared admiration for this American prodigy who had published his first collection of poems by age eighteen.

Poe was revered in French literary circles. Baudelaire called him "la tête forte des Etats-Unis"[31] and one of the greatest poets of his century. Paul Claudel compared him to Keats and published a translation of "Léonainie," a poem he mistakenly thought to be Poe's. (It is actually a pastiche by James Whitcomb Riley.) Paul Valéry joined the chorus by citing Leonardo da Vinci and Poe as the two major influences on his own literary and philosophic career.

One of the oldest books in Leger's library, now at the Fondation Saint-John Perse, is an annotated copy of Poe's *Poems and Essays*, signed "Alexis Leger, Pau, –06." Many other editions, in French and English, lined his bookshelves, and he often referred to Poe in letters, wishing him still alive. As a young man, Leger kept a photograph of Poe on his desk and even imitated the pose for his own portrait in 1906.[32] In 1911, he wrote of Claudel's *Vers d'exil:* "Il y avait, dans le poème liminaire, des strophes si belles [. . .] que j'eusse voulu Edgar Poe vivant pour, un soir, en parler avec lui" (720). A few weeks later, he remarked to Gide in a parenthetical sentence he later omitted from his published correspondence: "J'ai parfois regretté qu'Edgar Poe fût mort, que je ne puisse un soir lui parler d'André Gide."[33] Leger's first words on meeting Paul Valéry in 1912 are reported to have been: "Edgar Poe et vous, les deux hommes que j'ai le plus souhaité connaître."[34] Throughout his life,

---

[30] It was, after all, in "Le Tombeau d'Edgar Poe" that Mallarmé defined poetry's mission to give new meaning to everyday language, to offer "un sens plus pur aux mots de la tribu." *Œuvres complètes*, ed. Y.-A. Favre (Paris: Garnier, 1985), 71.

[31] Baudelaire, "Introduction à Bérénice," *L'Illustration,* 17 avril 1852, reprinted in *Edgar Allan Poe,* ed. C. Richard (Paris: L'Herne, 1974), 287.

[32] Perse owned at least five postcards depicting the writer, his wife and cottage. Katherine Biddle, a close friend, even claimed a physical resemblance between the two writers: "Il y a, dans l'aspect physique de Saint-John Perse, un je ne sais quoi, sous ce front très vaste et ces yeux très perçants, qui fait penser d'abord au visage de Baudelaire ou d'Edgar Allan Poe. Mais là s'arrête la ressemblance" (1248). A picture of Poe hung in the entryway of Perse's home in Georgetown, the first image a visitor would see.

[33] Fondation Saint-John Perse, Gide correspondence, June 1, 1911. The rest of the letter appears in the Pléiade edition, pp. 770-771.

[34] Paul Valéry, *Œuvres 1* (Paris: Gallimard, Bibliothèque de la Pléiade, 1957), 36.

Perse maintained a continuing companionship with this American ancestor, so enthusiastically adopted and even re-invented by French. [35] In a 1949 letter to the poet-critic Allen Tate, he affirmed: "Vous savez qu'envers et contre Eliot, je garde mon affection à Poe, pour tout ce qu'il porte en lui de virtuel" (977). A few months later, he again evoked their shared admiration for Poe:

> J'ai aimé la dernière chose que vous m'ayez fait lire de vous, cette conférence sur Edgar Poe, où votre beau sens humain nous a valu enfin, comme une réparation, cette juste appréciation qui n'omet rien des dons exceptionnels de Poe (fussent-ils virtuels) sans ignorer ses faiblesses et la limite de ses réalisations. (981)

In a footnote, composed in the third-person for the Pléiade edition, Perse repeats his esteem for "la langue d'Edgar Poe, dont il appréciait la sensibilité intellectuelle et la parfaite 'propriété'" (1294). The tribute is genuine, but Perse's repeated insistence on Poe's unrealized potential shows once again that even his warmest praise is not without reservations.

When *Images à Crusoé* was first published in the *Nouvelle Revue Française* in 1909, the poem carried an epigraph, in English, from Poe's "A Dream Within a Dream":

> O God! can I not grasp
> Them with a tighter clasp?
> O God! can I not save
> One from the pitiless wave?

These verses bring us to the central mystery of *Images à Crusoé*: the metamorphosis of Robinson into his twentieth-century descendant. *Robinson Crusoe* provides the mediating myth for the poet's coming of age in Europe after an Antillean childhood. Daniel Defoe thus occupies a privileged place in Perse's poetry as one of the rare pre-

---

[35] Many years later, Perse clipped from the *New York Times Book Review* an article about *The Portable Poe*. He also kept a photograph from the *New York Times* of June 27, 1945, depicting United Nations delegates signing the world security pact in San Francisco. Alluding to Poe's story, *The Tell-Tale Heart,* he pencilled his suspicions on the photo, and addressed it to Lilita Abreu: "Te souviens-tu de la photo représentant le pacte Germano-Russe. En la voyant j'avais pensé que ce pacte ne durerait pas. L'expression des Russes était très 'Tell Tale'. Cette photo ne m'inspire pas plus de confiance. Le Russe encore 'n'en est pas'."

decessors whose presence is explicit. But the privilege is ambiguous, for Defoe is reduced to anonymity, present only through his protagonists, Robinson and Friday, and it is Leger, the adolescent successor, who has the last word by writing a radically different ending to the story. Leger's poem depicts an aged Robinson, unhappily settled in England and nostalgic for his island. But, as readers of Defoe remember, Crusoe returns to Europe to discover that his investments have flourished in his absence. A rich man, he marries, fathers three children, and undertakes new voyages, including a return visit to his island. This upbeat trajectory makes him an odd model for Leger's protagonist. Daniel Defoe would surely not recognize either the corrupt Friday or the plaintive Robinson of *Images à Crusoé*. A French version of the story, edited for children in the "Bibliothèque Rose" collection offers a happy ending, as does Leger's schoolbook version, a standard text for ten-year-olds, *Vie et Aventures de Robinson Crusoé* (Hachette, 1895), which is still in his library. In this telling, Friday is killed on the return home, to Crusoe's sorrow, but the Englishman ultimately embarks on new voyages and a varied life before enjoying a peaceful retirement. Most of the intervening variations on the Crusoe story–those Leger might have read in his youth–also end well. Two popular ones, *The Swiss Family Robinson* by Johann David Wyss and *L'Ile mystérieuse* by Jules Verne both have happy conclusions, as does Verne's *Deux ans de vacances* (translated as *School for Robinsons)*. Another positive outcome closes *The Arctic Crusoe* by Percy Saint-John, which Joëlle Gardes Tamine has brilliantly identified as childhood reading for Leger and a possible element in the alchemy of his pseudonym. [36]

None of these latter-day Robinsons offer models for Leger's unhappy protagonist, although we come closest with the writings of poet Francis Jammes, Leger's early friend who loved Crusoe and often evoked his saga. Jammes had a particular affinity for Robinson's old age. In his poems, "Amsterdam" and "Sur Robinson Crusoé," he depicts the traveler's return to Europe. Although Jammes imagines an aged Robinson in his dark little London room, he endows the seemingly bleak portrait with a kind of wisdom and harmony.

---

[36] Joëlle Gardes Tamine, *Saint-John Perse ou la stratégie de la seiche* (Aix-en-Provence: Université de Provence, 1996), 19. She suggests that the poet's pseudonym might be understood as a homage, not only to Percy Saint-John but to Crusoe and all who resemble him.

Despite nostalgia for his island, Robinson is joyful to be home. In the 1906 poem, "Je fus à Hambourg," Jammes' septuagenarian Robinson reminisces with equanimity about his travels and looks ahead to a serene retirement in London. He is hardly a double for our baleful protagonist.[37]

Defoe would have been puzzled by Leger's hero. But not Edgar Allan Poe, for in this poem Crusoe is reborn in the spirit of Poe's protagonists. In the early version of the poem, the epigraph in English from "A Dream Within a Dream" helped signal this unexpected reincarnation. In Leger's own copy of Poe's verses, he specifically annotated this poem with diacritical marks, indicating the correct English pronunciation for a recitation. It is revealing to look at the verses immediately preceding this epigraph, for they sum up well the spirit of the Frenchman's Crusoe:

> I stand amid the roar
> Of a surf-tormented shore,
> And I hold within my hand
> Grains of the golden sand–
> How few! yet how they creep
> Through my fingers to the deep,
> While I weep–while I weep![38]

Leger's poem begins, as if in dialogue with this speaker and in compassion for his tears and empty hands:

> Vieil homme aux mains nues,
> remis entre les hommes, Crusoé!
> tu pleurais, j'imagine, quand des tours de l'Abbaye, comme
> un flux, s'épanchait le sanglot des cloches sur la Ville . . . (11)

The original epigraph flagged this deliberate rewriting of Defoe, but when the poems were collected in 1911 into the volume entitled *Eloges*, the poet chose to exclude this signal. He also erased another essential clue at the end of the poem. The manuscript of

---

[37] See Claude Thiébaut, "Rôle et influence de Francis Jammes sur Alexis Leger/Saint-John Perse," *Souffle de Perse* 5-6, 1995, 106-137, and Jacqueline Picard, "Les *Images à Crusoé* comme variation textuelle et picturale, *Souffle de Perse*, 7, 1997, 102-120, and 8, 1998, 65-66.

[38] Edgar Allan Poe, *The Complete Tales and Poems of Edgar Allan Poe* (New York: Modern Library, 1938), 967.

Images à Crusoé ends with a verse that emerges from–and plunges back into–the universe of Poe: "jusqu'au gouffre effroyable où l'on plonge." By withdrawing these final words and the epigraph, Leger hid Poe's explicit presence from the poem and thereby withdrew a guidepost to *Images à Crusoé*. As with many other revisions, the erasure removed an element of specificity and set the poem free for wider interpretations.

In a long letter to Monod, dated 1909, Leger explained the importance of reticence in art: "L'essentiel ne se dit pas, et bien plus, n'a jamais désiré se dire. Et c'est un fou, atrocement symbolique, qui dans le conte d'Edgar Allan Poe, du vêtu voulait faire un vêtement" (658).[39] Having learned from Poe that obliqueness and ellipse are the fundamental devices of art, Perse seems to have applied the lesson immediately by revising Poe out of his own work. The epigraph to Poe might have been read as a homage to an elder. (And what nineteenth-century French writer could avoid paying homage to Poe, who was already a hero to Baudelaire, Mallarmé, Gide, and the literary establishment?) But the absence of the epigraph in later editions is consonant with Leger's distrust for direct revelation in art, lest it offer too clear a key. This too-evident tribute had to be removed, but *Images à Crusoé* remains haunted by Poe.

The poem is also haunted in other ways. Like Poe's works, it achieves much of its power from the dialectics between presence and absence and the prospect of imminent departure. Like Leger's sea that is "hantée d'invisible départs" (28), his poems are permeated by mourning for a place and a person. King Light's Settlement may be a paradise, but the important fact about any paradise is that it is lost. Indeed, what is sought must needs be lost. This is the intuition of Gaston Bachelard, who has shown that we must lose our childhood in order to relive it in dreams, since we do not dream of what we already possess.[40] In two curious lines the narrator of *Pour fêter une enfance* evokes the lost tranquility of his youth: "Pentes! Pentes! Il y / avait plus d'ordre!" (25). The typography of his exclamation contributes to its meaning. Harmony has been lost, and the fractured world is transposed on the page by the rupture of *Il y /*

---

[39] The Poe tale to which Perse alludes is "The System of Dr. Tarr and Prof. Fether," which Baudelaire translated, keeping the puns, as "Le Système du Docteur Goudron et du Professeur Plume."

[40] Gaston Bachelard, *Poétique de l'espace* (Paris: Presses Universitaires de France, 1957), 100.

avait, an expression rarely divided in French. This division con-
trasts sharply with the past when "l'ombre et la lumière alors
étaient plus près d'être une même chose" (25). The seeds of destruction are already growing on Leger's island and the idyll of
childhood is threatened even as it is recounted.

In *Images à Crusoé* the island is explicitly mourned, but loss
pervades all the *Eloges* poems, if more obliquely. A cemetery dominates Leger's geography: "Car c'est le Cimetière, là, qui règne si
haut, à flanc de pierre ponce" (43); in an otherwise luminous setting, death is never far away:

> Vagissement des eaux tournantes et lumineuses!
> Corolles, bouches des moires: le deuil qui point et s'épanouit! (14)

Even the affirmation that "Ce navire est à nous et mon enfance n'a
sa fin" (40) is undermined by the surrounding verses, which evoke
ending. When the Uncles come to confer with the narrator's mother, their conversation appears peaceful: "Or, les Oncles parlaient
bas à ma mère. Ils avaient attaché leur cheval à la porte. Et la Maison durait, sous les arbres à plume" (30). But we know the House
will not endure. Its "arbres à plume" too closely resemble the feath-
ery trees which grow in the cemetery (43) not to foreshadow death.
The narrator's affirmation of permanence is undermined by his
awareness of rupture: "Sinon l'enfance, qu'y avait-il alors qu'il n'y a
plus?" (25). His world is also permeated by violence: a deranged
person, "envahi par le goût de tuer" (46) gets the idea of poisoning
the cistern, and even children must be kept from killing: "Et il ne
fallait pas tuer l'oiseau-mouche d'un caillou" (24).

In this setting of a soon-to-be-lost paradise, a Flood is forecast;
there is "un parfum de Déluge" (29). In *Genesis,* the best hope for
the future lies in an ark and in a new lineage descending from
Noah. In *Eloges,* a new Noah (29, 41) will also have an ark, as the
collection plays out a dialectic of beginnings and endings, reverence
and rejection of elders. Questions of genealogy are ever-present, not
only in Leger's subtle conversations with his ancestors, but also in
an ambiguous thematics of filiation which accompanies his rewriting of the ancestors. On the surface *Eloges* seems to celebrate the
ancestral ties, with veneration for the oldest members of the community, "Ceux qui sont vieux dans le pays" (48, 49), and for the old
man who resembles Tiresias (49). Family ties seem to confer a no-

ble, almost mythological status, conveyed in the capitalization of Uncles (30), Princes and Sons-in-law (29). These relationships create a kind of dynasty, where roots are respected and where wisdom specifically takes the form of a "bel arbre" (51). The family tree is a repository of knowledge and continuity.

But if *Eloges* is a homage to a family tree, it is fraught with hints of revolt against tradition and sterility. On the one hand, there is a nobility in roots–at least for literal roots–, a reverence for the "douceur de la vieillesse de racines" (23, 29) and the nourishment of roots: "alors, de se nourrir comme nous de racines, de grandes bêtes taciturnes s'ennoblissaient" (23). But we also sense a suspicion of "des arbres trop grands" (23). In the world of *Eloges,* "Des arbres pourrissaient au fond des criques de vin noir" (40), and the narrator, progressively impatient with his elders, ultimately elects to go off alone.

The poems evolve from reverence to revolt. In *Pour fêter une enfance*, the child explains: "On appelle. J'irai" (25). By the end of *Eloges*, he has declared his independence: "A présent laissez-moi, je vais seul" (52). As if mirroring the "enfance agressive du jour" (38), the child affirms his own aggressivity in the scene of the sailboat ride:

> . . . Oh finissez! Si vous parlez encore
> d'atterrir, j'aime mieux vous le dire,
> je me jetterai là sous vos yeux (41)

Or, again, in the famous scene of the coiffure:

> Ne tirez pas ainsi sur mes cheveux. C'est déjà bien assez qu'il faille qu'on me touche. Quand vous m'aurez coiffé, je vous aurai haïe (51)

As innocuous as these childlike threats may be, they are nevertheless symptomatic of the tensions between the narrator and his elders and of the more radical separation to occur in future poems.

When Leger's Crusoé was most in despair, he turned to a Book for solace. This Book enabled him to do what his own thoughts and dreams could not accomplish. The first poem of the collection thus ended with a celebration of reading. Progressively, though, books disappear, as do ancestors, replaced by a celebration of nature and the self: the insect, the rock, and "l'amitié de mes genoux" (52). Leger's revisions to the *Crusoé* manuscript, changing the Bible into a Book and erasing the Poe epigraph, are the first signs of a distancing from ancestors through rewriting and erasure. In *Eloges* the father's companions have the quasi-divine stature of Angels but they are, nevertheless, "des Anges dépeignés" (29). We return to the primal scene of the coiffure. When in *Vents* Jacob wrestles with the Angel, his combat will be reminiscent of the poet's own ongoing struggle with the "Anges dépeignés" of the literary canon.

While commemorating roots and honoring elders, both biological and literary, Leger enters into multiple dialogues in an effort to locate his own place in a literary genealogy that extends from Aristotle and the psalmists to Defoe, Rimbaud, Baudelaire, Mallarmé, Edgar Allan Poe, Francis Jammes and beyond. *Eloges* offers an ambiguous homage to these predecessors and provides the first hints of dissent from tradition. The poet quietly reverses roles by proposing a model in which the elders praise their descendants. In traditional genealogies, a family tree is rooted in the person of the founding ancestor. Perse's metaphor inverts this process and shifts the honor from the roots to the branches. Roots are made to celebrate the offshoots:

> Et les hautes
> racines courbes célébraient
> l'en allée des voies prodigeuses, l'invention des voûtes et des
> nefs (23)

Leger transforms the family tree and creates a new order of time where the past celebrates the future. *Eloges* may be a poem of praise, but it is a paradoxical praise, for it celebrates what has been lost while at the same time questioning what has come before. To forge his literary genealogy, Leger undertakes a deliberate "invention" of the branches that will constitute his own new tree.

CHAPTER 2

LA GLOIRE DES ROIS AND THE WEIGHTY
DYNASTY OF KING LIGHT

"Qu'est-ce que ce torrent de rois?"

Victor Hugo, *La Légende des siècles*

W HEN Saint-John Perse was offered the grandiose title of
Prince of Poets in 1960, he declined the honor, declaring: "je
n'accepterais, en aucun cas, de porter un titre auquel je n'ai point
vocation" (574). But the demurral does not negate a fascination
with royalty on the part of this Frenchman who once described
himself, rather wistfully, as a "démocrate de fait ou de logique, aris-
tocrate de regret." [1] Such a fascination is not surprising in a poet
preoccupied with genealogy, since royal lineage is genealogy writ
large. Peopling his early poems with kings and queens, Leger takes
on the largest subjects of epic and scriptures and matches himself
to literary elders in the tradition of the Bible, Homer and Shakespeare.

In a letter dated 1914, he invites André Gide to join him in recalling Shakespeare's *Richard the Second*, III: 2.

Je m'ennuie si grandement . . . Récitez avec moi ces deux vers,
qui sont beaux :

For God's sake let us sit down upon the ground
And tell sad stories of the deaths of Kings (786)

Telling stories of kings–whether sad or happy–was a familiar activity for Leger, beginning with King Light in *Pour fêter une enfance*

---

[1] *Lettres d'Alexis Leger à Gabriel Frizeau*, ed. A. Henry (Bruxelles: Académie
Royale de Belgique, 1993), 155-156.

and Queen "Heavy" (59) in *Récitation à l'éloge d'une reine*. Both poems were published in the April 1910 issue of the *Nouvelle Revue Française*, along with *Ecrit sur la porte*. King and Queen were thus joined between the covers of the journal. Only much later, in 1948, were they parted: the King remained in *Eloges* while the Queen introduced a whole new cycle devoted entirely to royalty.

In the separation of King Light and the "reine parfaitement grasse" (60) lies a crucial tale. Displacing the Queen from one setting to another, from one collection to the next, transforms her poem and at the same time reflects the poet's evolution. Reading the *Récitation à l'éloge d'une Reine*, first in its original context and then in its new milieu, we can follow the changes in the poem itself and in Perse's poetry more broadly, across almost forty years of writing and re-arranging these poems, from 1910 to 1948. Composed at different times, they traveled between the first and second collections in a path that is recapitulated in this brief tableau:

> *L'Animale*, dated 1907; unpublished in the poet's lifetime.
> *Récitation à l'éloge d'une reine*, dated 1907; published in the NRF 1910; in *Eloges,* 1911, 1924, 1925, then in *La Gloire des Rois* in 1948.
> *Amitié du Prince*, not dated; published in *Commerce* and as a separate volume in 1924; then in *La Gloire des Rois,* 1948.
> *Histoire du Régent*, not dated; published in the NRF, 1910; in *Eloges*; 1911, 1924, 1925; then in *La Gloire de Rois,* 1948.
> *Chanson du Présomptif*, not dated; published in *Commerce* and *Eloges,* 1924; then in *La Gloire des Rois,* 1948.
> *Berceuse,* not dated; published in *Mesa,* 1945; then in *La Gloire des Rois,* 1948.

Pour fêter une enfance, first published in 1910, portrays a seemingly idyllic childhood in a "blanc royaume" (23), bathed in light, even if shadows and darkness, death and departure, are all subtly present and fleetingly evoked. Sensuality and sexuality are never far away from this world which is attuned to nature. Even the child's sleep contains impulses and violence that are interrupted only when his mother wakes him: "perçant un rêve aux ombres dévoué" (27). The opening scene depicts a ritual bathing of the young protagonist: "Alors on te baignait dans l'eau-de-feuilles vertes; et l'eau encore était du soleil vert; et les servantes de ta mère, grandes filles luisantes, remuaient leurs jambes chaudes près de toi qui trem-

blais . . ." (23). The narrator twice describes the black servant wom-
en as shining or *luisantes,* referring to the perspiration on their skin.
For him they embody a female sensuality to which he is not indif-
ferent, at least retrospectively.

The sensuality that permeates this poem of childhood, whether
in dreams, in nature, or in the women of the household, also pervades the *Récitation à l'éloge d'une reine,* published at the same
time. It, too, opens under the sign of bathing, although here, as
throughout the poem, hopes are frustrated:

> ô Reine, romps la coque de tes yeux, sois-nous propice, ac-
> cueille un fier désir, ô Reine! comme un jeu sous l'huile, de nous
> baigner nus devant Toi,
>   jeunes hommes! (57)

From the child of *Enfance* to the adolescents in *Récitation* there is a
continuum; the "rêve aux ombres dévoué" (27) of the first poem
leads naturally to the "transes nocturnes" of the second, where
slightly older narrators are still dreaming about female sensuality.

The child narrator trembles at the "jambes chaudes" (23) of the
servant women, but the young man of *Récitation* implores the Queen
to lift her leg:

> soulève
> cette jambe de sur cette autre; et par là faisant don
> du parfum de ton corps,
> ô Affable! ô Tiède, ô un-peu-Humide, et Douce (60)

The same word *tiède* figures in both poems, describing both the
Queen of the *Récitation* and the servant woman of *Enfance,* whose
mouth is tepid: "–et si tiède, sa bouche avait le gout de pommes-
rose, dans la rivière, avant midi" (26).

Pour fêter une enfance concludes at night, with an image of
moons: "les lunes roses et vertes pendaient comme des mangues"
(30). *Récitation* also ends with the moon and the Queen's alliance
with cosmic forces:

> et la Lune qui gouverne les marées est la même que commande,
> ô Légale! au rite orgueilleux de tes menstrues! (61)

The two poems are linked by common themes and words. Read in
sequence, they narrate the story of a child narrator growing into

adolescence. The sensual dreams and desires hinted in the story of childhood become explicit in the young warriors whose Queen, "couleur d'écorce" (58), could well belong to the same race as the "grandes filles luisantes" of *Enfance*. Like them, her skin is characterized by its shine and by the same adjective *luisant:*

> ici et là, où brille et tourne
> le bouclier luisant de tes genoux (59)

The glistening servant women and the "idole à robe de gala" (29) evolve into the rituals of *Récitation*.

Each of the five sections of the *Récitation* concludes with a pivotal refrain, in a separate font: "–Mais qui saurait par où faire entrée dans Son cœur?" In this context, *cœur* is best equated with *corps*, for we know little of the Queen's heart, but much about her body. In the short space of the poem are portrayed all of the following: body (three times), eyes, shoulder (twice), side, hands, legs (twice), knees, womb (twice), navel. What the warriors seek is not so much entry into the regal heart as access to her body. They implore an opening, a welcome: "accueille un fier désir, ô Reine!" (57), but the secure fortress remains inaccessible. Much of the tension of the poem comes from this juxtaposition of *corps* and *cœur*, sensual and spiritual.

Language of Old and New Testaments is used here in a context of sensuality when the narrator describes this Queen as a sacrificial table and table of laws (58) and appeals for her favor: "sois-nous propice" (57). He borrows words and rhythms traditionally addressed to the Virgin Mary and directs them to the sensual queen of a pseudo-paradise on earth. In French missals, the litany enumerates 49 different attributes of Mary, grouped into clusters that celebrate her as mother, virgin, and queen of heaven. Participants in religious ceremonies recite them all. The narrator of this poem performs a similarly exhaustive enumeration, "ne comptant point ses titres sur mes doigts" (58). But if his praise echoes the litany, it often reverses or deflects the attributes. While Mary is usually the Queen of Peace, the Queen in this poem is "plus Paisible qu'un dos de fleuve" (58). Where Mary is the Throne of Wisdom, this Queen is, more prosaically, "O bien-Assise, ô Lourde!" (59). Mary is hailed in the litany as the Virgin. Her sensual counterpart in the pagan setting of *Récitation* has a "ventre infécond" (59). Like Mary, fortress and refuge, the Queen is also a place of protection for the warriors, but she is an "Haut asile des graisses" (57). Usually a recitation is an act of ritual or rote; here it becomes a more subversive (or creative) activity where the speaker borrows words traditionally recited in the litany to address a human and hardly-regal Queen. She, in turn, is more opportuned and berated than extolled.[2] This Queen, a contradictory alliance of voluptuousness and refusal, is the antithesis of Mary. To what royal family might she belong, and through what lineage can we trace her? How did Queen "Heavy" evolve into a work to be taken seriously, a poem Leger would include in *Eloges*, telling Gide in 1911: "Si vous jugez que je n'ai pas à redouter, de ce poème 'à l'éloge d'une Reine,' qu'il me fasse trop d'ennemis, je veux bien le laisser figurer là." (773).

Some clues to these puzzles are suggested by the general atmosphere of turn-of-the-century France, where two figures, Pierre Loti and Paul Gauguin, influenced the cultural horizon. During Leger's years in Pau and Bordeaux, Loti was the grand old man of exotic literature, living in the Basque country after a lifetime of travel and writing about Asia, Africa, the Middle East and Iceland. His immensely popular saga of Tahiti, *Rarahu*, later entitled *Le Mariage de Loti*, had appeared in the early 1880s, and earned him a seat in the French Academy (where he edged out Emile Zola that year). Loti introduced French readers to idyllic Polynesian islands, mythical goddesses, and the royal family of Tahiti, headed by Queen Pomaré IV, whom he portrayed as "la lourde personne royale."[3] This heavy royal personage is not the only memorable Loti monarch. On another Polynesian island lived Queen Vaékéhu and her court, whose days were characterized by long hours of immobility and rest.[4] Vaékéhu was as enigmatic as she was immobile. Loti believed her thoughts and secret reveries to be impenetrable.[5] Both Polynesians could have been worthy ancestors for Leger's Queen who combines in a single figure the weight of Pomaré and the impenetrability of Vaékéhu.

The very project of writing about a tropical island meant following in the path of literary forebears who had visited this terrain, if

---

[2] Mireille Sacotte, "Comment peut-on être un enfant?," *Saint-John Perse: Les années de formation*, ed. J. Corzani (Paris: L'Harmattan, 1996), 52.

[3] Pierre Loti, *Le Mariage de Loti–Rarahu* (Paris: Calmann Lévy, 1886), 84.

[4] *Ibid.*, 104

[5] *Ibid.*, 104.

only in imagination. Baudelaire and Rimbaud were among them, and their presence is felt throughout *Eloges*. But the renowned Loti was also a formidable and inevitable ancestor for any writer evoking the tropics. Precisely because of this, he was a model whom the younger poet needed to keep at bay for artistic and personal reasons.

By the end of the nineteenth century, romantic exoticism had been discredited. Any resemblance to Loti was to be shunned, lest a writer be guilty of what was disparagingly called "lotiform" writing.[6] In the *NRF* circle to which Leger aspired, it was imperative not to echo anyone else's nineteenth century, especially Loti's. Early correspondence underscores Leger's fear of writing in a borrowed voice. In 1909 he claimed to have rejected a collection of prose works "parce que j'ai craint subitement, deux ans après, que tout cela ne fût pas toujours absolument mien (exactement et uniquement), j'entends dans la forme."[7]

Leger's perilous project of writing about Guadeloupe required him to portray an exotic island while avoiding exoticism, to inhabit Loti's latitude while distancing himself from his predecessor. This may be one reason for Leger's subversion of Loti's poignant, respectful portraits in favor of more irreverent, sensual portrayal of a Queen as the object of adolescent longing. This transformation allowed him to remain in a lush locale while maintaining an aesthetic distance from Loti, the only feasible strategy for creating a new poetry of the tropics.

If artistic goals required Leger to rewrite Loti, psychological factors also compelled him to ward off a potentially overpowering predecessor. Loti's portrait of Pomaré IV ends in the realization that her Polynesian world is disintegrating. Queen and narrator share a sadness as the country degenerates to what he calls a place of prostitution.[8] The Queen presides over the end of a kingdom, and her pained awareness pervades the novel.

Leger could have written a similar account of Guadeloupe, depicting the disintegration of the old order and the unsettled social and economic conditions that prompted his family to emigrate.[9] He

---

[6] Jean-Marc Moura, *Lire l'Exotisme* (Paris: Dunod, 1992), 173.

[7] *Lettres d'Alexis Leger à Gabriel Frizeau,* 96.

[8] *Ibid.,* 154.

[9] See Claude Thiébaut, *Guadeloupe 1899: année de tous les dangers* (Paris: L'Harmattan, 1989).

could have given voice to the regret and alarm of French colonial-
ists over growing racial tensions and an increasing American presence in the island's economy. But it was not his goal to relate this
decline–at least not directly–and he takes pains to tell his story in
ways that mute the socio-economic woes of the Antilles.

Leger's early poems are nostalgic, to be sure, but in a way that is
less sociological and more psychological than Loti's novel. While
his island recalls those of Defoe, Baudelaire, and Rimbaud, it rises
above any specific place or historical plight, for Leger aspired to a
universal depiction both of islands and, more symbolically, of childhood. Not incidentally, he also had the last word over a literary elder of redoubtable repute, the writer who had probably done the
most, along with Bernardin de Saint-Pierre, to instill in French consciousness the exoticism of faraway places.

Half a century after these early poems, Perse still had Loti in
mind when composing his autobiography. The entry for 1899
records the Leger family's definitive return to France on the same
boat as admiral Pottier and his wife, "protecteurs de Pierre Loti"
(xi).

French writers of the late nineteenth century set to exploring
the "Orient"–a space that extended in the popular imagination
from Egypt and Palestine to China and Japan. Among them was
Paul Gauguin, whose presence hovers over the *Récitation* for reasons that are both biographical and artistic. In the year of Leger's
birth, Gauguin sailed from France to the Antilles in a reverse trajectory from the one the Leger family later followed. As early as 1909,
Leger highlighted the cartographic intersection of their lives when
he described "Marie Galante (une petite île dépendante de la
Guadeloupe–à qq.s. milles de la Dominique où Gauguin écrivit son
Journal.)" [10] The shared Antillean connection was obviously mean-
ingful to the young poet of Pau.

After the Caribbean, Gauguin settled in Tahiti, painting and
writing about Polynesian life, customs, and people, especially wom-
en. When excerpts of his account appeared in 1897 in *La Revue
blanche*, they were welcomed as symbolist works. Mallarmé himself
helped find a publisher for the complete volume, which came out
in 1901 as *Noa Noa*, the Polynesian word for *scent*. Albert Henry

---

[10] *Lettres d'Alexis Leger à Gabriel Frizeau*, 91. Gauguin actually stayed on Martinique rather than Dominica (p. 93).

speculates that Leger's allusion to Gauguin's *Journal* might, in fact, refer to *Noa Noa*, the diary he kept on Tahiti.[11]

Gauguin's death, only two years after this publication, brought him once again to the public eye, thanks in part to Victor Segalen, poet, writer and, coincidentally, a naval officer on the ship that repatriated Gauguin's possessions. Segalen was one of the first to visit the artist's cabin, to read his notes and manuscripts, see the unfinished paintings and sculptures, and bring back works that were auctioned off with fanfare in France. Segalen's account of his visit to Gauguin's atelier, entitled "Gauguin dans son dernier décor," appeared in the June 1904 *Mercure de France* and fueled an already-existing public fascination for this artist whom he summed up in one sentence: "Gauguin fut donc un monstre, et il le fut complètement, impérieusement."[12]

The pervasive influence of this "monster" reached Gabriel Frizeau, the wealthy Bordeaux art patron, who owned and displayed several Gauguin works in his home. Leger's correspondence with Frizeau is threaded with allusions to this artist who shared Leger's passion for islands. Gauguin's paintings offered visual renditions of Leger's own poetic obsession. Meditating on the place of islands and specifically of Marie Galante in his psyche, the poet wrote to Frizeau:

> Comme vous avez su comprendre tout ce que cette île signifie de retranchement! <u>se</u>-creta><u>se</u>-clusa! d'où <u>o</u>missa–Ce sens, qui est celui même de la forme île, ne se retrouve-t-il pas tout entier dans Gauguin? *même dans une forme humaine*, prodige! comme dans cette toile que vous aviez, au salon [. . .]. Cette toile, que j'appelle l'Animale, m'a longtemps poursuivi: si un jour vous la faites photographier, songez à moi, je vous en prie.[13]

In this same letter of February 1909, Leger reveals that the painting he has dubbed *l'Animale* has inspired him to write a poem, which we now know to be the unpublished *L'Animale*, dated "Bordx. - Juin 1907," with the epigraph "Gauguin (Collect. Frizeau)."[14]

---

[11] *Ibid.*, 93-94.

[12] Victor Segalen, *Œuvres complètes*, I, ed. H. Bouillier (Paris: Laffont, 1995), 288.

[13] *Lettres d'Alexis Leger à Gabriel Frizeau*, 96.

[14] This text is reprinted in the *Cahiers Saint-John Perse* 4 with a helpful study by Albert Henry. References to the poem are drawn from the *Cahiers* and indicated as C and the page number.

Leger promises to send the poem to Frizeau, but with the caveat that it not be shown to others. A month later, judging more favorably, he asks advice about possible publication:

> Si donc vous jugez que le manuscrit que vous avez *puisse* (seulement), être publié, je m'aperçois, maintenant, que j'en serais *très heureux*, car, en y réfléchissant, j'y verrais maintenant la très grande *utilité* d'un jalon planté, c'est à dire *d'une contrainte pour plus tard.* Par là, sans doute, l'amour-propre, ou le regret, aux jours de loisir, me tiendrait: la paresse n'étant que manque d'obligation derrière soi. [15]

Leger's new inclination to publish *L'Animale* turned out to be just another step in a long back-and-forth. When Frizeau responded encouragingly, Leger retreated and forcefully rejected the idea. "Si j'avais un jour de quoi publier, je reprendrais peut-être, avec d'autres, cette ancienne page, mais en la modifiant et l'aérant d'une façon plus personnelle, plus étroitement personnelle. Je crois depuis deux ans, pouvoir écrire *mien*." [16] After a long period of worrying about not being original, the poet now felt more confident about having a distinctive voice and relegated *L'Animale* to the earlier period.

Taken at face value, Leger's reticence could reflect a genuine assessment of the poem, but his explanation is disingenuous, for in the same letter where he speculates about a future rewriting of *L'Animale*, he announces that *Récitation à l'éloge d'une reine* will appear in the upcoming *NRF*. This chronology suggests that, during the period when he was sorting works, judging their originality, and sending *L'Animale* to Frizeau, he was also composing *Récitation*. A comparison of the two poems invites us to wonder if the newer work is not precisely the kind of rewriting of *L'Animale* that Leger had so recently (and hypothetically) imagined.

There are many branches in the genealogical tree of *Récitation*'s Queen. We have seen possible links to Loti's Pomaré and Vaékéhu. Critics have also traced her to Rimbaud, Baudelaire and Hugo, to the Hindu goddess Kali, Pindar's Nemean and Isthmian goddesses, the Queen of Sheba, Lia, and the wife of Lot. [17] But one branch of

---

[15] *Lettres d'Alexis Leger à Gabriel Frizeau*, 107.
[16] *Ibid.,* 141.
[17] Jacques Robichez traces some of the paths that link the Queen to Rimbaud,

her ancestry surely leads back to Leger's own Gauguin poem, and Renée Ventresque is correct to see the *Récitation* as a magnified image of *L'Animale.* [18]

Several themes carry across from one poem to the other. The heroine of *L'Animale*, twice described as "Onéreuse, ô grande fille sans mémoire!" (C12, 13), clearly belongs to the same family as the "Reine parfaitement grasse" of *Récitation,* who is hailed as "O bien-Assise, ô Lourde!" (59). In both poems, the protagonist plays a necessary role, simply by being. In *L'Animale:* "Elle témoigne. / Et la trombe solaire a besoin, pour virer, de son / inertie" (C13). Similarly, the Queen of *Récitation* does not need to act or do, but simply to be still and visible to the male gaze: "sois immobile et sûre, sois la haie de nos transes nocturnes" (61). The narrator of *L'Animale* finds reassurance in her presence: "Ici le gisement de toute sécurité" (C12). The speakers of the later poem find the same kind of security: "Ha Nécessaire! et Seule! . . . il se peut qu'aux trois plis de ce ventre réside / toute sécurité de ton royaume" (61). Roots are important in the thematics of *L'Animale.* The word recurs three times (C12) along with related notions of sources (C13) and seeds (C14). Both poems are founded on the antithesis of fertility and sterility; both protagonists are barren.

A fascination with exclusion and absence characterizes *L'Animale* where the Queen is defined by her absence: "Elle est omise" (C14). She twice proclaims this exclusion herself: "Je suis omise, et me réjouis dans l'absence" (C14, 15). But she does not disappear, even if she is proclaimed absent: "Elle est la terre même, et n'a point cessé d'être là" (C11). Similarly, in the evolution from *L'Animale* to *Récitation,* Gauguin and his subject may be omitted, but

---

Baudelaire and Hugo and others. *Sur Saint-John Perse* (Paris: Société de l'Enseignement Supérieur, 1982), 122-129. Anne Léoni and Antoine Raybaud compare her to the Hindu goddess Kali, "La Référence absente: une lecture de *Récitation à l'éloge d'une reine*," *Espaces de Saint-John Perse*, 1-2, 1979, 61-72. May Chehab describes Pindaric antecedents in "Saint-John Perse et la Grèce," doctoral thesis, Université de Provence, mai 1999, 112-115. Elisabeth Coss-Humbert traces links to the Ethiopian *Kebra Nagast* and the Queen of Sheba. *Saint-John Perse: Poésie, Science de l'être* (Nancy: Presses Universitaires de Nancy, 1993), 18. Judith Kopenhagen-Urian adds other biblical models, including Lia and Lot's wife in "La Condition de la femme biblique dans la poésie de Saint-John Perse," *Souffle de Saint-John Perse* 4, 1994, 55-66.

[18] Renée Ventresque, *Les Antilles de Saint-John Perse* (Paris: L'Harmattan, 1993), 45.

they never stop being present. In the early poem, Gauguin figured explicitly, both in the epigraph ("Gauguin [Collect. Frizeau]") and ostensibly as the "bon Peintre," whom the narrator addresses. In the transmutation from one poem to the other, these references are erased, but subtle traces of Gauguin stay behind.

Written explicitly about a painting, *L'Animale* is Leger's earliest known foray into ecphrasis, the time-honored form of writing about works of art. When *Récitation* is read as a revision of *L'Animale*, we can discern vestigal connotations of painting showing through the literal meanings of descriptions. Beneath the Queen's body and the "jeu sous l'huile" (57) lies another, more technical and painterly meaning left over from its earlier habitat in a poem about Gauguin. Other descriptions with residual meanings from painting are the "grand corps couleur d'écorce" (58), the "crin splendide et fauve" (58), and the injunction to remain "immobile et sûre" (61).

If the Queen of *Récitation* is in fact a painted one, like her predecessor in *L'Animale,* we understand all the better why her power is spiritual rather than physical and why no fruit can ripen within her. As a figure on a canvas, she becomes a new Olympia, subjugating viewers while remaining physically unattainable.

In *L'Animale*, all of nature is called to chant: people and palms, rivers and sea, and the widest variety of individuals, but the universal chorus is ominously joined by "un chœur d'adolescents tueurs de femmes!" (C15) and the poem closes with a plea that the warriors sail away and leave the woman in peace (C13-14). Could these murderous adolescents have migrated from *L'Animale* to the *Récitation*? Could they constitute the "peuple de guerriers muets" (57) that surrounds the Queen and gives such a menacing tone to that poem? The continuity between the two works heightens the disquieting atmosphere of the second. The Queen who is acclaimed in *L'Animale*, seems, in the sequel, to be harassed if not actually threatened by the annoying and perhaps even dangerous warriors pleading for access to her body and soul.

When the *Récitation* is read in its original context, as a part of *Eloges*, it continues Leger's early practice of paradoxical praise. Echoes of the Litany to the Virgin Mary undercut the tribute to the Queen; Loti is rewritten and Gauguin erased, as Defoe, Baudelaire, and Rimbaud before them. But when the Queen moves out of *Eloges* to become the cornerstone of a new collection, the poem takes on different attributes in its new context. We are compelled to take the poem seriously.[19]

She who was infertile in *Eloges* becomes a genitrix for *La Gloire des rois*. The poems that emanate from her, about prince and princess, regent and heir, retroactively illuminate her. Transplanted from one volume to the other, the *Récitation* looks back on the preoccupations of the young poet and ahead to a new phase in the narrator's life. After childhood and adolescence comes the movement from adolescence to adulthood, with this poem serving as a threshold between two periods and two collections.

Originally the *Récitation* belonged to the cycle that evolved from King Light to Queen Heavy; it wound up in a series with the reverse movement, from the "reine parfaitement grasse" (60) to a prince who is "plus maigre qu'il ne sied au tranchant de l'esprit" (65). This reversal reflects Leger's own preoccupations between the explicit date of the poem, 1907, and its publication in 1910. During that period family questions took on a heightened urgency as the twenty-year-old suddenly became responsible for his mother and sisters on the death of Amédée Leger. *La Gloire des Rois*, chronicle of a fictional dynasty, reflects the transformations of a real family as written by a son for whom questions of parents and children suddenly take on new importance. Given Leger's premature role as head of a family, his preoccupation with kings and lineage is undoubtedly more than purely literary.

There were in fact two losses: first a father, then a grandmother: "j'ai un nouveau deuil, très lourd: j'ai perdu la mère de mon père, mon père même, mon vrai sang, dont j'avais encore besoin pour me comprendre."[20] Leger's correspondence during these years attests to an interest in Shakespeare. He owned many editions and translations from different eras. Some of them, now at the Fondation Saint-John Perse, bear revealing annotations, like the nineteenth-century edition of *Cymbeline*, translated by Victor Hugo, where a hand that is visibly Leger's has underlined the following passage from scene XI:

---

[19] The fact that *Récitation* was so little revised during its many reeditions is another indication that the poet was satisfied with the poem in its early form. Roger Little has shown that the revisions are largely typographical, reflecting Perse's ideas about prosody. "La Disposition d'un texte: *Récitation à l'eloge d'une reine* à la recherche d'un rythme," *Etudes sur Saint-John Perse* (Paris: Klincksieck, 1984), 107-125.

[20] *Lettres d'Alexis Leger à Gabriel Frizeau*, 75.

> Les hommes ne peuvent donc pas être créés sans que la femme
> y soit de moitié. Nous sommes tous bâtards; et l'homme si
> vénérable que j'appelais mon père était je ne sais où quand j'ai
> été fabriqué; c'est quelque faussaire qui m'a frappé de son coin. [21]

Shakespeare's words obviously resonate with the poet's genealogical
preoccupations even as they point toward our larger investigation
of forgery and forging. Concepts of race and purity pervade Perse's
prose and poetry with an almost obsessional frequency, as if to belie
a deep-seated fear of impurity in his own genealogy. Among his
highest tributes to a person or a work is to be "très racé, très
français," an "œuvre de race et de lignée." [22]

Leger's early correspondence constantly circles back to questions of fathers and sons. [23] In a March 1907 letter to Gabriel
Frizeau he acknowledges his lack of first-hand experience at child-
rearing, but is not deterred from offering advice about parenting.
His suggestions are both amusing and ambiguous, for he is alternately a jocular grandfather and a docile son. After counseling
Frizeau about how to raise a healthy son, Leger avows: "Et à la mort
de mon père, c'est à vous que j'ai écrit, tout de suite, et à la façon
d'un enfant." [24]

Across the letters, Leger goes out of his way to stress his depen-
dence on Frizeau and others. A revealing passage specifically omitted from the Pléiade edition, focuses on Frizeau's paternal role after
the death of Leger's father:

> Un homme prie pour mon père, et ce n'est pas son fils: cher ami!
> il y a donc une amitié qui est continuité! [. . .] Aujourd'hui, j'ai
> rejeté mon père: et soudain vous êtes là, derrière moi!–C'est la
> même ambiance, avec exactitude. [25]

Casting Frizeau as a father-substitute makes Leger a son and suggests some of his peculiar attitudes about both sonship and father-

[21] William Shakespeare, *Cymbeline*, tr. V. Hugo (Paris: Alphonse Lemerre, n.d.,
v. 12), scene XI.

[22] *Lettres d'Alexis Leger à Gabriel Frizeau*, 171, 165.

[23] Mireille Sacotte studies the correspondence in "Comment peut-on être un
enfant?," *Saint-John Perse: Les années de formation*, ed. J. Corzani (Paris: L'Harmattan, 1996), 45-58.

[24] *Lettres d'Alexis Leger à Gabriel Frizeau*, 60.

[25] *Ibid.*, 106.

hood. For the young Leger, being a son means being puerile, a word that recurs frequently in his relationship with Frizeau. He closes a 1908 letter by declaring: "Je ne sais pourquoi je vous dis tant de choses, puérilement, sinon pcq. je vous aime. Tendez-moi la main." [26] The next year, when returning a book, Leger admits: "J'ai hésité qq. temps à vous adresser cet exemplaire: j'avais oublié qu'il fût tout crayonné, bien puérilement, sinon indiscrètement; et prendre une gomme eut été un travail de palimpseste." [27] Leger returns to the idea of puerility when debating about whether or not to publish *L'Animale:* "et songez enfin que j'ai l'orgueil assez puéril encore pour ne pouvoir envisager un refus quelque part." [28]

Throughout the letters, Leger insists more than necessary on his immaturity in relation to Frizeau and other adults. This one, dated October 2, 1908, is revealing:

> Vous, gardez toujours à l'esprit et dans le cœur que l'âge le plus atroce et le plus *gravement* stupide, oui le plus gravement, est cette adolescence d'où j'ai tant de peine à sortir. Mon âge est respectable, et respectable toute sottise qui résulte d'une disproportion entre le faix et l'épaule. [29]

At age twenty and twenty-one, shouldering family burdens, Leger describes himself to Frizeau as an irresponsible "petit jeune homme" [30] and almost simultaneously to Monod as a "père noble" who oversees the family finances (660). With a certain bravado he brags about his enduring adolescence: "Qd. j'aurai 800F, je publierai qqch., si j'en trouve encore le goût; ou bien je ferai un voyage qui me tente; ou bien tout autre chose, s'il ne m'est réservé que de finir par la femme.–Vous voyez que j'ai toujours 16 ans!" [31]

In subsequent letters, the poet continues to project himself as immature, explicitly using the word child, even as he discusses his legal studies, investment strategies and future career. In 1910, Leger proclaims: "Au surplus, c'est moi qui suis trop enfant, de partir toujours sans donner d'adresse." [32] He returns to the leitmotif a year

---

[26] *Ibid.,* 69.

[27] *Ibid.,* 115.

[28] *Ibid.,* 107-108.

[29] *Ibid.,* 86.

[30] *Ibid.,* 92.

[31] *Ibid.,* 124.

[32] *Ibid.,* 144.

later: "Je suis confus envers vous comme un enfant qui n'ose plus se montrer. J'aurais dû vous remercier tout de suite de la feuille finan- cière qui m'a aidé à prendre une détermination au sujet des valeurs mexicaines de ma mère."[33]

In all these letters, Leger calls attention to his supposed imma- turity in radical contradiction to the ambitions he harbors and the responsibilities he actually carries. He portrays sons as irresponsible and juvenile, weighing upon fathers for whom paternity is a bur- den. Learning that Claudel has become a father, Leger expresses a dismayed compassion in separate letters to Frizeau and Rivière: "Claudel me fait part de la naissance de son fils–Un fils! . . . la proie que son Dieu fait peser à ses mains!";[34] "Claudel m'annonce la nais- sance d'un fils. Quelle proie pour cet homme!" (650). In this metaphor of weight, one might expect the word *poids*. In its place, the twice-repeated homonym *proie* says volumes about the young poet's disquieting picture of fathers and sons preying on each other, a tableau of torment that is quite at odds with typical images of pa- ternity. This depiction and Leger's seemingly gratuitous references to his childishness suggest complicated feelings which undoubtedly include guilt and at the same time resentment against a father who can no longer carry his own share of responsibility. When Leger writes in 1909 "j'ai rejeté mon père,"[35] the choice of verb is reveal- ing.

The kinds of family dramas that pervade Leger's correspon- dence are also perceptible, though very much muted, in *La Gloire des Rois,* whose poems record the progressive autonomy of a narra- tor, gradually outgrowing his immaturity and evolving into a Prince. When Leger chooses, like Shakespeare, "to tell sad stories of the deaths of kings," the tales are inseparable from his own: the sad sto- ry about a father's death and the happier one about a son's matura- tion. *La Gloire des Rois* chronicles a narrator's transformation from an adolescent in a world of women to the Prince he seeks to be.

This Prince, the protagonist of *Amitié du Prince,* has a long and distinguished lineage, being "lourd d'ancêtres et nourrisson de Reines" (71), but that is freight from the past; he must begin his own dynasty. The task is urgent as we can see from the cycle's con-

---

[33] *Ibid.*, 169.
[34] *Ibid.*, 79.
[35] *Ibid.*, 106.

clusion. Here in *Berceuse* a baby princess is killed because the first-born heir must be male. Although first published in 1945, this haunting poem, filled with orioles, has an oriental atmosphere that harks back to Leger's reading of Chinese classics during his years in the East. It juxtaposes the reassuring form and title of a lullaby with the cruel, terrifying story of an infanticide performed in the name of family lineage. The princess's tragedy comes from having upset the birth order; harmony can only be restored by a son. In 1956 Perse clarified the plight of this royal child in response to his German translator: "L'enfant de sang royal, sacrifié, parce que fille, est livrée, dans la tombe, à l'éternité d'ennui et d'accablement lumineux de la solitude royale." [36] When the poem first appeared, Perse predicted to Lilita Abreu: "*Berceuse* [...] déconcertera, j'espère, mes amis." [37]

La Gloire des Rois is a long meditation about varieties of power: sensual and spiritual, public and private, legitimate and illegitimate, political and artistic. With a precision that is worthy of Machiavelli's *Prince*, different vignettes portray the ways power is gained and lost, used and abused. The Queen's attraction is physical and sexual while the Prince's sway is more mysterious and spiritual. The Regent acquires dominion through violence and revolution, while the heir respects his followers: "J'honore les vivants, j'ai grâce parmi vous" (79). [38] As the narrator passes his spotlight across regal figures, he also explores the poet's own place in the spectrum of authority.

Although *Amitié du Prince* ostensibly praises the taciturn Prince (69), its ultimate hero is the friend who travels to visit and dispense wisdom. The Prince's beard is "poudrée d'un pollen de sagesse" (68), but the true source of wisdom is the Poet. As the title suggests, both the friendship and the friend are more important than the Prince himself, and the Prince's greatest sign of nobility is his respect for the Poet: "je recueillirai le fruit de ta sagesse" (69). [39]

---

[36] Response to Friedhelm Kemp, "Annotations de Saint-John Perse," *Cahiers Saint-John Perse* 6, 1983, 48.

[37] Saint-John Perse, *Lettres à l'Etrangère,* ed. M. Berne (Paris: Gallimard, 1987), 99.

[38] Claude Thiébaut convincingly sees in the *Histoire du Régent* a veiled account of the 1847 earthquake in Guadeloupe. "L'Antillanité à tort contestée d'*Histoire du Régent,*" *Saint-John Perse: Antillanité et Universalité,* ed. Levillain and Sacotte (Paris: Editions Caribéennes, 1988), 89-115.

[39] Albert Henry sees this as a key to *Amitié du Prince*: "La substance de tout le message–le thème du poème si l'on se place sur un autre plan–c'est l'éloge d'un

The poet-protagonist mirrors Leger himself, progenitor of imaginary kings and queens and founder of a dynasty made of words. At a deep level *La Gloire des Rois* is a meditation about the power of the poet and his ways of holding sway over readers. The cycle evolves from the sensual to the prophetic. Its opening poem, in praise of the Queen, has a sometimes puerile tone, to borrow Leger's word from that era. By contrast, the homages to Prince and Poet, published more than a decade later, bear the ritual solemnity of wisdom literature, sprinkled with what he called the pollen of wisdom. *Amitié du Prince* is a mature, moving work, one of the poet's own favorites, set in a place he imagined to resemble Borneo. [40] Writing to the translator Louise Varèse in 1941, Leger called it the most important poem in the collection. [41] When the Queen of *Récitation* is brought into contact with the Prince and Poet, their presence gives her a role as founder that she did not have in the earlier context of *Eloges*.

In *La Gloire des Rois* (as later in *Anabase*), the poet merges his own poems with the masterpieces of wisdom literature. Words and rhythms echo classic texts–the Hebrew Scriptures, the New Testament, the Egyptian *Kebra Nagast*, Tacitus' *Germany*, various of Sallust's texts, Chinese poems and documents, Hindu myths. The Prince may like "l'odeur de ces grands Livres en peau de chèvre" (68), but Perse himself clearly has an affinity for the *sound* of wisdom texts. He assimilates their resonance and tone, their cyclical structure of rising and falling dynasties, and even specific words and images from ancestral literature, whether from ancient epics and the "plus vieilles Chroniques" (68) or from works by more recent predecessors like Baudelaire, Rimbaud and Loti.

In the course of the *Gloire des Rois* the narrator grows from a young man unsuccessfully soliciting royal attention to a mature poet, summoned by royalty. In this same period, the author himself evolves from the Saintleger Leger of *Récitation à l'éloge d'une reine*, to the St. J. Perse of *Amitié du Prince*. His rebaptism, prompted by

---

Prince suffisamment sage, par delà sa Naissance, pour accorder son amitié à un sage sans Naissance." "Servitudes de l'écrit et construction poétique dans *Amitié du Prince*," *Travaux de linguistique et de littérature*, XXX, 1, 1974, 393.

[40] In conversation with Arthur Knodel, Perse called *Amitié du Prince* "un de mes préférés."

[41] Daniel Aranjo, "Deux lettres inédites de Saint-John Perse," *Arts, Sciences, Techniques* 3, mai 1992, 9.

a practical desire to separate his literary and diplomatic careers, has wider symbolic repercussions, for it signals a new birth.

In 1907 Alexis Leger inherited, unexpectedly and perhaps somewhat resentfully, his father's role in the family. By 1924, St. J. Perse had founded his own poetic kingdom. Reaching beyond the settlement of King Light, he was now Prince of a wider poetic domain. *Amitié* portrays the ideal form of power, both of a sovereign over his people and a poet over readers. The narrator has heard good things about the monarch and twice repeats: "j'ai entendu parler de toi de ce côté du monde, et la louange n'était point maigre" (65, 69). This tribute could be applied equally well to poets, both the one inside the poem and the author of the cycle. Like the Prince, a poet is clothed in words, "vêtu de [ses] sentences" (65). And surely the poet casts as magical a spell as the Prince who is hailed as "l'Enchanteur aux sources de l'esprit!" (65). *Amitié* is a primer on why and how to praise a poet. It is also a self-fulfilling prophecy. In the act of portraying power, the poem becomes a tool for exercising authority, a place where Perse can have the same effect on his readers as the Prince upon his subjects, for whom: "Ton nom fait l'ombre d'un grand arbre" (70). [42]

The image of a tree has particular resonance in a cycle of poems about royalty and lineage. Just as the Prince has illustrious forebears, so the poet–any poet–is burdened with literary ancestors, whose voices and presence weigh upon him. He may choose to revolt openly against the tradition, in the manner of the Regent or the young warriors of the *Récitation*. Or he may devise strategies for assimilating the many strands of tradition. In *La Gloire des Rois* Perse undertakes a double movement of tradition and innovation. Deriving authority from works of earlier times and traditions, he gathers a "pollen de sagesse" (68) that links this cycle to the long tradition of wisdom literature, while at the same time beginning a new genealogical tree, rooted in his own new name.

---

[42] This idea is not unrelated to Steven Winspur's conception of the "Saint-John Perse effect" by which the poet shapes readers' interpretations, although Winspur sees the process as beginning in *Exil. Saint-John Perse and the Imaginary Reader* (Geneva: Droz, 1988).

CHAPTER 3

REVISIONARY REPUBLICS: *ANABASE*

> There are three or four books in a writer's
> life which are like the changes of direction in
> a long valley–the cols where the world opens
> up again and you take a break and go on.
> *Anabase* is such a book to me. I believe it is
> very great poetry.
>
> Archibald MacLeish to Princess Bassiano, 1927[1]

WHEN T.S. Eliot reminisced in 1949 about his first encounter
with *Anabase*, a quarter of a century earlier, he remembered
being struck by a sense of Saint-John Perse's utter singularity: "il ne
s'inscrivait dans aucune catégorie, il n'avait en littérature ni liens ni
ancêtres: son poème ne pouvait s'expliquer que par le poème lui-
même" (1105). *Anabase* may well give the impression of standing
outside all categories, and Eliot was surely right in urging readers to
seek its meaning from within, but this is nonetheless a poem where
ancestors are ever-present.

When the narrator exclaims: "O généalogiste sur la place! com-
bien d'histoires de familles et de filiations?" (113), he raises a question the reader must ask of the poem itself: how many stories of
families and filiations are woven into the genealogy of *Anabase*?[2]
And what role do they play in its shape and meaning?

The poem is, by most accounts, Perse's most enigmatic work,
and one that has fascinated readers and critics from the beginning.

---

[1] *Letters of Archibald MacLeish 1907-1982,* ed. R.H. Winnick (New York:
Houghton Mifflin, 1983), 194.

[2] In the manuscript of *Anabase*, this question is elaborated upon in a long parenthetical passage that indicates an even greater preoccupation with lineage than is
apparent in the poem: "(le généalogiste sur la place et le vieillard qui perd le fil de
sa lignée, parce que la veuve fut aux mains du régisseur et la servante avait rejoint le
maître dans la vigne)." Albert Henry, *Anabase de Saint-John Perse* (Paris: Gallimard, 1983), 62.

T.S. Eliot prefaced his translation with the caveat that he was "by no means convinced that a poem like *Anabase* requires a preface at all. It is better to read such a poem six times and dispense with a preface."[3] While Eliot nevertheless went on to offer a testimonial and some explanatory remarks, his suggestion about reading the poem six times is one signal that it can indeed appear bewildering. Renato Poggioli compared *Anabase* to "a necklace made of strong thread, but which has lost many pearls or gems along the way."[4] The opening and closing Songs act as clasps and the cantos as beads, separated by certain lacunae for the reader to supply.

Saint-John Perse once wrote of the poem:

> *Anabase* a pour objet le poème de la solitude dans l'action. Aussi bien l'action parmi les hommes que l'action de l'esprit; envers autrui comme envers soi-même. J'ai voulu rassembler la synthèse, non point passive mais active, de la ressource humaine. (576)

His succinct summary and the ambitious goal of synthesizing human potential leaves virtually intact the task of deciphering this much-commented and memorable work.

Anabase is enigmatic in part because it is an antiphonal poem, responding to off-stage words that are distant and muffled. Voices murmur on the horizon of the text; we listen to one side of a conversation, obliged to reconstitute the other. In a celebrated enumeration, the narrator relates all that he has beheld in his city, including "les conversations muettes de deux hommes sous un arbre. . ." (113). The scene is an apt image for the poem itself, where readers also witness and strive to overhear silent but crucial conversations that inform the poem. It is essential to discern some of the many dialogues and to understand the poet's complicated relationship to these voices.

While authors are not able to choose their biological ancestors, they can select their literary ones. In this poem we feel the presence of certain intellectual forebears "comme un frémissement du large dans un arbre de fer" (102). In the desert geography depicted in the poem, earlier generations can easily disappear beneath the sands,

---

[3] Saint-John Perse, *Anabasis*, tr. with preface by T.S. Eliot (New York: Harbinger, 1949), 9.

[4] Renato Poggioli, *The Spirit of the Letter* (Cambridge: Harvard UP, 1965), 233.

without a trace: "Hommes, gens de poussière et de toutes façons
[...] ô gens de peu de poids dans la mémoire de ces lieux" (94). But
this is decidedly not true in the text itself, where the memory of ancestors is always felt and carries great weight.

A story of expedition and foundation, this poem depicts the human adventure in its physical, spiritual, and poetic dimensions. Its
hero-narrator is a multi-faceted leader who cannot be readily identified with any historical figure. Jacques Charpier depicts him as the
anonymous hero of an epic in an imaginary country, placed under a
title from Xenophon, but who isn't Cyrus.[5] Across time, critics have
proposed different accounts of the poem's meanings, but most con-
cur that there are at least three principal readings. On a literal level,
Anabase narrates the epic adventure of a person, traveling across
space, founding a new city, looking ahead to a new departure. On
another level, it can be read as a chronicle of the human community
and the rise of civilizations.[6] Finally, the poem suggests the spiritual
adventure of a poet creating a new work. Although the title denotes
movement, much of the poem is about foundations, such that it is
balanced precariously, like its narrator, on the threshold between
motion and stasis.

The title seems to have haunted Leger from an early date, roam-
ing around his psyche in search of a poem. He described its magnetism in a famous letter to Paul Claudel: "J'aimerais seulement
qu'il me fût donné un jour de mener une 'œuvre,' comme une *Anabase* sous la conduite de ses chefs. (Et ce mot même me semble si
beau que j'aimerais bien rencontrer l'œuvre qui pût assumer un tel
titre. Il me hante.)" (724). The idea of the writer as a military com-
mander, leading his work like an expedition, recurs in another letter
in which Perse comments on Claudel's new play, *La Ville,* and observes how difficult it must be to "conduire à sa fin une œuvre
comme la vôtre" (722).

For Perse the word *anabasis* denoted the journey not only of
writers but also of critics. His ideal reader, imagined in a 1910 letter
to Jacques Rivière, is a person who recreates a work of art by restor-
ing its framework and context. In this way

---

[5] Jacques Charpier, *Saint-John Perse* (Paris: Gallimard, 1962), 63.
[6] Shlomo Elbaz presents a useful summary of major interpretations, as well as
his own, in *Lectures d'*Anabase *de Saint-John Perse: le désert, le désir* (Genève:
L'Age d'Homme, 1977). He discusses enumerations on pp. 107-108.

> la critique peut accomplir un acte propre, cesser d'être un para-
> sitisme pour devenir un compagnonnage; une 'anabase,' si vous
> voulez, ou retour à la Mer, à la commune Mer d'où l'œuvre fut
> tirée (dans sa définitive, et peut-être cruelle, singularité). (677)

In this image of a common Sea, from which a unique text emerges, Perse offers the best approach to his own poem, for although it is as singular as T.S. Eliot proclaimed, it nevertheless belongs to a literary tradition. This *common Sea* functions as a kind of "sociolect" [7] –an idiom that is shared by a group of people and encompasses their language, literary tradition, primitive archetypes and mythic structures, as well as their images, clichés and stereotypes. A work of art is nourished by the sociolect, but it must forge its own particular language, or in Leger's terms, its definitive and even cruel singularity. The reader's task is to uncover the ties that link a specific text to the broader sociolect and to see how elements borrowed from the shared language and culture become kernels of meaning capable of generating a new text.

Although Perse acknowledged the common Sea of language from which all texts emerge, he also–and almost always–denied specific ties to individual authors or schools within the tradition. He claimed the French language and literary heritage as his patrimony, but repeatedly denied links to particular writers. Alain Girard has speculated that the poet's repeated claims of kinship with Pindar were a way of leapfrogging the entire French tradition and portraying himself as rooted directly in Greek antiquity. [8]

The drama of *Anabase* lies in the complicated relation between a singular text and its literary patrimony. When Perse describes the cruel singularity of a work of art, he hints at a muted violence that is never far below the surface of *Anabase*. "Ce n'est pas une œuvre de douceur ni d'abandon, de rêverie ni de langueur," he wrote to the Swedish composer Karl-Birger Blomdahl, "mais de conquête et d'action: une œuvre dure, volontaire, plus elliptique qu'on ne croit [. . .]." [9] This description may apply to all great poems, but it aptly depicts the drive and determination of this one.

---

[7] Michael Riffaterre, "La Trace de l'Intertexte," *La Pensée*, 215 (Octobre 1980), 4.

[8] Alain Girard, "Le Mallarmé de Saint-John Perse," *Souffle de Perse* 5/6, 1995, 82.

[9] Letter to Blomdahl, cited by Marie-Noëlle Little, *Saint-John Perse: Correspondance avec Dag Hammarskjöld, Cahiers Saint-John Perse* 11, 1993, 216.

Most accounts of its genesis take their cue from the poet's romanticized account of writing *Anabase* in a disaffected Taoist temple, a day's horseback ride from Peking, during his years as Secretary of the French delegation in China, 1916 to 1921. The opening Song was published after Perse's return to Paris in 1922 and the complete work in 1924, although it may have been composed before *Amitié du Prince*.

Perse's years in China had an undeniable influence on his poetry, despite his vigorous disavowal of a Chinese setting or of any other precise geography. Indeed, he disclaimed any kind of orientalism or exoticism in his work, which he envisaged to be outside of time and space. These caveats have not kept critics from trying, perhaps all the more assiduously, to locate *Anabase* in some specific place and epoch, whether in China, Babylon, Mexico, the Antilles, or elsewhere.[10] Yet, what may be most significant about the poem's geography is its capacity to evoke and synthesize the foundations of all celebrated cities in the epic tradition–Troy, Babylon, Alexandria, Jerusalem, Rome–as well as other sites on the human trajectory, from China to Guadeloupe, according to Perse's expressed aim that the poem be a synthesis of human activity (576).[11]

To move forward through *Anabase* is, at the same time, to go back in time and find many different traditions coexisting within it. Notable among them are classical antiquity, the Bible, and travel literature about China, both Perse's own accounts and those of others writing about the Orient, from Marco Polo to more modern French predecessors: Jules Verne, Pierre Loti, Victor Segalen and Paul Claudel. Each strand of the poem, classical, biblical and oriental, represents a branch of the genealogical tree that links Perse to his predecessors.

Saint-John Perse's commentary about the title of the poem is well known:

---

[10] Marcelle Auclair sees in *Anabase* the Mexico of Bernal Díaz del Castillo's *Conquête de la nouvelle Espagne,* as she relates in *Mémoires à deux voix* (Paris: Seuil, 1978), 253. On the Antilles, see Jack Corzani, *La Littérature des Antilles-Guyane françaises,* t. 2 (Fort de France: Desormeaux, 1978), and Régis Antoine, "Une Echappée Magnifiante sur la Guadeloupe," *Saint-John Perse: Antillanité et Universalité,* ed. H. Levillain, M. Sacotte (Paris: Editions Caribéennes, 1988), 28.

[11] Jean-Michel Le Guen identifies allusions to different civilizations in *L'Ordre exploratoire: L'*Anabase (Paris: Sedes, 1985).

> Le mot est neutralisé, dans ma pensée, jusqu'à l'effacement d'un
> terme usuel, et ne doit donc plus suggérer aucune association
> d'idées classiques. Rien à voir avec Xénophon. Le mot est em-
> ployé ici abstraitement, incorporé au français courant avec toute
> la discrétion nécessaire, dans le simple sens étymologique de:
> 'Expédition vers l'intérieur,' avec une signification à la fois géo-
> graphique et spirituelle (ambiguïté voulue). Le mot comporte
> aussi, de surcroît, le sens étymologique de: 'montée à cheval,'
> 'montée en selle'. (1145)

Despite this claim that the poem has nothing to do with the famous
Anabasis (or presumably with Arrian's work of the same title), critics have long been tempted to seek keys in Xenophon (430-350
B.C.), and it is difficult not to see a relationship with this disciple of
Socrates who served as a mercenary in the Persian army of Cyrus
the Younger. When Cyrus was killed in 401 at the battle of Cunaxa
and his Army of Ten Thousand was forced to retreat, Xenophon
became both a participant and a chronicler of the flight, recorded
in his *Anabasis*. Later he composed a paean to Cyrus The Great,
the *Cyropedia*, in which he traced the lineage of Persians and Cyrus
back to the mythological Perseus. The descendants of Cyrus went
on to found Persepolis, one of the marvels of the ancient world,
which flourished for two centuries until Alexander's army plun-
dered and buried it in 330 B.C. as punishment for the Persian inva-
sion of Greece.

The family of Cyrus was present in Perse's spirit from an early
date. In *Eloges* two monarchs from Cyrus's lineage, Cambyses and
Xerxes, merge into a bird that is "sauvage comme Cambyse et doux
comme Assuérus" (39). Much later, in 1967, the landscape of southern France prompts Perse to note in his journal: "Retraite des
10.000." [12] It is thus not surprising to find traces of Xenophon in a
French work of the same title, and especially in the one by which
Saint-John Perse inaugurates his full pseudonym. In *Eloges* he
played with his civilian identity, Leger / Light. In a bilingual pun on
the double meaning of the word light, he founded a poetic realm
playfully called King Light's Settlements. Now, in *Anabase,* under a
title reminiscent of Xenophon and the Persians, Saint-John Perse
founds his own poetic Persepolis. [13] Yet, if the title of this poem

---

[12] "Croisière aux Iles Eoliennes," *Cahiers Saint-John Perse* 8-9, 1987, 19.

[13] Jean-Pierre Richard proposes an interpretation of the pseudonym based on
the verb *percer. Microlectures* (Paris: Seuil, 1979), 199.

beckons us unmistakably into the Greek world, it invites us beyond Xenophon to his master, Socrates, as portrayed by Plato.

Perse's philosophy led inexorably to discord with Plato. The poet's favorite philosophers were the pre-Socratics, especially Heraclitus. His annotations in *La Naissance de la philosophie* suggest to what extent he shared with Nietzsche both a predilection for the early thinkers and an aversion to the author of the dialogues. Given Perse's passion for multiplicity and for the process of becoming, rather than a static being, it is not surprising that he felt an affinity with Aristotle. [14] Perse's wariness of metaphysics naturally pitted him against the inventor of ideal forms; Plato's condemnation of poetry in the *Republic* only fueled an ongoing quarrel destined to last all of Perse's life. Some thirty-five years after *Anabase*, Perse again alluded prominently, if anonymously, to Plato in his Nobel Prize acceptance speech, giving Plato the dubious distinction of being the ancient philosopher to whom poetry was the most suspect (444).

In the *Theaetetus* (155d), Plato identifies philosophy as the daughter of wonder; for Perse, by contrast, the true "fille de l'étonnement" (444) is poetry–a legitimate and even privileged instrument of knowing, superior to discursive thought. But however much Perse disagreed with Plato, about art as about metaphysics, he could not avoid him, any more than Alfred North Whitehead, who once quipped that wherever he went in his mind, he always met Plato coming back. When Perse set about founding a city, he necessarily met Plato returning from his own attempt to construct an imaginary republic.

The idea of founding a community intrigued Perse from a young age. In his autobiography, he cites three early experiences that reflect this interest: 1910 in the Béarn (xv); 1912 in England (xvi); and his elected office in China as a quasi-mayor of the diplomatic compound (xvii). Some of the earliest verses, "Des villes sur trois modes," which he claimed to have written "sur les bancs du lycée de Pau" (1194), and later denounced as "insupportables" (735), already prefigure the city-building of *Anabase*. Perse was particularly curious about communities founded by European settlers. Régis Antoine has documented how, in books about these settle-

---

[14] On Perse and Aristotle, see Steven Winspur, *Saint-John Perse and the Imaginary Reader* (Geneva: Droz, 1988), 154, 176-181.

ments, he specifically underlined accounts of founders and of arrival scenes. [15] Marcelle Auclair remembers the vivacity with which Perse encouraged her to read Bernal Díaz del Castillo's account of the Mexican conquest. [16]

Many cities preside over *Anabase*, some real, some fictive, but one of the most powerfully present is the theoretical city created in Plato's *Republic*. Perse pursues, even as he disputes, Plato's meditation about ideal forms of government, the nature of leadership, and the relation of knowledge to experience. He addresses the relations between politics and imagination in a modern dialogue with his predecessor.

In the *Republic* Socrates proposes to study justice by enlarging it to the scale of a country. He imagines the birth of a nation, beginning with a few indispensable people: farmer, mason, weaver, shoemaker. Socrates predicts that inhabitants will soon want more comfort than these workers can furnish; the population will inevitably grow to include hunters and artists, poets, actors and dancers, nurses, nannies and tutors, chefs and doctors (373b). [17] His imaginary extrapolation leads to a bustling city that is filled with variety, although extravagant in Socrates' eyes. In a spirit of poetic revelry, Perse outdoes Socrates by creating his own enumeration of human activities broad enough to embrace "toutes sortes d'hommes dans leurs voies et façons" (112-113). While echoing and amplifying Socrates' list, Perse adds a playful dimension to Plato's seriousness by expanding the repertoire of citizens to include "l'homme de nul métier." If in Plato's *Republic* there is no room for inactivity, Perse mischievously places near the top of the hierarchy an individual who does nothing at all: "bien mieux, celui qui ne fait rien." While Socrates' inhabitants are defined by their work, those in Perse's city can be portrayed equally well by what they do not do, or by their

---

[15] Régis Antoine, "Une Echappée magnifiante sur la Guadeloupe," in *Saint-John Perse: Antillanité et Universalité,* ed. H. Levillain, M. Sacotte (Paris: Editions Caribéennes, 1988), 28. Yves Bonnefoy witnessed Perse's fascination with the details of communities when the two poets toured George Washington's home in Mount Vernon, a site Perse often visited during his Georgetown years. *Le Nuage rouge* (Paris: Mercure de France, 1977), 231.

[16] Marcelle Auclair, Françoise Prevost, *Mémoires à deux voix* (Paris: Seuil, 1978), 253.

[17] Plato, *Republic,* tr. R. Waterfield (Oxford: Oxford UP, 1994), 59. All references to the *Republic* are drawn from this edition, with paragraph numbers in parentheses in the text.

thoughts ("celui qui pense au corps de femme, homme libidineux"), or by everyday acts ("qui porte une conque à son oreille").
They can forge their identity in past experience ("celui qui a vécu
dans un pays de grandes pluies") or in future plans ("celui qui a fait
des voyages et songe à repartir").

Socrates' hierarchy of professions is headed by the chief of
state, while Perse's encyclopedic list leads to a very different culmination: "soudain! apparu dans ses vêtements du soir et tranchant à
la ronde toutes questions de préséance, le Conteur qui prend place
au pied du térébinthe . . ." The one character with a capitalized
name occupies a place of honor beneath the sacred tree. By assign-
ing the privileged space to a storyteller, Perse specifically flaunts
Plato's dire warnings about the dangers of literature. According
to Plato's criteria, "the only poems we can admit into our community
are hymns to the gods and eulogies of virtuous men" (607a). *Eloges*
might gain admittance into Plato's city, by virtue of its title, but
lyrics and epics (including *Anabase*) would surely be banned. The
only acceptable poets for Plato are those who play a role in governing the city-state. Homer would be ineligible, although Perse might
have had a chance, in recognition of his diplomatic role in China.

In opposition to Plato, Perse creates his own poetic Republic, a
new Persepolis, governed by a storyteller. Then he goes a step further and reverses Plato's question about whether the poet is good
for the state and asks instead if governance is beneficial to the poet.
The question had particular relevance for Perse at the time, given
his responsibilities. One of the central, unresolved tensions of the
text is whether the poet must ultimately leave behind the city he has
founded to concentrate on the "Terre arable du songe!" (114), a
space conducive to artistic creation.

The best-known episode of the *Republic* is the allegory of the
cave in Book VII. In this one episode (and nowhere else in the book)
the word *anabasis* occurs three times (515e, 517b, 519d), to denote
the climb from the darkness of the cave to the light of knowledge.
(The noun recurs only one other time in all of Plato's known works,
in the *Symposium* 190d.) In Plato's allegory, anabasis is the process of
rising from shadows toward light, following a path from the lowest
kind of knowledge, perception of shadows and images, to the highest–understanding of the ideal forms, symbolized by the sun.

Perse's *Anabase* calls this hierarchy into question and charts a
new kind of expedition. From the very first canto the sun is prob-

lematical; it is present, but immediately contested: "Va! nous nous étonnons de toi, Soleil! Tu nous as dit de tels mensonges!" (96). While Plato advocates an ascent up from representation and the material world toward an ideal form of reality, Perse questions this trajectory and the metaphysics it implies. His poetry is, above all, an affirmation of the exhilarating diversity of the inhabited world, independent of ideal forms in another realm.

In the archaeology of *Anabase*, the *Republic* coexists with another classical city, waiting to be uncovered. This is Troy itself, the site of Homer's epics and point of departure for Virgil's saga of the founding of Rome. As the classical empire moved west from Greece to Rome to France, the epic voice also moved west, from Greek to Latin to Italian. Whether or not it is true, as Voltaire is said to have remarked, that "Les Français n'ont pas la tête épique," French literature has been seen by many as a series of attempts, by trial and error, to create an epic voice in French. The authors of the medieval *Roman de Troie* and the *Chanson de Roland* may have been the first to write epics in French. Ronsard certainly tried in his *Franciade*, and Victor Hugo in his *Légende des siècles*. But Perse shared the belief that France had not yet found its Homer or Virgil, that the art of the epic was still to be perfected, and that a great French epic remained to be written. Throughout his career, and most fully in later poems, *Vents* and *Amers*, he attempted to bring an epic breath to French poetry. We can already discern this ambition in *Anabase*, whose ships seek to rival and even surpass those of Troy: "Et les vaisseaux plus hauts qu'Ilion" (98).

Behind Perse's poem about the founding of a city lies Virgil's epic about Aeneas' journey to found Rome. The *Aeneid* opens with a poet's famous announcement: "I sing of arms and of a man." [18] Arms also figure in the first stanza of *Anabase*, where "Les armes au matin sont belles et la mer" (93). Reminiscences of the *Aeneid* and other Latin texts continue throughout the poem. In Virgil's epic, Jupiter prophecies that Aeneas shall establish his city and govern for three summers and three winters (I:369-372). His son shall reign for thirty years, and his descendents for three hundred more, until Romulus and Remus inaugurate the Roman "empire without end"

---

[18] Virgil, *The Aeneid*, tr. A. Mandelbaum (New York: Bantam, 1981), 1. All references to the *Aeneid* are drawn from this edition, with citations by book and verse in parentheses in the text.

(I:390). This emphasis on the number three finds its immediate echo in the opening declaration of Canto I: "Sur trois grandes saisons m'établissant avec honneur, j'augure bien du sol où j'ai fondé ma loi" (93). [19] In the bustle of foundation one finds the "Maître du grain, maître du sel, et la chose publique sur de justes balances" (93). This French translation of the *res publica*, along with allusions to grain and salt, to the literal scales of merchants and the metaphorical scales of justice, are reminders of that particular configuration of goods and values in Roman civilization.

Another prominent city of the *Aeneid* is Dido's kingdom in Carthage, which Aeneas observes in amazement on his arrival:

> The eager men of Tyre work steadily:
> some build the city walls or citadel –
> they roll up stones by hand; and some select
> the place for a new dwelling, marking out
> its limits with a furrow; some make laws,
> establish judges and a sacred senate;
> some excavate a harbor; others lay
> deep foundations for a theater,
> hewing tremendous pillars for the rocks,
> high decorations for the stage to come
>
> (I: 601-610)

This ebullient, creative activity is a worthy precedent for the specific tasks enumerated in *Anabase*, but strikingly absent from the modern poem is any equivalent of Dido, although she is mentioned later, in *Pluies*, where rain is compared to "Didon foulant l'ivoire aux portes de Carthage" (143). In the city of *Anabase* all leadership belongs to men.

Aeneas, founder of Rome and ancestor of Caesar, is the putative protagonist of Virgil's epic, but the poem is ambiguous, for it ends in a terrible carnage that prompts us to ask, as the *Aeneid* subtly does, whether the true hero is the warrior-leader, Aeneas-Caesar, or the poet-chronicler, Virgil. Whatever Aeneas' feats, only the writer

---

[19] Joëlle Gardes Tamine has interpreted the three seasons as winter, spring and summer, based on Perse's reading of Tacitus. *Saint-John Perse ou la stratégie de la seiche* (Aix-en-Provence: Université de Provence, 1996), 65-66. May Chehab shows that the Greeks also had three seasons, spring, summer and fall, since Apollo was absent in winter. "Saint-John Perse et la Grèce," doctoral thesis, Université de Provence, mai 1999, 232-239.

can immortalize them, as he is well aware in his apostrophe: "If there be any power within my poetry, no day shall ever erase you from the memory of time" (IX:592-594). The last word belongs to the poet. In *Anabase* a narrator hesitates between the roles of Aeneas and Virgil, statesman and artist. With the *Aeneid* acting as watermark beneath the poem, Perse renews a perennial (and personal) question while placing his work in an epic lineage.

If the title and opening canto of *Anabase* echo classical texts, from Rome and Greece, the poem's liminal song ushers us into the biblical space of the New Testament. We know how important the Scriptures were for Perse as a treasury of images, expressions and stories. The Crampon translation was his favorite, and a letter in the Pléiade volume, dated 1917, asks his mother to send him this edition in China (850). [20]

Perse told T.S. Eliot there were no biblical allusions in his poetry (1145), but this is hardly true. They are explicitly present in the Flood and Ark of *Eloges* (29, 41) and abundantly perceptible in rhythms and allusions of later poems. Despite Perse's reservations about institutional religion and rituals, he clearly used the Scriptures as a linguistic resource. Annotations in his own copy show how carefully he mined the Bible for vocabulary and images.

The Hebrew Scriptures offered him rich and unusual lore about laws and practices, including sexual taboos, which he frequently underlined. While Perse did not annotate the New Testament as copiously, he was familiar with its cadence and metaphors from his childhood classes with the priests of Guadeloupe and from years of hearing passages read aloud. The Bible provided a compendium of images and a tone of solemnity he could draw upon to give his own poems an aura of wisdom literature, a "pollen de sagesse" (68), to borrow the expression from *Amitié du Prince*. [21]

At the threshold of *Anabase,* the opening song twice proclaims:

[20] In the light of Catherine Mayaux's studies, we know that letters from this period were largely reconstructed by the poet in the late 1960s, but if this request is indeed a belated re-creation, it becomes an even more significant sign of the Bible's ongoing importance in his writing. "Les Lettres d'Asie," *Cahiers Saint-John Perse* 12, 1994, 19.

[21] For studies on biblical language in Perse's poetry, see Diane Nairac, "Valeur des réminiscences bibliques dans l'œuvre de Saint-John Perse," *Cahiers Saint-John Perse* 7, 1984; Judith Kopenhagen-Urian, "La Condition de la femme biblique dans la poésie de Saint-John Perse," *Souffle de Perse* 4, janvier 1994, 55-66; and Mireille Sacotte, *Saint-John Perse* (Paris: Belfond, 1991), 214-230.

Je vous salue, ma fille, sous le plus grand des arbres de l'année (89)
Je vous salue, ma fille, sous la plus belle robe de l'année (89)

Rhyming with the angel's Annunciation to Mary from Luke's Gospel: "Je vous salue, Marie" (1:29), this refrain heralds the presence of a most special messenger. By echoing the sound and tone of the Ave Maria, outside a specifically Christian context, the poet confers special stature and a prophetic, if secular authority upon his Stranger/Narrator.

It is appropriate that a poem which specifically evokes "histoires de familles et de filiations" (113), should begin with an allusion to that most extraordinary genealogy by which a son is born without human paternity. Echoes of this biblical moment of Annunciation recur in the refrain of Canto 9:

> Je t'annonce les temps d'une grande chaleur (109)
> Je t'annonce les temps d'une grande faveur (109)
> Je t'annonce les temps d'une grande chaleur (109)
> Je t'annonce les temps d'une grande faveur (110)
> Je t'annonce les temps d'une grande faveur (110)

In Luke's Gospel, Mary's response is the Magnificat (1:46-47), translated in Perse's Crampon Bible as:

> Mon âme glorifie le Seigneur
> Et mon esprit tressaille de joie en Dieu, mon Sauveur
> [. . .]
> Parce qu'il a fait en moi de grandes choses, Celui qui est puissance
> Et dont le nom est saint

In *Anabase* the language of this hymn is echoed in the response: "Mon coeur a pépié de joie sous les magnificences de la chaux" (96). It is, of course, a male narrator, speaking in a very different context, but the rhyming of *Je vous salue, ma fille* with the Gospel phrase *Je vous salue, Marie;* the refrain *Je t'annonce;* and the parallelism between *Mon cœur a pépié de joie* and *Mon esprit tressaille de joie* all gesture toward the Bible. This suggestion is enhanced by a vocabulary of thanksgiving, soul and vocation in the following stanza: "grâces, grâces lui soient rendues [. . .]. Mon âme est pleine de mensonge, comme la mer agile et forte sous la vocation de l'éloquence." (96). We are far from the meaning of the Gospel, but the echo of its language gives an aura of ritual to the scene. However much the meaning of these biblical expressions is transformed or even deformed in the borrowing, their very sound bestows on a modern, secular text the tone of an ancient scripture.

After these resonances of the New Testament, *Anabase* moves back in time to the Hebrew Scriptures, a locus for so many of the questions that pervade the poem: genealogy, leadership, creation. The most annotated books in Perse's Crampon Bible are Genesis, Exodus, Leviticus, Numbers, Deuteronomy, Joshua, the Song of Songs, Joel, Amos, Micah, Nahum, Zachariah and Malachi. The poet's underlinings reveal a constellation of preoccupations, many of which recur in his poetry. One is a nexus of allusions to generation, sources, and seed. Variations of the word *semence* are often underlined. Another network of annotations highlights biblical laws, especially sexual interdictions. They are reflected in *Anabase* where "Le prêtre a déposé ses lois contre le goût des femmes pour les bêtes" (97). Perse also noted biblical judgments, whether rewards or, more often, punishments by violence, sterility or destruction. In a letter to Gustave-Adolphe Monod, Perse cited his favorite episode from the Bible, Genesis 18, where Abraham bargains with God on behalf of Sodom:

> Il y a, ne trouves-tu pas? dans ce marchandage juif défendant pied à pied le divin contre l'humain (si ce n'est déjà tout l'humain contre le divin), quelque chose de cette prodigieuse 'spéculation' juive qui terminait l'intercession d'Abraham en faveur de Sodome (Genèse): Abraham rusant avec son Dieu, le pressant âprement, ou même, transigeant! (Non, je ne vois pas de page plus extraordinaire dans toute l'histoire humaine: plus compliquée, plus humblement hautaine ou plus sublimement basse!) (657)

Stories of laws, expeditions and foundations permeate *Anabase,* recalling the biblical Chronicles, prophets and Exodus, but the poem's ultimate model is Genesis. It is easy to understand why Perse favored this text, since it is a paradigm for all poetic activity. Words suffice to create the universe; God creates all things, which Adam can then name. Every poet seeks to play both roles.

When Perse read the Bible, he also annotated unusual names of people and places as well as episodes illustrating the thematics of naming. This predilection dates back to *Eloges* where a community bears the name of its monarch and incidentally of the poet: "King Light's Settlements." *Anabase* opens with an anonymous Stranger and an unnamed force, twice acknowledged: "Et le soleil n'est point nommé, mais sa puissance est parmi nous" (93, 94). What will they call the new city? When they do find a word, it is so "pure" that we never hear it: "Ainsi la ville fut fondée et placée au matin sous les labiales d'un nom pur" (98).[22]

Through language the poet of *Anabase* brings a community into being and then has the power to bestow–or withhold–names. It is not accidental that in the long enumeration of citizens, "l'homme en faveur dans les conseils" is precisely "celui qui nomme les fontaines" (112).

A modern poet has few opportunities to create new names, but he can at least revel in the multiplicity of nouns that exist, and juxtapose the familiar with the surprising, like "l'agriculteur et l'adalingue" of *Anabase* (112). The latter, translated by T.S. Eliot as "the young noble horsed,"[23] is a rare word, absent from most dictionaries; in the multi-volumed *Grand Larousse* it is defined as the son of a king, from the Anglo-Saxon *aetheling*. This example is emblematic of Perse's fascination with words. Like one of the inhabitants of his city, "l'homme versé dans les sciences, dans l'onomastique" (112), he delves into etymologies and renews language by calling upon multiple meanings of words, as when he hails the "inventions de sources en lieux morts" (111). The expression plays simultaneously on the Latin root, *invenire*, to find, and the modern usage, invention. The city, like the poem itself, is both found and invented, by a poet who is both discoverer and creator.

In Genesis, Yahweh sees his creation and deems it good (I:10); in Perse's new world, an unnamed witness also surveys the realm and finds: "choses vivantes, ô choses / excellentes!" (111). With this biblical affirmation in the last canto, Perse places his community in a long biblical tradition that begins with Genesis and continues to the Annunciation of the New Testament.

---

[22] Arthur Knodel sees in this verse an example of the "curious concreteness without specificity" that characterizes *Anabase* and much of Perse's subsequent poetry. *Saint-John Perse: A Study of his Poetry* (Edinburgh: UP, 1966), 45.

[23] *Anabasis*, trans. T.S. Eliot, *Saint-John Perse: Collected Poems* (Princeton: Princeton UP, Bollingen Series LXXXVII, 1983), 137.

The biblical and classical voices of *Anabase* are accompanied by a third set of crucial conversations. Traveling to China in 1916 to join the French delegation in Peking, Perse followed the path of predecessors who had chronicled their own journeys to Asia. In the early days of the twentieth century, as Catherine Mayaux has pointed out, the Far East was seen as an obligatory destination for writers in search of adventure or inspiration, and China was a key site for French poetry. [24] To Frenchmen of that generation, a voyage to the Orient offered escape and exoticism. For Perse it had the added dimension of a professional journey. In a 1917 letter, he thanked Philippe Berthelot for encouraging him to go: "Vous aviez raison de me dire qu'il n'y a pas de formation professionnelle, ni humaine, complète sans séjour en Extrême-Orient, et de cela aussi je vous suis reconnaissant" (812).

Everyone who writes about the Orient brings to the subject a set of associations. "Additionally," writes Edward Said, with particular emphasis on the Middle East, "each work on the Orient affiliates itself with other works, with audiences, with institutions, with the Orient itself." [25] Perse was no exception, bringing to China a cultural baggage of images and expectations acquired through depictions by earlier observers and dreamers.

One important predecessor was Pierre Loti, whom Perse seemed destined to follow on his multiple trajectories, although there is no evidence the two men ever met. Loti's exotic portrayal of Tahiti was already a model to be avoided when the younger poet depicted his own island paradise in *Eloges*. Now in China, Perse was in territory Loti had literally trod just a few years earlier, to write about the 1900 Boxer rebellion in *Les Derniers Jours de Pékin*. While following the same itinerary, Perse actively avoided Loti's style, writing *Anabase* in specific opposition to a romanticism of the Orient.

Two other French writers were equally problematic predecessors for the young poet. One was Victor Segalen, who lived in China from 1909 to 1914, a mere two years before Perse. The more recent arrival always denied having been influenced by this naval doctor

---

[24] Catherine Mayaux, "Les Illustres prédécesseurs de Michaux en Chine: Claudel, Segalen et Saint-John Perse," in *Henri Michaux: un barbare en Asie*, ouvrage collectif (Paris: Editions Marketing, 1992), 110.

[25] Edward W. Said, *Orientalism* (New York: Vintage, 1979), 20.

and chronicler of Gauguin's house in Tahiti, but his early poems share an unmistakable kinship of tone and theme with Segalen's volume of *Stèles*. Since Segalen himself found his sources among historic Chinese texts, they have an enigmatic and solemn aura that has prompted comparisons with Perse's Chinese poems. Segalen's homage to the Prince in "A Celui-là" is a typical example:

> [. . .] le Prince est là: je suis tout entier pour le Prince. La servi-
> tude glorieuse pèse sur chacun de mes gestes comme le sceau sur
> l'acte impérial et le tribut. [26]

This tribute, inspired by the Chinese work *Li ki,* does not begin to have the poetic rigor of Perse's phrases, but it creates an atmo-sphere that is not unlike the praise in *Amitié du Prince*: "une chose est certaine, que nous portons le sceau de ton regard; et un très grand besoin de toi nous tient aux lieux où tu respires" (65-66).

Perse energetically discouraged any comparisons between the two poets. In the 1950s, when Alain Bosquet was composing his *Saint-John Perse* for the "Poètes d'Aujourd'hui" series, one of the only revisions the poet requested on the manuscript was "la sup-pression de toute votre page de citations de V. Segalen" (1068). An-dré Brincourt observed: "Je n'ai connu que Perse pour se flatter, en priorité, de ce qu'il n'avait pas lu (Segalen, par exemple!)." [27] But Perse had obviously read his predecessor, as we can see from the annotated volumes in his library; he called Segalen "un poète livresque, qui a tout pris chez les autres et dans les chroniques an-ciennes. Il n'a pas vécu ses poèmes." [28] On another occasion, Perse dipped into English to describe his compatriot as "arty-arty." [29]

In 1960 Christian Murciaux acknowledged Segalen as the cre-ator of a new poetic climate—"le songe hiératique et ingénu que Gauguin a fixé sur les toiles" [30]—and observed: "Sans doute, Victor Segalen a aidé Saint-John Perse à déchiffrer la mystérieuse stèle gravée qu'était la Chine [. . .]" [31] This allusion obviously touched a

---

[26] Victor Segalen, *Stèles, Œuvres complètes*, t. 2, ed. H. Bouillier (Paris: Laffont, 1995), 68.

[27] André Brincourt, *Messagers de la nuit* (Paris: Grasset, 1995), 104.

[28] Henriette Levillain, *Sur deux versants, la création chez Saint-John Perse d'après les versions anglaises de son œuvre poétique* (Paris: Corti, 1987), 228.

[29] Perse related this to Arthur Knodel.

[30] Christian Murciaux, *Saint-John Perse* (Paris: Editions Universitaires, 1960), 10.

[31] *Ibid.*, 18.

sensitive chord in Perse, who deleted both passages in red pencil from his own copy of the book, too late, of course, to erase them from the published volume.

Perse resisted parallels to any recent predecessors, but his feelings about Segalen may have been colored by rivalry with this contemporary who (unlike Perse) had learned Chinese, who had participated in archaeological expeditions, acquired a reputation as a sinologist, and played a role in the Gauguin saga. His hostility may have been exacerbated by Segalen's close relationship to Paul Claudel, one of Perse's own early mentors. *Stèles* is dedicated to Claudel in a gesture that risked crowding out a newer, younger disciple.

For many reasons, Perse's relationship with Claudel was also complicated. [32] His autobiography dates their meeting as 1905 "Rencontre à Orthez, chez Francis Jammes, de Paul Claudel, qui lui offre un exemplaire de son *Ode: Les Muses*, dans l'édition grand format de la 'Bibliothèque de l'Occident'" (xii). The next year, in a startling expression of pain, the nineteen-year-old Leger wrote to Claudel, who was exactly twice his age:

> Si je songe à vous, c'est un peu avec une aigre détresse, qui est bien certainement de l'égoïsme, parce que vous êtes pour moi–et Jammes aussi, et votre ami Frizeau–celui qui a fini, celui qui est 'sorti,' qui est 'arrivé,' tandis que moi je commence. Et je serai seul sans doute jusqu'au terme. Vous êtes de ceux qui ont disparu pour moi derrière le lac de Soufre de vos Livres Saints [. . .]. Rappelez-vous votre jeunesse et vous retrouverez ce deuil que laissent ceux qui nous précèdent (712).

This bitterness is tempered in later correspondence, where Perse's letters are filial in tone, seeking advice and praising Claudel's works. Any lingering traces of the 1905 competitiveness are muted or, more probably, channelled away from the letters only to be subtly reenacted in Perse's poems. Throughout *Anabase* we can hear the presence of this giant who was Perse's predecessor in literature, in diplomacy, and specifically in the Orient, where he occupied diplomatic positions for almost fifteen years. Many of Claudel's

---

[32] An early study of the two poets is Michel Autrand's "Saint-John Perse et Claudel (1904-1914)," *Revue d'Histoire littéraire de la France,* 78:3 (mai/juin 1978), 355-378.

works were written in and about China, including *Connaissance de l'Est, Connaissance du Temps, Traité de la Co-Naissance au monde et de soi-même, Les Cinq Grandes Odes, La Jeune Fille Violaine,* and the second version of *La Ville*.

Claudel was an early confidant of Perse's desire to "mener une 'œuvre' comme une *Anabase* sous la conduite de ses chefs" (724). The completed poem begins with *naissance* and ends with *connaissance,* as if in echo of the famous essay where Claudel spun the link between these words: "Nous ne naissons pas seuls. Naître, pour tout, c'est connaître. Toute naissance est une connaissance." [33] Claudel endowed those two words with religious implications; Perse extracts them from a theological context to make them affirmations of human existence. Citation, homage, dialogue, rejoinder: this example is emblematic of the long, complex relationship between the two poet-diplomats.

In 1911, Perse praised Claudel's newest play, *La Ville,* as "une œuvre si hautement admirée qu'elle me semble parfois la plus grande journée de tout votre théâtre" (722). Portraying the willful destruction of a city and the promised establishment of another one, this drama about happiness and governance closes with the words of the new king Ivors: "Pour nous, nous établissant dans le milieu de la Ville, nous constituerons les lois." [34] *Anabase* opens with the same reference to establishment and law, as if it were a sequel to Claudel's drama. The city announced by Ivors is now being founded by the narrator of *Anabase,* whose law will prevail: "Sur trois grandes saisons m'établissant avec honneur, j'augure bien du sol où j'ai fondé ma loi" (93). Claudel's city is destroyed in the summer when "Mars entre au Lion"; [35] Perse builds his in the time when "le soleil entre au Lion" (91). In this intertextual conversation, Perse continues Claudel's work, but at the same time supersedes him, at least symbolically. The competition that could not appropriately be articulated in letters is transmuted into literature where the narrator of *Anabase* replaces the destroyed city of *La Ville* with a new one, over which he rules.

---

[33] Paul Claudel, "Traité de la Co-naissance au monde et de soi-même," *Œuvre poétique* (Paris: Gallimard, Bibliothèque de la Pléiade, 1967), 149.

[34] Paul Claudel, "La Ville," *Théâtre* I (Paris: Gallimard, Bibliothèque de la Pléiade, 1956), 490.

[35] *Ibid.,* 466.

In the same letter where Perse praised Claudel's play, he also reported that a young military officer named Alain-Fournier (soon-to-be author of *Le Grand Meaulnes*) had brought him a copy of *L'Annonce faite à Marie* (723). It is likely that this play, steeped in the imagery of the Annunciation, triggered some of the biblical resonances in *Anabase*. The Annunciation story figures in any missal, and Perse would have been familiar with it from Luke's Gospel, but his thoughts may well have been sparked by reading Claudel's play or his *Cinq Grandes Odes*, whose third ode, "Magnificat," opens with the biblical words "Mon âme magnifie le Seigneur."[36]

The correspondence between these two writer-diplomats is a fascinating chronicle of Claudel's efforts–and Perse's resistance–to engage in religious dialogue. The spiritual wrestling match between them seems to have ended, not unlike Jacob's struggle with the Angel, in a draw, signaled by Perse's declaration in 1908: "Mais pour arriver au christianisme, je n'arrive pas d'assez loin" (717). Raised by a devout mother, educated at an early age by Catholic priests, and attuned to Christian imagery through his reading of the Bible, Perse felt himself too close to Christianity to experience the kind of conversion Claudel had undergone, while too distant to share Claudel's faith. His statement marks a plateau in their overt religious dialogue. But a more covert, coded conversation continues on a literary plane. Given Claudel's insistent seriousness about religion and Perse's irreverent revision of his elders, the rewriting of the Annunciation in a non-religious context, with Mary's response attributed to a male narrator, seems like an unmistakable signal–to Claudel–of Perse's determination to keep his distance from the convert's faith and to seek the spiritual, instead, in the everyday realm. Across half a century, the two writers remained apart on issues of religion. Perse resolutely sought and found meaning within the world, in a spirituality of immanence that is best summed up, retrospectively, by a verse from *Chant pour un Equinoxe:* "Dieu l'épars nous rejoint dans la diversité" (437). By contrast with Claudel's faith in a transcendent God, Perse's poems, like his life, are explorations of the diversity that exists in the world and of the spiritual dimension within the human. Claudel and Perse never resolved their fundamental differences in religious outlook, although their lifelong conversation would resume, two decades later, in the

---

[36] Paul Claudel, *Œuvre Poétique*, 248.

Poème à l'Etrangère, through the prism of the biblical story of Tobias.

Claudel and Segalen were recent visitors to the Orient. Behind them lurks a more distant predecessor, who traveled through China in the multiple roles of explorer, ambassador, and chronicler. For seventeen years in the late thirteenth-century, Marco Polo served the Kublai Khan, descendent of Genghis Khan, on diplomatic missions around the country. His shadow extends across Perse's work, from *Eloges* to *Oiseaux*. The poet owned at least two editions of Marco Polo's memoirs in French, dating from 1865 and 1928. In the prologue, the scribe explains that Polo remained with the Lord ("Seigneur") for seventeen years, serving as his emissary to many different countries:

> Et lui, parce qu'il était sage et connaissait les manières du Seigneur, se donnait bien du mal pour savoir et entendre toutes choses qu'il pensait devoir plaire au Grand Khan. Si bien qu'à ses retours il lui contait tout avec ordre. Et pour cela, le Seigneur l'aimait beaucoup et l'affectionnait.[37]

This description of Marco Polo's travels, news-gathering, and reunions with a receptive monarch anticipates the meetings in *Anabase* between the Prince and the wise man who reports on the kingdom.

Given Marco Polo's exotic travels, his verve in relating them, and his intimacy with the Kublai Khan, it is understandable that he would capture the imagination of subsequent travelers, especially those en route to China. In a 1917 letter to foreign minister Alexandre Conty, Saint-John Perse compared himself to "un diplomate vénitien" (813), in a clear allusion to his Venetian model. Throughout Perse's poems there are echoes of this pivotal text of the European discovery of China.

Traveling across the Tonocain province, on the border of Persia, Marco Polo came upon an exceptional tree:

> [. . .] l'arbre-solque, que les Chrétiens appellent l'arbre-sec. [. . .] Il n'y a pas d'autre arbre à plus de cent milles, excepté à un en-

---

[37] Marco Polo, *Le Livre de Marco Polo,* tr. A. T'Serstevens (Paris: Albin Michel, 1955), 67.

droit, à environ dix milles. Les gens de la contrée disent que c'est
là que fut la bataille d'Alexandre contre le roi Darius.[38]

In *Anabase*, the narrator's reference to the "lieu dit de l'Arbre Sec"
(107) embraces a network of allusions, from Alexander and
Xenophon to Marco Polo. Similarly, when he describes the burning
of a woman: "On fit brûler un corps de femme dans les sables"
(99), the terse reference probably alludes to Marco Polo's account
of Canbaluc: "Sachez que dans la ville on ne peut ensevelir nul
corps mort; les idolâtres les portent, pour les brûler, en dehors de la
ville et des faubourgs, en un lieu éloignée qui est désigné pour
cela."[39]

From Perse's diplomatic career in China, the exploit he most
buoyantly related is his evacuation of President Li Yuan-hong's
family after the coup d'état of 1917. In a facetious account to Conty, he describes how he was able to transport the legitimate portion
of the household, but did not have room in his car for the innumerable concubines (815). This folkloric account has an amusing an-
tecedent in Marco Polo's own rescue of the Kublai Khan's wife, a
gesture that earned him lasting esteem.[40]

One of Perse's stated ambitions was to remain in Peking as a
special advisor to the President, in a role not unlike Marco Polo's.
When the growing Chinese nationalism and a change of régime after World War I made this impossible, he abandoned the idea and
returned to Europe. Taking the longer route, eastward, like Phineas
Fogg in *Around the World in Eighty Days*, Perse followed an
itinerary charted by Jules Verne, one of his favorite childhood authors and one of the few he is known to have read outside of
school.[41]

Unlike the other writers—Marco Polo, Pierre Loti, Paul Claudel
and Victor Segalen—who had actually been to China, Jules Verne
had visited the Orient only in books and dreams, but for nineteenth-century readers he symbolized adventure. Long before arriving in China, Perse had already seen the Celestial Empire filtered
through the eyes of Verne, who himself relied on Marco Polo. In

---

[38] *Ibid.*, 96-97.
[39] *Ibid.*, 168.
[40] *Ibid.*, 70-71.
[41] Pierre Guerre, *Portrait de Saint-John Perse,* ed. R. Little (Marseille: Sud, 1989), 188.

Les Tribulations d'un Chinois en Chine Verne cites his Venitian predecessor when describing Peking: "cette mystérieuse Kambalu, dont Marco Polo rapportait une si curieuse description vers la fin du treizième siècle, telle est la capitale du Céleste Empire." [42]

Some of the most memorable pages of Verne's novel describe the temples and inhabitants, sights, sounds and activities of the imperial city in long enumerations that seem to prefigure the one in *Anabase*. While Verne never saw the capital, he went to great lengths to describe "la ville Jaune" (V110) in its specificity. Perse, by contrast, was there, but his particular aim in portraying "la ville jaune" (99) (without capitalization) was to raise it above any particular city and thereby suggest all empires and peoples, "toutes sortes d'hommes dans leurs voies et façons" (112, 113). Nevertheless, Perse relied in part on Verne's technique of accumulated detail. The heroine of Verne's *Tribulations*, transported on a wicker chair, wends through streets crowded with people engaged in myriad occupations (V110-112). Saint-John Perse leads his reader through the same landmarks and activities, complete with "l'homme à la chaise de rotin" (113). Verne's "orateurs en plein vent" (V114) find their counterpart in Perse's "grammairien [. . .] en plein air" (97). Verne's Peking includes a host of marginalized people: "manchots, boiteux, paralytiques, files d'aveugles conduits par un borgne, et les mille variétés d'informes vrais ou faux, qui fourmillent dans les cités de l'Empire des Fleurs" (V114). This underside of society also exists in Perse's city, with "le malingre" (97), "l'homme libidineux" (112), "l'embuscade dans les vignes, les entreprises de pillards au fond des gorges et les manœuvres à travers champs pour le rapt d'une femme" (113).

What is significant about both writers' portrayals is not so much the overlap of elements, which might be expected, but their common technique of accumulating details to create a mosaic. Verne seems to have been fascinated by the challenge of finding words to capture a diverse, exotic city. What other place, he asks within the novel, can offer such a variety of forms and objects? "Quelle cité même, quelle capitale des Etats européens pourrait offrir une telle nomenclature?" (V111). The word nomenclature highlights Verne's

---

[42] Jules Verne, *Les Tribulations d'un Chinois en Chine* (Paris: Hachette, "Grandes Œuvres," 1979), 108. Subsequent references are indicated with a "V" in parentheses.

vocation as a writer. In the abundance of his enumerations, he sought to capture the prismatic reality of a specific city. Perpetuating Verne's fascination with words, names and details, Perse has the last word by visiting a place that Verne had only read about: "et que le mort saisisse le vif, comme il est dit aux tables du légiste, si je n'ai vu toute chose dans son ombre et le mérite de son âge" (113). When the twentieth-century poet arrived in China, he could hardly help measuring it against the template of his childhood reading of Verne.

While Verne was handicapped by not having seen China with his own eyes, he could find consolation in his belief that language is as important as action. In his non-fiction history of exploration, *Les Grands Navigateurs du XVIIIe siècle*, he makes a crucial point about the relation between traveling and telling. As Verne explains, the French explorer Bougainville was the first to circumnavigate the globe, but it was the skill and charm of his stories that made him famous. If he is better known than other sailors, it is not because he did more but because he knew how to relate his adventures in a captivating fashion. [43] Such an assertion undoubtedly betrays Verne's own desire to justify his literary vocation, but it also highlights the tension between explorer and writer, deeds and chronicles, a dichotomy that Marco Polo resolved in his dual life as diplomat-commentator and that Perse also sought to reconcile.

At the heart of *Anabase* lies the vocational dilemma that haunted Alexis Leger in the 1920s, between statesman and poet. Inside the text, poet, king and statesman cross paths. The poet makes the announcement: "Et voici que ces Rois sont assis à ma porte. Et l'Ambassadeur mange à la table des Rois. (Qu'on les nourrisse de mon grain!)" (96). The Kings come to the man of letters, who offers them sustenance. Here, as often in Perse's work, grain and seeds suggest poetry, in their capacity to travel through the air and take root in new lands: "Et la terre en ses graines ailées, comme un poète en ses propos, voyage . . ." (101). A tension that pervades this poem is the narrator's dilemma between staying and leaving, governing and writing. He is on a threshold, poised for departure:

---

[43] Jules Verne, *Les Grands Navigateurs du XVIIIe siècle* (Paris: Ramsay, 1977), 107-108.

Etranger. Qui passait (91)
Pour une année encore parmi vous! (93)
Nous n'habiterons pas toujours ces terres jaunes, notre dé-
lice . . . (105)
Qui parle de bâtir? - J'ai vu la terre distribuée en de vastes
espaces et ma pensée n'est point distraite du navigateur (114)

In this debate between practical and spiritual action, governance and poetry, *Anabase* works toward the protagonist's choice of an artistic vocation. Various intertexts constitute a kaleidoscope of options for resolving the tension between diplomacy and poetic creation. In the classical world, Xenophon combined action and reflection as soldier and narrator of the flight of the Ten Thousand, participant and chronicler of the original *Anabasis*. At the other extreme, Plato polarized the vocations of poet and statesman and exiled the artist from his city. Through conversations with multiple ancestors, Perse meditates on the precarious equilibrium of statesmanship and art. In the beginning of the poem the narrator proclaims a balance: "Maître du grain, maître du sel, et la chose publica sur de justes balances!" (93): the *res publica* occupies its fair weight on the scale. But such parity between soul and state is temporary: "Pour une année encore parmi vous!" (93). *Anabase* is the crossroad where poet and statesman diverge into the two separate names, Alexis Leger and Saint-John Perse. At this juncture, in 1924, Perse opts for statesmanship, largely out of financial necessity, and ostensibly abandons poetry for the (foreshortened) duration of his diplomatic career.

Through the conversations that make up the fabric of *Anabase*, where Perse examines his place in the literary tradition, motifs of generation abound. The poem opens under the sign of birth–"Il naissait un poulain sous les feuilles de bronze [. . .] Il naquit un poulain sous les feuilles de bronze" (91). Throughout the poem allusions to life and death, fertility and sterility, paternity and genealogy are never far away. The Stranger who arrives in the opening song is, by definition, someone whose genealogy is unknown. The rest of the poem, by contrast, is threaded with allusions to lineage: father (99), mother (100), daughter (95, 103), son (97), sister (99) and "tant de familles à composer comme des encagées d'oiseaux siffleurs" (103). A preoccupation with ancestry weaves itself through the poem from beginning to end, as the poet-narrator grapples with

questions of chronology and with his relation to an inherited culture. This drama is fraught with violence: "la violence au cœur du
sage, et qui en posera les limites ce soir?" (97).

When the wind begins to blow in section 2, it heralds the beginning of a conflict: "Il vient, de ce côté du monde, un grand mal violet sur les eaux. Le vent se lève. Vent de mer. Et la lessive part!
comme un prêtre mis en pièces . . ." (95). In this highly visual image, the clothing scattered by the wind is compared to the dismembering of a priest. Such a dispersion of the mantle of authority
threatens the traditional elders and refutes their preeminence, suggesting the particular love-hate ambivalence that characterizes relationships in the poem: "Je vous hais tous avec douceur" (100). Even
the simplest bond between a child and a colt presages destruction:
"et le poulain poisseux met son menton barbu dans la main de l'enfant, qui ne rêve pas encore de lui crever un œil . . ." (101). Neighboring tribes are warned to be wary of this people because of its
brutality (103). The most anxious relationships lie within families:
"de telle familles humaines, où les haines parfois chantaient comme
des mésanges" (107).

On one level of *Anabase* the poet converses with ancestors
whose voices are often silenced, whose works are rewritten and whose
names are erased. This same process is mirrored by the narrator
who reduces previous inhabitants to dust, "des morts sous le sable"
(97), "là où les peuples s'abolissent aux poudres mortes de la terre"
(105). Destined to be forgotten, these men are "gens de poussière et
de toutes façons (. . .) ô gens de peu de poids dans la mémoire de
ces lieux" (94); the women of the land are "veuves criardes sur la
dissipation des morts" (109), survivors of husbands the poet has
buried.

The poet's tools feature a dialectics of oblivion and remembrance, sterility and fertility. The conquered land of *Anabase* is a
place without memory on which the Stranger/Prince/Poet can
found his own creation, "un grand pays d'herbages sans mémoire,
l'année sans liens et sans anniversaires, assaisonnée d'aurores et de
feux" (108). It is a virgin territory, "la terre sans amandes" (93), in
which everything will be new. Among the people cited in the very
first enumeration are the "flaireurs de signes, de semences" (94);
this is the poet's cohort, those who are adept at finding springs in
barren places. In this revised version of Eden, paradise is not a land
of plenty, but a desert the narrator can fill with his own words.

It may be every poet's anguish that he comes too late in time. The narrator of *Anabase* seems acutely aware of this and struggles with his fate, both in and through his poem. A preliminary victory comes in Section 10, when the storyteller succeeds in reversing time. Arriving at the end of the celebrated enumeration of human beings, the last of a prodigious inventory of people, activities, and talents, he suddenly becomes the first: "ha! toutes sortes d'hommes dans leurs voies et façons, et soudain! a paru dans ses vêtements du soir et tranchant à la ronde toutes questions de préséance, le Conteur qui prend place au pied du térébinthe . . ." (113). The storyteller arrives late but takes the privileged space under the sacred tree. He creates a new chronology in which he is the beginning, and a new geography in which he is the center, with the world in concentric circles around himself (113).

As judge and measure of past and future, looking backward and forward, the narrator assesses the principal repositories of culture: "les entrepôts de livres et d'annales, les magasins de l'astronome et la beauté d'un lieu de sépultures, de très vieux temples" (113). Collectively these libraries, observatories, cemeteries and temples represent an inheritance: literature, history, science, religion and family traditions. All of them will be left behind as the narrator looks ahead: "et par delà le cirque de mon œil, beaucoup d'action secrètes en chemin."

To begin a new lineage, the narrator must erase, bury, or supersede the past: "Aux pays épuisés où les coutumes sont à reprendre, tant de familles à composer [. . .] vingt peuples sous nos lois parlant toutes les langues" (103). Over this disparate geography, spanning China and Jerusalem, Babylon, Rome and many other sites of human energy and imagination, the poet must establish his own authority.

It may seem paradoxical that a poem whose theme is the silencing of the past should echo so many voices from the literary tradition, but the process of writing necessarily involves re-writing. Perse's own definition of anabasis as a "retour à la [. . .] commune Mer" (677) suggests that for a new work to be unique, it must wrestle, sometimes even violently, with the elders and siblings who would contest the poet's birthright or "aînesse" (93). The poem is the site of agonistic combat. In battles waged within the boundaries of the poem, the victory is linguistic, won through metaphors by which Perse makes the narrator first and central rather than last and peripheral.

Anabase closes under the sign of an irresistible Pied Piper: "je siffle un sifflement si pur, qu'il n'est promesses à leurs rives que tiennent tous ces fleuves" (117). He has become the leader whom all of nature follows. It is the predecessors who are disadvantaged: "Et paix à ceux, s'ils vont mourir, qui n'ont point vu ce jour" (117). Perse creates a new *Republic* with a poet as head of state, a new *Aeneid* whose ships are "plus hauts qu'Ilion" (98), and where a single hero is both conqueror and poet, Aeneas and Virgil. This is a story of a new beginning: the creation of a poetic kingdom, where the poet can rewrite genealogy, including that of Alexis Leger, in order to begin anew, without ancestors, as Saint-John Perse.

CHAPTER 4

THE IMAGINARY ATLAS OF *EXIL*

I N the world of Saint-John Perse, the promised land is sometimes a desert. This is perhaps nowhere more true than in *Exil*, the first of four poems in the exile cycle. From the beginning, the hero is alone in the most desolate surroundings, yet he sees himself not as a victim but as a monarch: "Où vont les sables à leur chant s'en vont les Princes de l'exil" (124). There is a strong sense that this exile is not merely endured but actively elected, as indicated by the narrator's declaration: "J'élis un lieu flagrant et nul comme l'ossuaire des saisons" (123). The poem thus opens under the sign of paradox; the concept of exile, usually associated with banishment and exclusion, is linked here to choice and openness: "Portes ouvertes sur les sables, portes ouvertes sur l'exil" (123). On the literal level, the poet refers to the actual setting of the poem, in a house opening out to the beach of Long Beach Island, New Jersey. But the openness has existential and symbolic dimensions. Roger Little may have been the first to see in that first verse a parallel to the Roman temple of Janus, whose gates were closed in periods of peace but open in time of war.[1]

When this poem was published in 1942, during Perse's exile from an occupied France, many readers saw it as a *poème engagé* of the Resistance movement, but the poet specifically discouraged this interpretation: "*Exil* n'est pas une image de la Résistance. C'est un poème de l'éternité de l'exil dans la condition humaine."[2] In a fur-

---

[1] Roger Little, "The Image of the Threshold in the Poetry of Saint-John Perse," *Modern Language Review,* 64, 4 (October 1969), 778.

[2] Entretien avec Pierre Mazars, reprinted in Jacques Charpier, *Saint-John Perse* (Paris: Gallimard, 1962), 207. On another occasion, Perse wrote "*Exil* [. . .] traite seulement de l'exil humain, de l'exil terrestre, sous toutes ses formes" (553).

ther effort to refute what he claimed were erroneous rapproche-
ments to World War II, Perse elucidated the poem's first stanza by
explaining that the glass house belonged to his friends and hosts,
Francis and Katherine Biddle who, indeed, left a set of keys with
neighboring lighthouse keepers:

> Les clés aux gens du phare, et l'astre roué vif sur la pierre du seuil:
> Mon hôte, laissez-moi votre maison de verre dans les sables . . . (123)

Beyond these few references to a particular site, *Exil* unfolds on
a beach that could be almost any seashore.[3] But it is not without its
own special geography. The vague, deserted landscape seems, as the
poet claimed, to elude all historical and geographical references
(562), but this is only because *Exil* obeys other laws than those of
either an atlas or the travel brochures Perse collected. The poem is
best understood by looking beyond the scenery of New Jersey to a
landscape of prior texts. Its true map is not referential but intertextual. Its setting points beyond a specific site to cultural symbols that
are shared by author and reader. While *Exil* is undeniably inspired
by an intensely personal experience of exile, it is also and inevitably
set against a background of prior experiences and previous words.
Above Perse's sea and sand there hovers a seagull, "ralliant les
stances de l'exil" (126). His presence links the landscape of New
Jersey to a vaster map of exil and to all the "stances de l'exil" of the
human tradition.

Exil is built on ever-widening concentric circles of pain, going
from an individual to a specific country to the destruction wrought
by all wars. All three circles are present from the first stanza:

> Mon hôte, laissez-moi votre maison de verre dans les sables
> [. . .]
> L'Eté de gypse aiguise ses fers de lance dans nos plaies [. . .]
> Les spasmes de l'éclair sont pour le ravissement des Princes
> en Tauride (123)

In the center is the first-person narrator, referring to *my host.* The
next circle embraces *our wounds,* which are not only the narrator's
but those of a broader community of victims. Across the poem, the

---

[3] Henriette Levillain sees Guadeloupe in the shore of *Exil.* "Le Versant de la
Guadeloupe: L'Amérique," *Antillanité et Universalité,* ed. H. Levillain, M. Sacotte
(Paris: Editions Caribéennes, 1988), 164-166.

sufferings of an individual and a nation are elevated to universality through classical and mythological allusions. The world of Greek tragedy is ushered in through Euripides' Princes of Tauris, the place where Iphigenia was to have been sacrificed. [4] In the same strophe, the "dieu fumant" (123) points to the mythological universe of Mars, the God of War, who rose from his asbestos bed and brought to earth the perils of fire and destruction.

Alongside the classical and mythological allusions of *Exil* are references to sacred texts that contribute another dimension to the suffering. The "saintes écritures" (125), the "grands Livres" (126), and the "peuples en exode" (126) underscore the precedent of Old Testament exile which resonates with the poem's title, landscape and themes. Exodus, Euripides and Mars link the specific political circumstances of 1940s France to wider precedents from tragedy, mythology and religion.

The chorus of *Exil* is large, but it is dominated by one individual. Naturally, he is not named, but the poem's signature, *Long Beach Island (New Jersey), 1941,* offers a clue to his identity, for here, as elsewhere in Perse's poetry, the place name is more than a simple geographic indicator; it is charged with poetic resonance. At first glance, the parenthetical reference to New Jersey might appear redundant, since none of Perse's other exile poems specify a state, but the name plays a vital role in the intertextual atlas of the poem, providing a "semantic depth"[5] that extends well beyond the simple mention of a place. While signaling an objective reality, it also evokes a subjective one and gives a disproportionate power to this site by evoking another cultural tradition.

The geographical and biographical nexus of the poem brings an exiled poet-diplomat to the beach of a coastal island, where he hears the sound of waves and the inner voice of his own struggle to compose "un grand poème né de rien" (124). It is revealing to superimpose another configuration upon this ensemble, one that belongs to an earlier poet-diplomat, also in exile from France in an English-speaking land, not in New Jersey but on the island of Jersey. He is, of course, Victor Hugo, who spent the years 1852 to 1855 on that Anglo-Normand Channel island before settling in

---

    [4] Saint-John Perse, *Exil,* ed. R. Little (London: Athlone, 1995), 90.
    [5] J. Nicholas Entrikin, *The Betweenness of Place: Towards a Geography of Modernity* (London: Macmillan Education Ltd., 1991), 55.

Guernsey for fifteen more years of exile, until his triumphant return to France in 1870, after the fall of the Second Empire. Many of Hugo's poems from the *Châtiments* and *Contemplations* were composed during his years on Jersey. Striking parallels between the political and geographic circumstances of these two great poet-diplomats invite us to reflect on the links between them.

The toponymic similarity between Jersey and New Jersey is coincidental in the first instance but not without repercussions for a writer who is deeply involved in the meanings and connotations of words. To a twentieth-century French poet this overlap constituted a bridge to that near-legendary predecessor a century earlier. (Before Hugo, another eminent French writer-diplomat, François René de Chateaubriand, had also been exiled on Jersey, in the wake of the French Revolution. He spent four months on the island before going on to London for the remaining eight years of his exile.) Both Hugo and Perse ultimately waited some eighteen years before returning to France. The ties between them offer a privileged access to *Exil*.

For any French poet of the late nineteenth or early twentieth century, Victor Hugo represented a formidable ancestor of almost mythic stature. Perse's library contains numerous and much-underlined volumes of Hugo's works. Among his papers, he also saved, perhaps from an actual visit, an annotated brochure of Hauteville House, Hugo's home in Guernsey, along with three postcards, including a view of the writer's study that looks surprisingly like Perse's own room in Giens. Actual references to Hugo are rare in Perse's letters, and almost always negative, making them all the more revealing for their critiques. A characteristic assessment is the one he claimed to share with André Gide:

> Hugo, en somme, né poète, c'est-à-dire accessible malgré lui aux sources secrètes du subconscient, s'était aveuglément perdu, et, avec lui, avait perdu le Romantisme français, dans le verbalisme et la cécité, pour avoir sacrifié le mystère poétique à la conquête extérieure du succès et aux compromissions massives d'une grande carrière publique. Il nous avait valu une sorte de 'Perte du Rhône' du Romantisme, à l'issue de laquelle les meilleurs et les plus avertis avaient eu bien grand-peine à retrouver quelques brins du fil le plus précieux. (479-480)

This lucid inventory of Hugo's shortcomings did not prevent Perse from admiring the qualities and quasi-mythical stature of his illustrious predecessor. If he disdained Hugo's compromises, verbalism and rationalism, he nevertheless credited him with being a born poet. This ambivalence coincided with Paul Claudel's paradoxical affirmation that Hugo and others were "poètes de génie," but not "grands poètes." [6] No matter what ratio of genius or greatness one attributed to Victor Hugo, he was an ancestor who could not be ignored by any French poet aspiring to greatness or universality.

Claudel once claimed that a single plot pervades much of Hugo's work:

> C'est le Proscrit, un solitaire, un homme pour une raison ou pour·une autre éliminé de la société et livré au vent, à ces forces vagues, élémentaires et hostiles qui se donnent carrière au delà de l'abri humain. [7]

Claudel's summary also describes several of Perse's poems, especially *Exil*, where the protagonist is explicitly named the *Proscrit*, as if in direct lineage from his Hugolian forebear. The poem takes on deeper meanings when it is read as a conversation.

In the last section of *Exil*, the poet-narrator describes his effort to communicate across the vast distance imposed by exile: "ô pur langage d'exil! Lointaine est l'autre rive où le message s'illumine" (136). His words refer to loved ones who remain in France, but on a deeper level, that other bank–"l'autre rive"–might also suggest the shore of Jersey, where the poem finds a different kind of illumination. The dialogue between Hugo and Perse, initiated through the superposition of the two islands, is elaborated through lexical and thematic matrices that are common to *Exil* and to the poems of Jersey. Without seeking sources in the narrow sense, we can nevertheless trace implicit networks of transformations that lead from one poet to the other, from one island to the other, from one set of texts to another.

Perhaps the best way to follow these paths is to focus on one representative poem from Hugo's years in Jersey, in which the island is specifically named. Written at the beginning of Hugo's exile,

---

[6] Paul Claudel, "Introduction à un poème sur Dante," *Positions et Propositions I, Œuvres complètes,* v. 15 (Paris: Gallimard, 1959), 93.
[7] Paul Claudel, "Sur Victor Hugo," "Accompagnements," *Œuvres en prose,* ed. J. Petit (Paris: Gallimard, Bibliothèque de la Pléiade, 1965), 470-471.

in 1852, and published in *Châtiments*, the poem illustrates the constellation of elements that constitute the mythic presence of Victor Hugo in the French literary imagination. Whether or not Perse had this particular text in mind while composing *Exil*, he was acutely aware of the Hugolian precedent against which he, like any modern epic and lyric poet, was obliged to situate himself.

Hugo's poem, cited here in its entirety, is composed of ten stanzas of six verses. The *incipit* is also the title.

> Puisque le juste est dans l'abîme,
> Puisqu'on donne le sceptre au crime,
> Puisque tous les droits sont trahis,
> Puisque les plus fiers restent mornes,
> Puisqu'on affiche au coin des bornes
> Le déshonneur de mon pays;
>
> O République de nos pères,
> Grand Panthéon plein de lumières,
> Dôme d'or dans le libre azur,
> Temple des ombres immortelles,
> Puisqu'on vient avec des échelles
> Coller l'empire sur ton mur;
>
> Puisque toute âme est affaiblie,
> Puisqu'on rampe; puisqu'on oublie
> Le vrai, le pur, le grand, le beau,
> Les yeux indignés de l'histoire,
> L'honneur, la loi, le droit, la gloire,
> Et ceux qui sont dans le tombeau;
>
> Je t'aime, exil! douleur, je t'aime!
> Tristesse, sois mon diadème.
> Je t'aime, altière pauvreté!
> J'aime ma porte aux vents battue.
> J'aime le deuil, grave statue
> Qui vient s'asseoir à mon côté.
>
> J'aime le malheur qui m'éprouve;
> Et cette ombre où je vous retrouve,
> O vous à qui mon cœur sourit,
> Dignité, foi, vertu voilée.
> Toi, liberté, fière exilée,
> Et toi, dévoûment, grand proscrit!

J'aime cette île solitaire,
Jersey, que la libre Angleterre
Couvre de son vieux pavillon.
L'eau noire, par moments accrue,
Le navire, errante charrue,
Le flot, mystérieux sillon.

J'aime ta mouette, ô mer profonde,
Qui secoue en perles ton onde
Sur son aile aux fauves couleurs,
Plonge dans les lames géantes,
Et sort de ces gueules béantes
Comme l'âme sort des douleurs!

J'aime la roche solennelle
D'où j'entends la plainte éternelle,
Sans trêve comme le remords,
Toujours renaissant dans les ombres,
Des vagues sur les écueils sombres,
Des mères sur leurs enfants morts.[8]

The first three stanzas of Hugo's poem constitute one long sentence which enumerates the misfortunes of France. The nation's woes are articulated through a series of parallel grammatical structures introduced by the conjunction *since,* which is repeated eight times in the poem and five times in the first stanza alone. This accumulation of causal phrases builds to an unexpected crescendo, for the litany concludes with the narrator's surprising declaration: "Je t'aime, exil! douleur, je t'aime!" The last six stanzas recite all that the poet loves in his exile–paradoxical loves, since they include unhappiness, suffering, darkness, poverty, grief, and the desolate setting of his island. Hugo explicitly models his poem after a love song, singing the paradoxical praise of banishment: "Je t'aime, exil." Nine times the narrator repeats the verb *J'aime*, referring in each case to the circumstances of his exile.

The poem is a locus of many of Hugo's most characteristic themes–island, ocean and abyss, sea birds, exile, praise of liberty, resentment against illegitimate political power, the poet as witness and the immortal Pantheon of immortals. Together, these themes

---

[8] Victor Hugo, "Puisque le juste est dans l'abîme," *Châtiments, Poésie* I (Paris: Seuil, 1962), 514.

give a good idea of the Hugolian universe Perse chose to encompass and surpass.

"J'aime ma porte aux vents battue," declares Hugo's narrator a century before Perse's "Portes ouvertes sur les sables, portes ouvertes sur l'exil" (123). Beginning with this shared reference to open doors, the two poems have an interlocking system of thematic and lexical recurrences. Key elements of Hugo's text return, amplified and transformed, in Perse's poem, beginning with a rhythm of octosyllables at the very entrance to *Exil*, whose first canto contains seven octosyllabic segments that echo the rhythm of Hugo's poem.

A seagull figures prominently in Hugo's text as a privileged symbol of the human soul which can emerge from sorrow as a gull rises from the deep: "J'aime ta mouette, ô mer profonde." As we have seen, a seagull also hovers over *Exil*. It is not just any gull, but one specifically defined by his resemblance to an earlier though unspecified exemplar. Twice the poet calls him "la même mouette sur son aile, la même mouette sur son aire" (126). Perse's repeated emphasis on sameness–*la même mouette*–suggests a continuity with some unspecified past that we can only imagine to be as far as antiquity and as near as the nineteenth century.

On his shore, Hugo's narrator listens to the incessant sound of waves: "Des vagues sur les écueils sombres." Perse, listening to waves on his own island, accentuates once again the sameness and continuity of wind, wave and inspiration:

> sur toutes grèves de ce monde, du même souffle proférée, la même vague proférant
>> Une seule et longue phrase sans césure à jamais inintelligible
> ... (126)

Hugo closes his poem with a reference to the plaintive sound of the waves:

> J'aime la roche solennelle
> D'où j'entends la plainte éternelle,
> Sans trêve comme le remords [. . .]

The poet of *Exil* also records a lament, using the same word *plainte* and once again specifying its identity to an earlier moaning: "la même plainte sans mesure / A la poursuite, sur les sables, de mon âme numide" (126). Perse's three-fold insistence on sameness, in the repeated configuration of *la même plainte, la même vague* and *la même mouette*, links his poem to a universal and "même souffle" (126) that inspires all the great texts, from the earliest epic and biblical stories of exile to the nineteenth-century shores of Jersey and the contemporary beach of New Jersey.

One of the long-standing puzzles of *Exil* is the apparent absence of anger or political commitment from the poem, by contrast with the *Châtiments*, where Hugo's outrage is palpable and where he repeatedly denounces Napoleon III for dishonoring the country. When Perse dismissed political interpretations of *Exil*, especially allusions to the French Resistance, his contemporaries wondered all the more about how a diplomat and patriot could, in 1941, omit from his writing his personal plight and that of his countrymen.

One possible answer to this puzzle lies in the presence of Hugo as a palimpsest, informing *Exil* from behind. The precedent of the *Châtiments* allows us to understand why it was unnecessary for Perse to explain the misfortunes of 1940s France: Hugo's depiction of 1852 still applied. His vehement denunciations, encapsulated in the five-verse sequence of *puisque* constituted a preamble to *Exil* and presaged the plight of occupied France. Once again, "le juste" had been hurled into the abyss, rights had been betrayed, the country had been dishonored. It was not in Perse's nature to explain the reasons for his exile or to lament his plight in personal terms. Had he been tempted to do so, the latent presence of Hugo's enumeration would have made such explanations superfluous. There was no need to repeat the misfortunes Hugo had powerfully explained; Perse had only to continue the saga of a century earlier. He could thus begin, as he often did, *in medias res*, skipping causal conjunctions to arrive directly at the consequence: "J'élis un lieu flagrant et nul comme l'ossuaire des saisons" (123). For readers attuned to Hugo, causes decried in Jersey could illuminate results endured in New Jersey.

Long before the *Châtiments*, Hugo had already depicted poets as voluntary exiles: "Le poète sur la terre console, exilé volontaire, les tristes humains dans leurs fers." [9] This conception of the artist

---

[9] Victor Hugo, "Le poète dans les révolutions," *Odes et Ballades* (Paris: Chabrol, 1821), 23.

was deeply anchored in the French romantic imagination and understood to be a necessary condition for creativity. Against such a background, it was doubly unnecessary for the hero of *Exil* to explain his choice, since exile was a pre-condition, a rite of passage for his poetic identity.

Joining in the long tradition of "stances de l'exil" (126) from the Bible and Homer to Ovid and Hugo, *Exil* renews *la même plainte, la même vague,* and *la même mouette.* In this way, Perse places his poem in a historic dimension that is underscored when the narrator observes: "Plus d'un siècle se voile aux défaillances de l'histoire" (131). Through the intermediary of earlier exiles, Perse makes room for the voice of history and for those specific lapses of history–personal and national, past and present–which are muted at first reading. These include the drama of one writer and an occupied France. Anger is attenuated in *Exil*, but it is not absent. Instead, it is elevated to a universal plane and linked to all past history. The poem closes with a reference to "un pur courroux" (137) which prolongs all previous outrage against war and dictators.

If similarities of context and language link Perse and Hugo, the differences between the two poets are equally significant and offer a guide to *Exil.* Hugo himself, when reflecting on the literary tradition, once explained:

> Flot sur flot, vague après vague, écume derrière écume, mouvement puis mouvement. [. . .] L'éternelle poésie se répète-t-elle? Non. Elle est la même et elle est autre. Même souffle, autre bruit. [. . .] Non! ni décadence, ni renaissance, ni plagiat, ni répétition, ni redite. Identité de cœur, différence d'esprit: tout est là. [10]

In "Puisque le juste est dans l'abîme," to take a representative example of Hugo's Jersey poems, a personal voice seems on the surface to dominate. The pronoun I recurs ten times in eight stanzas, and the level of indignation is high. But the poem is surprisingly abstract, addressed to a series of personifications: "Je t'aime, exil! douleur, je t'aime!" The narrator goes on to extol the qualities he reveres: poverty, grief, misery, dignity, faith, virtue, liberty, pride, and devotion. In *Exil*, by contrast, the messages are directed to

---

[10] Victor Hugo, *William Shakespeare, Œuvres complètes,* v. 18 (Paris: Hetzel et Quantin, 1882), 126-127.

more discernible recipients, whether individual women or the inner demon of inspiration, whom the poet depicts as a monster. Hugo's text ends with the grief of mothers, mourning lost sons. *Exil*, too, ends with a mother, but this is a more personal tribute to an individual, left behind in France. The contrast between these two maternal allusions mirrors distinctions between the two poets. Hugo and Perse use the same word *proscrit*, but in Hugo's poem, it is an abstraction, a metaphor for devotion: "Et toi, dévoûment, grand proscrit!" Under Perse's pen, the capitalized *Proscrit* is a specific victim, narrating his story. An idea that is abstract in Hugo's rhetorical poem becomes painfully personal in Perse's reflective text.

Hugo portrays France in masculine terms, as a patrimony and a locus of geniuses:

> O République de nos pères,
> Grand Panthéon plein de lumières,
> Dôme d'or dans le libre azur,
> Temple des ombres immortelles [. . .]

This metaphoric vision of the homeland as a Pantheon is hardly surprising from Hugo. Readers of his *William Shakespeare* are familiar with the skyline of geniuses he considers his true patrimony. Strikingly different is the country Perse evokes in Canto VII–not a fatherland with a golden dome, but a window where two specific women, mother and lover, watch and wait. While Hugo's poem hails the "République de nos pères, / Grand Panthéon plein de lumières," Perse's poem ends in a conversation with two women, "deux ailes de femmes aux persiennes" (136) on a far-away shore.

This rewriting of Hugo's vision is symptomatic of Perse's longstanding ambivalence towards his (predominantly male) ancestors in the French literary tradition. While the author of *Exil* aspired as deeply as Hugo to enter the Pantheon of literary geniuses, his desire is communicated through different, though equally revealing metaphors. Beyond the themes of war and separation, *Exil* chronicles the anxiety of a poet in the throes of writing, and reenacts multiple ingredients from which this or any text is created.

The narrator's explicit project is to create a "grand poème né de rien, un grand poème fait de rien" (124), like the God of *Genesis*. But Perse was well aware that poems do not come from nowhere. The whole history of civilization, along with all the resources of the human psyche, participate in the genesis of a work of art. A propos of Victor Hugo, he defined a poet as someone with special access to the subconscious. In a letter to Paul Claudel, he stressed the need to "concilier irrationnel et rationnel" (1017). All of these elements fuse in the crucible of art. *Exil* documents their complicated alchemy in the episode of the horseback rider, surveying the horizon:

> Comme le Cavalier, la corde au point, à l'entrée du désert,
> J'épie au cirque le plus vaste l'élancement des signes les plus fastes.
> Et le matin pour nous mène son doigt d'augure parmi de saintes écritures. (125)

The words *signes* and *écritures* place us in the semantic field of written texts. The verb *épie* echoes the opening declaration of the poem: "J'élis un lieu flagrant et nul comme l'ossuaire des saisons" (123). The paronomasia of *J'élis / J'épie* brings together two antithetical processes which lie at the heart of literary composition. At one pole is the explicit goal of a work "né de rien [. . .] fait de rien," symbolized by the verse "J'élis un lieu flagrant et nul comme l'ossuaire des saisons"–a virgin place, without a past, where the poet can create a new poem. At the other pole is a kind of phylogenesis by which any new work recapitulates all of literary evolution, incorporating the "signes les plus fastes" (125) and the "saintes écritures" (125). The two opposing conceptions are juxtaposed in the landscape of *Exil*, which is simultaneously a wasteland and a cornucopia, a desert and a repository of all that has come before. The beach appears desolate, but is really buzzing with voices from the past and echoes of earlier exiles, all of which reverberate in historical, geographical, mythological and biblical allusions: the princes in Tauris, the painted horn of the altars, the family of the Julii, the pretorian tumult, and the myriad references that critics continue to elucidate.

> L'exil n'est point d'hier! l'exil n'est point d'hier!
> 'O vestiges, o prémisses,'
> Dit l'Etranger parmi les sables . . . (125)

Vestiges of the western cultural tradition litter the sands of the text. Perse's chosen place is indeed an ossuary to the extent that it contains remains of so many epochs and cultures. The tension of the poem lies precisely in the distance between its desired genesis *ex nihilo* and its actual encyclopedic phylogenesis.

This same tension is mirrored in the protagonist's on-going debate with his monster-muse. The inner voice of inspiration connects modern poets with a long tradition of writing and with the "gonflement de lèvres sur la naissance des grands Livres" (126). Any such connection is fraught with apprehension. The poet portrays it as a struggle with a formidable opponent: "Je vous connais, ô monstre! Nous voici de nouveau face à face. Nous reprenons ce long débat où nous l'avions laissé" (126).

On an anecdotal level, this inner debate pits the poet's need to write against his determination to remain silent. But his dilemma is related to a broader conflict between past and future, between an inherited tradition and a work to bequeath. On one hand, the narrator reveres the rich tradition of human deeds and creations, especially the quirkiest endeavors and individuals. His admiration is coupled with an equally strong reticence. While part of him hails the person who deals in "très grands livres: almagestes, portulans et bestiaires" (134), another part, undoubtedly the poet in him, resists the weight of past books. At the heart of *Exil*, as of so many of Perse's poems, lies a preoccupation about inheritance and filiation, communicated through a constellation of references that include:

> né/ é/s/ naître/ naissance, naissante (124, 125, 126, 127, 129, 130, 131, 137)
> famille des Jules (124)
> alliances (124)
> castes (124)
> inceste (128)
> épouse (129, 136)
> déshérences (131)
> ses filles et ses brus (132)
> femmes d'autre race (132)
> hybride (133)
> mère (134, 136)
> héritage (134)
> fils (137)
> race (132, 137)

These allusions to birth and genealogy signal the poet's ambiguous relationship to his literary ancestors, including Victor Hugo.

This particular relationship is summed up well in an article Perse clipped and kept in his library. With a vertical line he highlighted a passage that had caught his attention: "Et quand l'orgueilleux poète (qui s'imagine naïvement avoir fixé la poésie) ose déclarer: 'Après Victor Hugo et moi, je ne vois pas ce qui reste à faire avec le vers!,' c'est d'un concert unanime que les jeunes poètes lui répondent: 'De la poésie.'" [11] All his life, Perse remained one of those young poets proclaiming the future of poetry, despite the legacy of any who might believe there remained nothing else to write.

Exil ends with the word *race* and the epic call, echoed from Homer and Virgil, that the protagonist identify his roots: "Et c'est l'heure, ô Poète, de décliner ton nom, ta naissance, et ta race . . ." (137). For a text that grapples ceaselessly with issues of lineage–of individuals and texts–these might be read as fitting last words for the poem. They have illustrious precedents in classical epics. In Homer, for example, Menelaos asks Odysseus and his crew to tell their names, forbears and families (IV:60-64), while in Virgil's *Aeneid,* the hero tells the Etruscan king his name and race (X:205). *La Chanson de Roland* concludes with the same verb as *Exil*: "Ci falt la geste que Turoldus declinet." But not all readers have been satisfied with a last verse that trails off in silence, leaving unresolved questions. Fortunately, these suspension points are not the conclusion of *Exil*. They lead, both visually and substantively, to the true ending, contained in the signature: *Long Beach Island (New Jersey) 1941.*

Since the signature and the dedication to Archibald MacLeish are the only words the poet addresses directly to readers, without the intermediary of a narrator, they carry special weight. It is in fact through the toponym that the poet proclaims his race and rank. In a tacit allusion to the poet of Jersey, he recalls an illustrious French predecessor in exile and letters, and takes his place in the genealogy of Victor Hugo and of their shared and admired forefather, Chateaubriand. With the same place name, Perse also proclaims the uniqueness of the work at hand. Inside the poem, the narrator stresses the continuity of tradition and the sameness of *la même plainte, la même vague* and *la même mouette.* But on its margins,

---

[11] Henri Dérieux, "Démarches de la poésie contemporaine," *Mercure de France* 15:IV, 1934, 253. Fondation Saint-John Perse, dossier Hugo.

when the poet speaks in his own voice, his message is newness. In this proclamation of a *New* Jersey, Saint-John Perse joins the pantheon of authors in the long tradition of "stances de l'exil" (126) while at the same time allowing the Muse to speak, in French, from the shores of the New World.

CHAPTER 5

A POETICS OF THE NEW WORLD: *PLUIES*

W HEN Paul Claudel first read Saint-John Perse's exile poems in 1945, he noted in his journal: "On a un peu la sensation d'un avion q[ui] se prépare à atterrir au-dessus d'une grande ville. Etourdissement, manque de repères, confusion d'images, on est au centre de toutes espèces d'horizons en proie au virage." [1] Of the four poems in the collection, Claudel's description most aptly describes *Pluies,* whose difficulty and complexity readers are not apt to underestimate. The poem figures second in the exile cycle, although it was written after the *Poème à l'Etrangère,* which Perse placed last. Unlike that love poem which solicited unwelcome inquiries into the poet's life and the identity of the "Foreign Lady," *Pluies* was meant to be less personal. As Perse himself confided to his Washington companion, Lilita Abreu: "je défie bien cette fois que l'on viole rien de personnel, car c'est certainement l'œuvre où j'aurai porté le plus loin, spirituellement, ce qui me tient à cœur contre le public." [2]

Arthur Knodel singled out *Pluies* as one of Perse's most inaccessible texts: "I do not feel that any commentator has yet seized on the total configuration, the *gestalt* of the poem, that will make all the details fall into place." [3] In the decades since this assessment, few critics have taken on the challenge of finding the "total configuration" of the poem. And yet, paradoxically, *Pluies* is the poem

---

[1] Paul Claudel, *Journal* (Paris: Gallimard, Bibliothèque de la Pléiade, 1968), II, 513.

[2] Saint-John Perse, *Lettres à l'Etrangère*, ed. M. Berne (Paris: Gallimard, 1987), 86.

[3] Arthur Knodel, *Saint-John Perse* (Edinburgh: UP, 1966), 80.

whose context and composition we know the most about. Its genesis is chronicled by the writer, Charlton Ogburn, who was present
when Perse began the poem during a tour of the southern United
States as a guest of Attorney General Francis Biddle and his wife,
the poet Katherine Garrison Chapin (1115-1119). In Ogburn's detailed account of the journey, he recounts the fervent legal discus-
sions that took place en route to Wilmington Island, Georgia. He
relates the pilgrimage to a plantation on Sapelo Island, where one
of Perse's royalist ancestors settled after the French Revolution, and
the search for his tombstone, long-since covered by the sea. Above
all, Ogburn narrates the extraordinary storm over Savannah that is
said to have inspired Perse's sleepless night, during which he composed lines that would later become *Pluies.*

The poet himself confirms the core of this story in a lapidary,
third-person autobiographical entry for 1942: "Voyage dans le Sud
avec Francis Biddle, Attorney général des Etats-Unis: séjour en Ca-
roline du Sud et en Géorgie, où il visite d'anciennes plantations et
retrouve les traces d'émigrés français de sa famille, au XVIIIᵉ siècle.
Ecrit, aux environs de Savannah, le poème *Pluies,* qui sera publié
en Argentine et en Amérique, reproduit à Alger et à Paris dans la
revue *Fontaine*" (xxiv). This spare account omits most of the details, notably the rainstorm and the other travelers, but it does situate the genesis of *Pluies* in this voyage-*cum*-pilgrimage to an ancestral plantation, in search of family origins.

In one sense, *Pluies* is surrounded by reassuring signs. Its title,
dedication and signature–the elements belonging to what Gérard
Genette calls the "paratexte"–[4] suggest a familiar geography and a
specific moment in history. The title, *Pluies,* in its meteorological
meaning, denotes a common, everyday reality. The dedication to
Katherine and Francis Biddle, Perse's traveling companions and
close friends, seems a further anchor in an amiable time and space.
Indeed, their presence on the threshold of the poem suggests that
Pluies is one more link in a warm friendship, chronicled in Perse's
long correspondence with each of the Biddles about law, poetry,
America, human emotions and loneliness. The abundant legal vocabulary of *Pluies* makes it all the more fitting as communication

---

[4] Gérard Genette, *Palimpsestes* (Paris: Seuil, 1982), 9. Genette defines "paratexte" as those elements that accompany a text, notably "titre, sous-titre, inter-
titres, préfaces, postfaces, etc."

with the Attorney General in the language of his métier, while as poetry, *Pluies* is a communion with Katherine Chapin in the language of her art. The signature, *Savannah, 1943*, reinforces our impression of the specificity of the poem, composed in a designated New World locale, in a precise moment during a world war.[5]

But if these signals situate the text in an exact time and space, the poet takes pains on other occasions to stress the universal dimension of his work. Writing to Adrienne Monnier in 1948 to correct what he felt to be Maurice Saillet's misreadings of this and other poems, he condenses the work into a sentence: "*Pluies* [. . .] traite seulement du ressentiment général de la condition humaine et de ses limites matérielles" (553), as if one of his poems could plausibly have *only* one meaning! At least two others are evident. One is the poetic description of a tropical storm, from the arrival of the rain until its departure, leaving behind a glistening, fragrant landscape. Closely linked to this is the comparison of rain to a Muse, descending unexpectedly upon the poet, only to disappear as suddenly as it came. *Pluies* portrays a poet in the throes of creation, exhilarated and then dejected. These literal, philosophical and metatextual readings offer multiple paths through the poem, but none really resolves the tension we feel between geography as we live it and the poetic space of the poem.

If Paul Claudel felt a dizzying displacement of expected landmarks when reading the poem, this may be because *Pluies* obeys the laws of a very particular poetic geography that lies beyond meteorology and travelogue. Its true topology reaches beyond Perse's travels to Georgia and South Carolina to embrace a written landscape of the United States. Besides the American south that Perse saw and experienced in the 1940s is the land that had been depicted in prior texts. Voices from these works inhabit the poem.

The same paratextual signals that anchor *Pluies* in a particular time and place also link it to a long history of writing in and about the New World. The Savannah of the signature evokes a whole tradition of American literature of the south, both in English and in French, and, perhaps most immediately, Margaret Mitchell's *Gone With the Wind,* which was published in 1936 and became a film in 1939. Set in Atlanta, this work created an almost mythic vision of

---

[5] Steven Winspur, "Le Signe Pur," *Cahiers Saint-John Perse* 4, 1981, 45-63. Winspur discusses the signatures of each of Perse's exile poems.

plantation life at the time of the Civil War. Perse's modern pilgrimage to the "anciennes plantations" of Georgia, in search of his own ancestors, was a return of sorts to this century-old world. Perse alluded to Mitchell's title, many years after *Pluies*, when thanking Jacqueline Kennedy for retrieving a piece of iron grillwork from his grandparents' plantation in Guadeloupe: "Vous m'appreniez qu'il ne reste plus rien de la vieille demeure familiale sur l'ancienne plantation 'La Joséphine.' Comme il est bien qu'il en soit ainsi! 'Gone with the Wind . . .' Est-il un plus beau sort?" Enclosing a photograph of himself as a child at the plantation, he added: "'Gone with the Wind . . .' Lui aussi!"[6] Perse used the same terms when relating the incident in his autobiography: "'Tant mieux, tant mieux! Rien derrière moi! Qu'autant en emporte toujours le vent! . . .'" (1101).

As Saint-John Perse traveled through the South in the footsteps of familial ancestors, he was also following the French explorers, travelers, exiles and writers who had shaped and been shaped by myths and realities of the New World. Perse's library testifies to his own special interest in French settlers and visitors in America.[7] Jean Ribaut, Huguenot leader of the first French expedition in 1562, was one of his favorites. In the 1950s, when Perse was looking for possible homes in France, the property that most tempted him was Jean Ribaut's island, near Giens, owned for centuries by the explorer's descendants and, in a more recent past, by relatives of Perse's own family.[8]

Eighteenth-century French travelers in America include St. John Crèvecœur, the marquis de Lafayette, the abbé Prévost, and the botanist-explorer André Michaux. They were followed by Chateaubriand, Alexis de Tocqueville, Jules Verne and Paul Claudel, among others. The presence of French predecessors is palpable in *Pluies*. They inhabit the margins of the poem, like the people the narrator senses on the borders of his own writing: "Tout un peuple muet se lève dans mes phrases, aux grandes marges du poème" (146).

---

[6] Fondation Saint-John Perse, letter 7, 1 mai 1967.

[7] Among Perse's possessions in Georgetown was a 1941 article from the *New York Times Book Review* entitled "When Emigrés from Another Europe Sought Refuge." Among the notable émigrés are Louis XVII, whom some say was smuggled to America after his father was guillotined in the French revolution, and Joseph Bonaparte, brother of Napoleon, who came to America after Waterloo.

[8] These details figure in an undated letter to Mina Curtiss, presumably from 1956, now at the Pierpont Morgan Library, New York.

Among these presences, Paul Claudel comes first to mind, given his weight–as diplomat, writer and believer–for Perse, who once called him: "seul grand de mon temps, et seul investi pour moi de l'autorité lyrique" (1019). On their shared itinerary, Claudel seems always to have arrived first. He preceded Perse to China, then to America, and even to Savannah, where in 1928 he placed wreaths on the tombs of French exiles from Santo Domingo who may have been related to Leger.[9] Not only had Claudel already traveled through America but he had even composed a play inspired by the New World, *L'Echange,* which opens, like *Pluies,* under the sign of rain:

> Dis, Louis, toute la nuit il a plu
> A verse, comme il pleut ici, et j'écoutais l'eau,
> songeant à tous ceux qui l'écoutent
> A ce même instant . . .[10]

In the first verse of *Pluies* an oriental banyan tree metaphorically conquers the American landscape: "Le banyan de la pluie prend ses assises sur la Ville" (141). Like this curious tree whose drooping branches take root in the earth around them, the avalanche of raindrops seems to take root in the soil. Banyan trees are not unknown in the American south, but this one arguably grows much farther away, amid the flora of Claudel's *Connaissance de l'Est* and in his poem "Le Banyan." The link is heightened by the fact that Claudel and Perse are among the few to replace the common French spelling, *Banian,* with the more exotic, anglophone *Banyan.*

Perse's same opening verse contains "la Ville," title of the famous Claudel play he had praised in 1911 and cited again, half a century later in his notebook: "Rome illuminée (cf. *La Ville* de Claudel)."[11] The proximity of *la Ville* and *banyan* at the beginning of *Pluies* alerts us to listen for other echoes of Claudel.

---

[9] Charlton Ogburn alludes to Leger's ancestors, including his great grand uncle and namesake, Alexis de Leyritz, whose family settled in Baltimore (1117).

[10] Paul Claudel, *Théâtre* I (Paris: Gallimard, Bibliothèque de la Pléiade, 1956), 729.

[11] "Croisière aux Iles Eoliennes," *Cahiers Saint-John Perse* 8-9, 1987, 209. Catherine Mayaux discusses Perse's admiration for Claudel's early poetry and theater in "Saint-John Perse, lecteur de Claudel," *Claudel Studies* XXIV, 1-2, 1997, 110-116. The first verse of *Pluies* may also be a quiet homage to Rimbaud, whose poem "Après le déluge" begins: "Aussitôt que l'idée du Déluge se fut rassise [. . .]." The diluvian rain of *Pluies,* along with "L'Idée nue comme un rétiaire," and the word *assises,* echoing Rimbaud's *rassise,* suggests a tribute to Perse's admired predecessor.

A short prose poem, "La Pluie," also in *Connaissance de l'Est* relates the process of writing. On a rainy day, a poet works in his study: "j'écris ce poëme." [12] In *Pluies* Perse takes up the subject in greater detail, chronicling a poem in the making and concluding with a paradoxical lament for the poem that was not written: "qui ne fut pas écrit!" (153). Although the two poems share a kinship of title and subject, *Pluies* has less in common stylistically with "La Pluie" than with another, more significant work, Claudel's "L'Esprit et l'eau" from the *Cinq Grandes Odes,* which resonates across Perse's ode to Savannah.

In Claudel's poem the world is suddenly nourished by the "lait de la pluie." [13] *Pluies* opens with a similar "lait d'eau vive" (141). This water will vivify the people and landscapes: "L'argile humaine" in Claudel, "l'argile veuve" (141) for Perse. The earth is "bien chauffante, tendre-feuillante et nourrie" [14] for one; for the other it is "fumante au goût de venaison" (141). Both poems have metatextual dimensions. "Voici L'Ode, voici que cette grande Ode nouvelle vous est présente," [15] declares the narrator of "L'Esprit et l'eau." His counterpart in *Pluies* begins with a twice-repeated call "Chante, poème" (141). Both poems declare the sensual aspect of creation: for Claudel "l'esprit liquide et lascif"; [16] for Perse, "la rose obscène du poème" (141). Yet neither themes nor images are the most important links between the two poems, since both are rather commonplace. Ultimately, Claudel had most to teach by the very form of his prose poems and his odes, which are liberated from rhyme and advance with their own inner rhythms of sound and silence. "L'Esprit et l'eau" opens with verses of varying lengths, divided into segments of six to eight syllables. The first is short: "Après le long silence fumant"; others are longer. The word "Soudain," repeated seven times in the opening section, dramatically accentuates the contrast between the long silence of the first verse and the sudden apparition of a new spirit. Claudel's play on rhythms offered a model for effects Perse also wished to create in verses supple enough to express both continuity and surprise. A typical example

---

[12] Paul Claudel, *Œuvre poétique* (Paris: Gallimard, Bibliothèque de la Pléiade, 1957), 63.

[13] *Ibid.,* 234.

[14] *Ibid.,* 234.

[15] *Ibid.,* 235.

[16] *Ibid.,* 235.

is this passage of *Pluies* where segments of different lengths communicate both the immediacy of the lightning bolt and the continuous action of rain:

> Vienne l'éclair, ha! qui nous quitte! . . . Et nous reconduirons aux portes de la Ville
> Les hautes Pluies en marche sous l'Avril, les hautes Pluies en marche sous le fouet comme un Ordre de Flagellants. (152)

Echoes of *Cinq Grandes Odes*, as of *La Ville* and *Connaissance de l'Est*, are an implicit homage to the earlier French diplomat-poet who opened up French verse to new rhythms.

One of the most colorful characters on the roster of French visitors to America is Michel-Guillaume-Jean de Crèvecœur (1735-1813), whose biography is as varied as the permutations of his name: J. Hector St. John, John Hector St. John and, as he is best known, St. John de Crèvecœur. This native of Caen preceded Perse in the French diplomatic career, serving as one of the first French consuls to the United States and authoring three books. One is the fictional account of a voyage; the others, better known, are *Sketches of Eighteenth-Century America* and *The Letters of an American Farmer*. Fascinated by botany and horticulture, Crèvecœur created one of the earliest botanical gardens and lived a sort of Robinson-Crusoe existence, not unlike the one Perse claimed to lead during summers on Seven Hundred Acre Island. [17] Crèvecœur's *Letters* had an enormous impact in Europe, where they confirmed the dream of a primitive America that a writer like Chateaubriand would later translate into the exotic, lush landscapes of *Atala, Les Natchez* and the *Voyage en Amérique*.

Chateaubriand looms large, of course, in the literary genealogy of the New World. Both his writing style and his colorful existence attracted the poet of *Pluies*. [18] In Perse's library there is a heavily-annotated 1931 edition of *Atala, René,* and *Le Dernier Abencérage* along with a sextant, compass, scale and cup that Chateaubriand is said to have given to one of Perse's ancestors (1340). As with many of Perse's kinships, however, the admiration was largely tacit. The

---

[17] These frontier-like activities are related in a 1942 letter to Katherine Biddle (904).

[18] Perse once recited by heart to Arthur Knodel lines from the *Mémoires d'Outre-Tombe* to illustrate Chateaubriand's innovative style.

eminent predecessor figures in only one curious sentence of the
autobiography, where Perse's great grandfather, Paul-Etienne Dormoy, adventurer and sailor "avait connu à Paris M. de Chateaubriand vieillissant qu'il amusait de ses histoires d'Amérique" (x). By
this off-hand mention, Perse turns the tables on the great French
writer. The bard of Saint Malo, often known as *L'Enchanteur*, famous for his tall tales, is reduced to a passive listener, to be amused
and perhaps even enchanted by the poet's forefather.

If the creator of *Atala* is silenced in this anecdote, his voice can
nevertheless be heard in the Savannah of *Pluies*, with its echo of
Chateaubriand's *savane* and his much-anthologized, though ficti-
tious description of the Mississippi:

> Les deux rives du Meschacebé présentent le tableau le plus ex-
> traordinaire. Sur le bord occidental, des savanes se déroulent à
> perte de vue; leurs flots de verdure, en s'éloignant, semblent
> monter dans l'azur du ciel, où ils s'évanouissent. [19]

Chateaubriand's works offer numerous accounts of travels through
the American south, along an itinerary so ambitious that it borders
on the mythical. [20] His lush depictions of landscapes, fauna and native inhabitants figured in the cultural baggage of all *lycéens,* and a
twentieth-century French observer would naturally see America, at
least in part, through the eyes and across the pages of Chateaubriand. Master of a sentimental exoticism, the nineteenth-century
Enchanter created a series of famous storm scenes, situated in the
New World and functioning almost as set pieces to heighten the
psychological and emotional dramas they accompany. [21] Saint-John
Perse, while resolutely distant from both sentimentality and exoticism, especially in *Pluies,* nevertheless reflects these celebrated
pages. In one of the most dramatic scenes of *Les Natchez*, René's
bride, *l'Indienne*, holds vigil during a violent rainfall outside the
prison where her husband is held. A local resident rescues her and

---

[19] François-René de Chateaubriand, *Œuvres romanesques et voyages* (Paris: Gallimard, Bibliothèque de la Pléiade, 1969), 34.

[20] Chateaubriand could not possibly have covered all the terrain he claimed to
have traveled; his sweeping account, from Florida to Niagara Falls, necessarily relied on the writings of other explorers, notably William Bartram.

[21] The most dramatic storm scenes are in *Atala*, 61-63; *Les Natchez* 416-419;
Voyage en Amérique, 732-733, in Chateaubriand, *op. cit.*

takes her in: "Oh! pauvre Indienne, s'écria-t-elle, descends vite ici." [22] When, in *Pluies* III "L'Indienne ce soir logera chez l'habitant" (143), the enigmatic allusion may point to Chateaubriand's famous heroine and to his pioneering scenes of New World rain.

The list of French visitors to America also includes a famous cousin of Chateaubriand's, none other than Alexis de Tocqueville, who arrived on an official mission in 1831 to study the judicial system. He traveled around for nine months, learning about laws and penal institutions in preparation for his foresighted *De la Démocratie en Amérique,* which shaped French perceptions of America and American perceptions of itself. As Alexis Leger traveled through the south, discussing law with Attorney General Biddle and attending a trial at the Savannah court house (1117), he was retracing the itinerary of Tocqueville and other predecessors who had shaped French perceptions of the New World. Years later, in 1966, when Perse's exile ended and he divided his time between France and America, he complained to Mina Curtiss about the stifling atmosphere of French politics under General de Gaulle and claimed that he felt liberated, as well as more French, in the United States: "Je comprends de plus en plus ce qu'a pu être pour un Tocqueville cette atmosphère américaine face à la France du Second Empire." [23]

Like Tocqueville and other French observers, Perse sought to translate an American experience into French, to make the French Muses sing of the New World. This effort takes on a special character because his birth and self-declared identity as an "homme d'Atlantique" (xl) made him a "native," in some sense, of the New World he was exploring. Perse's exile from France marked a return to the American hemisphere of his birth and to the torrents that wash both the *savane* of Guadeloupe and the Savannah of *Pluies.*

Through Perse's pilgrimage in the footsteps of ancestors, both literary and familial, he sought not only his origins as a French writer in America but, above all, the sources of inspiration itself. *Pluies* is a genesis narrative, fraught with tensions between remembering and forgetting, writing and erasing, creating and destroying. As the poem opens, a violent rainstorm is unleashed upon the city.

---

[22] Chateaubriand, *op. cit.*, 419.
[23] Letter to Mina Curtiss, January 9, 1966. Pierpont Morgan Library, New York.

Swelling across cantos II and III, the power of the rain rises, quickens, and unfurls until its peak in canto IV. Then, as abruptly as it began, the rain subsides. "Le banyan de la pluie perd ses assises sur la Ville" (152). In this echo of the poem's opening verse, a single word, *prend,* is transformed into *perd.* The storm is over.

Through multiple images the rain is depicted as an ambiguous and even contradictory force, sometimes masculine, sometimes feminine, life-threatening but also life-giving. Its destructive power may even be its most creative, for by destroying what exists, rain makes way for the new. In a single canto the verb *lavez* is repeated twenty-six times, as in a religious or magical incantation. Rain, as Arthur Knodel has pointed out, is not the substance of poetry, but it is a necessary prelude, washing away the impediments–regrets, memories, or distant ideals–that keep us from living in the present moment. [24] The narrator imagines a purification of all textual memory, all traces of the recorded past: "terre abluée des encres du copiste" (149). Specifically, he exhorts the rain to wash away "tous les vélins et tous les parchemins [. . .] les plus beaux dits de l'homme [. . .] les phrases les mieux faites, les pages les mieux nés" (151). The presence here of "well-born" pages betrays the poet's longstanding preoccupation with the cultural tradition he has inherited. In this poem, as in earlier ones, an anxiety about literary ancestors is often conveyed through images of birth and lineage, ranging from the "argile veuve sous l'eau vierge" (141) to the "Semeuses de spores, de semences et d'espèces légères" (144). Frequent allusions to generation and genealogy communicate the poet's preoccupation with creation–whether sexual or poetic. The desire to create poetry is, inevitably, a striving for originality, in the deepest sense of the word, and for a brand-new language, like the one seemingly promised by the rain: "Une langue nouvelle de toutes parts offerte!" (144).

An extended vocabulary of sensuality and sexuality runs through *Pluies*, beginning in the opening verses where a hurried polyp "monte à ses noces de corail" (141). This leads directly to the "Idée nue comme un rétiaire" (141) of the third verse, where sword-like rains penetrate the earth. Within the imagery of sexuality one set of metaphors depicts the narrator's struggle to capture inspiration.

---

[24] Arthur Knodel, *op. cit.*, 77.

Here, the rain is feminine, a Muse who comes in the form of nurse-maids (142, 144), women in waiting (142), sisters of Assur's soldiers (143), the wife of Cortés (143), women warriors (143), helmeted women, sowers, dancers (143) and mestizos (149). Rain itself is a half-breed, daughter of sky and earth, intermediary between matter and spirit, human and divine. It intimates and even seems to herald a divine message. To the narrator's disillusion, there is no revela-tion, but the rain does restore and renew the human realm. While it does not offer a sustained exaltation, it helps us accept our earthly fate.[25]

A rhythm of tension, paroxysm, and release is common to rain, sexuality and creativity. Through parallel networks of images, Perse brings together the sexual and creative acts under the common "umbrella" of a tropical rainstorm. In all three, there are hopes for illumination and permanence that cannot be fulfilled, despite the genuine benefits and joys they do bring. After a time of intensity there is a disappointing return to normalcy. *Pluies* traces this arc and the narrator's reaction at finding himself once again on the hu-man plane after exhilarating moments of love and creativity.

Pluies, by its very title, implies a return to origins, inviting us to "remonter au déluge," to the time of *Genesis,* Noah and the flood, and a world where Adam could name all of creation. In a letter to Jacques Rivière, dated 1910, Perse defined writing as the art of naming (675). A year later he elaborated on the idea when confid-ing to Valery Larbaud:

> Je n'ai jamais aimé nommer que pour la joie, très enfantine ou ar-chaïque, de me croire créateur du nom. Pensez avec moi à toute l'extrême différence qu'il y a entre le 'mot' et le 'nom'. (793)

If there is a chasm between words and names, writers can try at least to bridge it. Like the Socrates of Plato's *Cratylus,* they can re-motivate the arbitrariness of inherited words and restore them to fuller meanings, linking them vertically to their etymology and hori-zontally to allusions and resonances of their context.

Among the different kinds of words, Perse clearly favored nouns. According to Pierre-M. van Rutten, his poetry consists of 48.9% nouns, by contrast with a 40.5% average for the French lan-

---

[25] Anne Berrie, "Une Lecture de *Pluies,*" *Cahiers du XXe Siècle* 7, 1976, 77-89.

guage. [26] Given this predilection for *noms*, in the double sense of nouns and names, we can understand Perse's poetics as a continuous effort to transform words into nouns and nouns into proper names. Throughout his poetry there are intimations of the power that can reside in a specific name. "Honneur au Prince sous son nom" (69) is the greeting of *L'Amitié du Prince*; "Ton nom fait l'ombre d'un grand arbre" (69-70).

When Perse was preparing the Pléiade edition of his works in the 1960s, he reworked one of his earliest, unpublished poems, *Cohorte*, expanding and improving this youthful text from the vantage point of a lifetime of writing. The original poem was a prosaic compendium of birds that Perse fortunately prevented André Gide from publishing in the *NRF* in 1911. Not surprisingly, the rewritten version of *Cohorte* is much improved. Notable among the additions is a meditation on the poetics of naming and an exclamation that was absent from the original poem: "Nommer, créer! Qui donc en nous créait, criant le nom nouveau?" (683).

Perse's fascination with names receives full expression in his 1965 tribute to Dante, which opens with a meditation on naming and anonymity: "Se lever aujourd'hui en l'honneur du Dante, c'est s'exprimer anonymement au nom d'une immense famille: celle pour qui le nom, le mot Dante, puissant vocable, tient la plus haute résonance au fond de l'antre poétique" (449). Perse suggests here that the very word *Dante* possesses a power that goes beyond the contingent: "Il y a, dans l'histoire d'un grand nom, quelque chose qui s'accroît au-delà de l'humain: '*Nomen, numen . . .*' imminence sacrée–frémissement d'âme dans le bronze et comme un son d'éternité" (450).

If poetry is, for Perse, the alchemy by which every word becomes *le mot juste* and every noun becomes, in a sense, a proper noun, it is particularly revealing to look at the status of proper names, which are rare in his work, but all the more significant. As he confided to Jean Paulhan, "Les noms sont pour moi choses vivantes." [27] In his poems we find few names, but much onomastic fantasy. The transformation of a single name can offer a paradigmatic example

---

[26] Pierre-M. van Rutten, *Le Langage poétique de Saint-John Perse*, published by the author, n.d., 79.

[27] *Correspondance Saint-John Perse - Jean Paulhan*, ed. J. Gardes Tamine, *Cahiers Saint-John Perse* 10, 1991, 78. Michèle Aquien explores the poetics of naming in *Saint-John Perse: L'être et le nom* (Seyssel: Champ Vallon, 1985), 41.

of the mission of poetry. And what better name to choose than Saint-John Perse's own pen name?

In a famous litany, the narrator of *Pluies* mentions "ceux-là qui n'ont point cure de leur nom dans les trompettes d'os . . ." (150). The poet, by contrast, was intensely preoccupied with his name during the period when he was composing *Pluies*. As he confided to Archibald MacLeish:

> C'est bien la pire torture pour un homme, de ne pouvoir, pratiquement, rien pour des êtres, pour des femmes, qui dépendent entièrement de lui, et pour qui son nom même est néfaste. (543)

In wartime, the diplomat worried that his very name could endanger his mother and sisters. But even before then, his name may not have been a happy burden. He once quipped to André Gide: "votre nom connaîtra la joie, quelque part, de ne signifier rien!" (768). This was obviously not the case of Leger, an adjective serving as a proper noun. Two of his best friends had names that could be extolled. Of Larbaud he wrote: "Les deux syllabes de son nom sonnaient un bel aloi au trébuchet des Lettres" (497); and later, "Fargue! . . . L'éclair du nom tient vive en nous sa trace" (507). When Alexis Leger traded his given name for a chosen one, he entered into a realm of poetic resonances like the ones he admired in others.

Widespread are the speculations about Saint-John Perse's pseudonym, whose mysterious origins continue to fascinate readers, despite (or perhaps because of) the poet's specific caveats:[28]

> Le nom choisi ne le fut point en raison d'affinités, réminiscences, ou références d'aucune sorte, tendant à rien signifier ni suggérer d'intellectuel: échappant à tout lien rationnel, il fut librement accueilli tel qu'il s'imposait mystérieusement à l'esprit du poète pour des raisons inconnues de lui-même, comme dans la vieille onomastique: avec ses longues et ses brèves, ses syllabes fortes ou muettes, ses consonnes dures ou sifflantes, conformément aux lois secrètes de toute création poétique. (1094)

---

[28] Roger Little has traced the affinity between Saint-John Perse and James Joyce's character Persse O'Reilly in *Finnegan's Wake. Etudes sur Saint-John Perse* (Paris: Klincksieck, 1984), 199-203. Joëlle Gardes Tamine, in *Souffle de Perse* 1, 1991, suggests an echo of the poet's childhood reading of Percy Saint-John, 17-24. Claude Thiébaut evokes Spencer Saint-John, author of *Haïti ou la République noire*, as another possible precedent for the name. *Souffle de Perse* 2, 1992, 30-31.

While the origin of the pseudonym is shrouded in a mystery that the poet was careful to maintain, its genesis is less pertinent than Perse's later efforts to remotivate it, long after it had been chosen. *Pluies* is one atelier for this effort.

The poem's title is a matrix of resonances. From the annotations in Perse's library we know how assiduously he read Charles Maquet's *Dictionnaire analogique*, underlining the many reverberations of a single, usually very common word. He owned two editions of this dictionary, published in 1936 and 1971. In the later one he specifically annotated the description of kernel words linked to myriad others by relations of synonymy, analogy, extension, derivation, nuance or detail. This predilection for exploring different associations can be seen all across Perse's poems whose very titles are kernels of multiple meanings. *Pluies* is a typical example. From the flood of Genesis to New Testament baptisms and purification, the poem is a foyer of biblical evocations of water. The "lait d'eau vive" (141) of the opening lines suggests a life-giving, nourishing water that links body and spirit. A constellation of religious images reinforces the spiritual nature of the water. Water creates "une fraîcheur d'haleine par le monde / Comme le souffle même de l'esprit" (144) and transforms the earth into a landscape of golden bibles (146). The rain is even seen as divine: "l'affusion du dieu salubre sur nos faces" (144). Underlying these images is the ritual of baptism and the unspoken name of the prophet and precursor of Jesus: Saint John the Baptist. In the poetic liturgy of *Pluies* the poet performs a special kind of baptism, a poetic re-naming, in which the Saint-John of his pseudonym merges with his biblical namesake.

The multivalent matrix of *Pluies* contains both biblical and mythological connotations. The title also beckons us into the world of Zeus, who transformed himself into golden raindrops to fecundate Danae and thence to father Perseus. (This is the Perseus who would later behead the Medusa, marry Andromeda and reign over Mycena.) Zeus, as seducer *par excellence*, god of thunder, lightning and rain, is ominously present in the seductive imagery of *Pluies,* beginning with the "noces de corail" (141) of the opening lines; the "éclair salace" (145); the "grandes aubes lacérées, / Au pur vélin rayé d'une amorce divine" (145); and that great flash in the sky: "la grande onciale de feu vert" (145). He is perhaps most dramatically visible in the precise reference to golden ovules: "Une éclosion d'ovules d'or dans la nuit fauve des vasières / Et mon lit fait, ô fraude! à la lisière d'un tel songe" (141). [29] Like Zeus, the rain arouses suspicion, especially about sexual designs: "Convoitiez-vous nos femmes et nos filles derrière la grille de leurs songes?" (148). Like Zeus, it is accused of "inlassables semailles" (152).

Among Zeus' characteristic attributes is a lightning bolt, reminiscent of the ones that figure in *Pluies:* the "beaux veuvages de l'éclair" (146); "Vienne l'éclair, ha! qui nous quitte!" (152). When the god appeared as lightning to Semele, she perished before giving birth to Dionysus, god of wine and laughter, who is also present in *Pluies.* He is addressed as the "Seigneur terrible de mon rire" in a refrain, five-times repeated (141(2x), 142(2x), 154), while the aroma of rain-soaked earth is likened to wine: "Et, flairée de plus près comme un vin, n'est-il pas vrai qu'elle provoque la perte de mémoire?" (141).

In the kingdom of words that constitute a poem, the writer is a kind of Zeus, with the power to accomplish and reenact exploits. Just as Zeus can father Perseus, the poet can father Perse. While the pen name may originally have been chosen because of melodic echoes or unconscious associations, *Pluies* is an opportunity, two decades later, to explore its implicit connotations. The poet remotivates his name by weaving a web of analogies around it and, in a poetic sense, giving birth anew.

The dual components of the poet's *nom de plume* are never explicitly written in the poem, but they exercise a power beneath the surface of the text. [30] *Exil* closed with the well-known exhortation: "Et c'est l'heure, ô Poète, de décliner ton nom, ta naissance, et ta race . . ." (137). In *Pluies* the name itself, Saint-John Perse, functions as a "puissant vocable" (449). This continuing pursuit of a name may in fact help explain why *Pluies* came to be placed second in the collection, immediately after *Exil,* since it enacts the action ordered by the preceding work.

Perse's onomastic quest took him to curious crossings. Through a kinship of names, Alexis Leger is linked to his predecessor, Alexis de Tocqueville. Another configuration pairs him with that earlier writer-diplomat, Crèvecœur; the path is short from St. John Crève-

---

[29] In Ronsard's famous sonnet, the poet also dreams about imitating Zeus' seduction of Danae: "Je voudrois bien, richement jaunissant / Goutte à goutte descendre / dans le beau sein de ma belle Cassandre."

[30] Michael Riffaterre would call this a "hypogrammatic" power. "L'Illusion référentielle," *Littérature et réalité,* ed. Roland Barthes et al. (Paris: Seuil, 1982), 105.

cœur to St.-John Perse, requiring the merest semantic shift from *crever* to *percer* and *percer le cœur*. For a French writer in America, the desire to be a new voice inevitably meant surpassing Crèvecœur and all the other French predecessors in order to begin a new genealogical tree. Here, the banyan of the opening verse is emblematic. Most trees are land-bound and even enchained, like the one in Canto VI: "un vieil arbre chargé des chaînes de la terre" (148). Offshoots depend on roots. But *Pluies* reverses this through the intermediary of a curious species whose branches and offshoots can become new roots and new trees. At the threshold of the poem, it is an appropriate metaphor for the poet's effort to create a new lineage and a new work.

At one point in the poem, the whole creative process seems to come to naught: "Et vous ne nierez pas, soudain, que tout nous vienne à rien" (152). *Pluies* appears, for a moment, to conclude under the sign of nothingness, disappointment and despair. The inspiration that accompanied the rain has ceased as abruptly as it came. The promise of exaltation and insight is dashed: "Promesses non tenues!" (152). But this is not the poem's final word or its ultimate meaning. In early versions, canto VIII ended with regret over lost inspiration and the poem "qui ne sera pas écrit!" (153). But Perse later transformed the meaning of the verse by revising a single tense: "mon poème, ô Pluies! qui ne fut pas écrit!" (153). This substitution leaves open the possibility of texts to come, for although the poem of that particular storm may not have been written–*ne fut pas écrit*–future works are not precluded.

T.S. Eliot wrote in his *Prelude:* "You had such a vision of the street / As the street hardly understands." Saint-John Perse had a vision of Savannah such as Savannah would hardly understand. The city of his poem is a place where arbitrary, inherited words are remotivated through etymologies, resonances and allusions. The real geography of *Pluies* is the poetic space where the poet can be both Saint John of the baptismal waters and Perseus, son of Jupiter's golden rain. It is a privileged locus where he can master time and space, capturing the transitoriness of inspiration and rendering necessary the arbitrariness of everyday words and names, beginning with the emblematic example of his own name. It is the place where he can follow in the footsteps of French ancestors, the silent figures at the margins of the poem, while at the same time forging his own path in the New World.

CHAPTER 6

NEIGES AND THE SNOWS OF YESTERYEAR

B Y its title, *Neiges*, and its signature, "New York, 1944," this
poem might seem, at first glance, very much anchored in a particular time and a specific New World site. But as with all of the exile poems, its cartography is more complex than that. The snow
that covers all roads and landmarks resembles a blanket of forget-
fulness falling upon the landscape and erasing all paths to the past.
Yet this distance is more apparent than real, for if the snow is a
force of rupture, it is also, on a deeper level, a privileged link to the
past. The narrator's contemplation of a modern city triggers a meditation about the past and about poets' ways of capturing the snows
of yesteryear.

Many clues about *Neiges* are already offered in its margins, in
the significant surrounding elements that Gérard Genette calls the
paratext.[1] From the beginning, *Neiges* announces a precise geography amid the skyscrapers of a winter's dawn. In the early 1940s
Perse witnessed the spectacle of a snow-covered New York and
kept souvenirs of the sight among the innumerable newspaper clippings in his dossier about America. These *New York Times* photos
of January 1941 depict the city by day and night under the first
snowstorm of the year. Since the poet was living in a New York hotel at the time and alludes to the "premières neiges de l'absence"
(157), it is possible that he conceived the poem during this first
American winter, only to complete it later.

---

[1] See Gérard Genette, *Palimpsestes* (Paris: Seuil, 1982), 9, and *Seuils* (Paris:
Seuil, 1987).

Although third in the exile collection, *Neiges* actually bears the latest date–1944–a dramatic year for a world at war and a poet in exile. On first reading, the paratextual specifications invite us to read this as a poem about a specific city, the Manhattan that Blaise Cendrars immortalized in his 1912 poem, "Pâques à New York." The narrator of Cendrars' work, like his counterpart in *Neiges*, relates meditations inspired by a stay in a New York hotel. But it is soon apparent that if New York triggered this poignant meditation, the poet has other aims than the depiction of a city.

The signature, "New York, 1944," may suggest a referential text, but the poem's opening verses offer a surprising contrast. From the beginning, we are ushered into a world of "choses insignes" (157) where "de tous les côtés il nous était prodige et fête" (157). The evocation of an actual city suddenly becomes a fantasy as poetry annuls everyday geography and offers a new reality with its own laws and logic. Against the backdrop of skyscrapers unfolds a spectacle where buildings defy the laws of gravity and seem to float, "dans l'oubli de leur poids" (157), in a mythical mid-winter night's dream where mundane realities like garbage are cloaked in a blanket as white as manna. In this enchanted landscape, Alice in Wonderland cedes to Snow White in a setting closer to *The Arabian Nights* than to modern Manhattan. A fabulous owl inhabits this fairy-tale realm, where readers happen upon events as unexpected as the dancing toys of the *Nutcracker Suite*: "Nous en dirons merveilles . . ." (157).

What kind of reading can reveal the laws that govern this land, or its logic if it has one? In Leger's 1901 letter to Jacques Rivière, he confided his dream of finding an ideal reader for his works, someone capable of accomplishing a return to origins, to "la commune Mer d'où l'œuvre fut tirée" (677). A work of art is nourished by this "sociolect" or common Sea, but it must forge its own particular language, in Leger's terms, its definitive and even cruel singularity. The reader's task is to see how elements borrowed from the shared language and culture become kernels of meaning capable of generating a new text. When we approach *Neiges* from this perspective we confront two such kernels on the very threshold of the poem. The first is the title which, while denoting the wintry climate of New York, is charged with innumerable connotations beyond meteorology. A second semantic kernel is the poet's dedication to his mother: "A Françoise-Renée Saint-Leger Leger."[2] These two matrices, mother and snow, are interlaced in complex patterns. Each one has numerous ramifications. They operate like the "mots-centres" that attracted Perse to Charles Maquet's *Dictionnaire analogique* and illustrate the process of crystallization by which the poet shuttles among different semantic fields of snow.

Perse once remarked, à propos of Léon-Paul Fargue's writing, that every page of poetry resembles a "tissu vivant parcouru d'un seul spasme" (518). This image of a living fabric applies equally well to *Neiges,* as the poet himself suggests by introducing weaving and looms in the very first verse: "les grands lés tissés du songe et du réel" (157). Perse weaves his text from multiple threads of images and associations, some of which are drawn from other literary works. The presence of these prior texts invites us to shuttle back and forth between the poem we are reading and those with which it converses.[3]

One of these works, dating back to the origins of French poetry, is François Villon's celebrated "Ballade des Dames du temps jadis." The specifically plural snows of *Neiges* recall the medieval poet's famous refrain: "Mais où sont les neiges d'antan?"[4] Villon left a lasting mark on French letters, not only because of his colorful life ·(complete with condemnation and exile) but above all because he helped forge the French poetic voice through his ballad form and lyric tone. A forefather of later French poets, he was an early figure in Perse's library, where there is a volume of his poetry, signed "Alexis Leger 1904 Pau." Much later Perse honored the medieval bard in his 1963 homage to Fargue: "Et qui donc, après Villon, pouvait écrire aussi simplement de soi: 'né a Paris, rue Coquillière . . .'?" (527). Villon's presence transforms *Neiges* from a simple evocation of New York into a pilgrimage to the sources of French verse and a quest for the "neiges d'antan."

---

[2] In the manuscript of *Neiges,* Madame Leger's name has the accent, Saint-Léger Léger, which is still present in the 1960 Gallimard edition of the *Œuvre poétique* but does not figure in the Pléiade edition, 1973.

[3] Michael Riffaterre describes this as a "dialectique mémorielle entre le texte qu'on déchiffre et ces autres textes qu'on rappelle." *Sémiotique de la Poésie* (Paris: Seuil, 1983), 128.

[4] François Villon, *Œuvres poétiques,* ed. A. Mary, D. Poirion (Paris: Flammarion, 1965), 59.

Villon placed his *Testament* under the sign of a double maternity–mother and madonna–as he prayed to the Virgin Mary for his
own mother:

> Item, donne a ma pauvre mere
> Pour saluer notre Maitresse,
> Qui pour moi ot douleur amere,
> Dieu le sait, et mainte tristesse;[5]

In a similar fashion Saint-John Perse pays explicit tribute to his own
mother and places her in the same biblical context. At first, the
dedication to Françoise Renée Saint-Leger Leger seems surprising
from a man who shunned biographical detail and studiously dis-
joined the civil identity of Alexis Leger from the poetry of Saint-
John Perse. Here at the threshold of *Neiges* he unexpectedly proclaims his genealogical links to the Leger family and calls attention
to his identity as son. But even in this gesture of filial devotion, he
remains a poet, for he attributes to his mother a poeticized version
of her name. Saint-Leger Leger was one of his own earliest
pseudonyms, but it was not Madame Leger's civil identity. When
Perse gives his mother this name, he sets up a network of associations related to birth and origins, both human and literary.

The maternal presence, inscribed at the threshold of *Neiges,*
turns this poem into a modern "Ballade des Dames du temps jadis."
The mother who was young and beautiful in *Eloges* (26) is now a
"Dame de haut parage" (160), with a medieval aura suited to
Perse's conversation with his fifteenth-century predecessor. The son
pays tribute to his mother in her "grand âge" (160) and to a *temps
jadis* that seems as distant as Villon's.

In Perse's well-known letter to André Gide, dated 1911, he bap-
tised his first collection, *Eloges,* and deemed the title: "si beau que
je n'en voudrais jamais d'autre, si je publiais un volume–ni
plusieurs" (769). In *Neiges* the poet continues this impulse toward
praise by rewriting his first collection to reflect the accumulated
wisdom and suffering of the intervening years. Separated by three
decades, *Eloges* and *Neiges* are joined by ties that are affective, linguistic and, more unexpectedly, visual, harking back to the world of
Guadeloupe.

---

[5] *Ibid.,* 82.

In the collective imagination, the Antilles are most often seen as lush and exotic, in colors from the palettes of Paul Gauguin or Henri Rousseau. What is thus surprising about Perse's early depiction in *Eloges* is the striking whiteness of its landscape. We expect Guadeloupe to be a "vert paradis des amours enfantines" (a verse Perse underlined in his copy of Baudelaire's works).[6] Certainly, *Eloges* does depict a lush Caribbean landscape, but what is less predictable is the luminous and even diaphonous nature of this "blanc royaume" (23) surrounding the narrator's childhood. In *Eloges*, green is present, of course (nineteen times), but white is also cited nine times in crucial descriptions. Mornings in the Antilles are bathed in white: ". . . Or ces eaux calmes sont de lait / et tout ce qui s'épanche aux solitudes molles du matin" (37). By a poetic alchemy, the ocean is transformed into reassuring, maternal milk, in accord with the entire atmosphere: "l'air laiteux enrichi du sel des alizés . . ." (12). It is as if the affective memory of a maternal presence and its association with milk transformed the landscape in its wake. White is also associated with other maternal women and the fabrics of female clothing: petticoats, muslins, white stockings. Of his grandmother, the narrator observes:

> je dirai qu'on est belle, quand on a des bas blancs, et que s'en vient, par la persienne, la sage fleur de feu vers vos longues paupières / d'ivoire (26-27)

The child's father and friends are also remembered as "de grandes figures blanches" (29). The realm of childhood is an "havre de toile" (49), a haven of wind and sails, inspiration and reassurance. The same word *havre* becomes a kind of refrain in *Neiges*, as the poet evokes "un havre de fortune, un lieu de grâce et de merci" (157). New York and Guadeloupe thus merge in a shared symbolism of protection by which Perse seeks to render his mother as nearby as she was in his childhood.

While snow threatens to erase all paths to the past, it ultimately becomes the conduit for memory. The "blanches fêtes" (158) of Manhattan recall the "blanc royaume" (23) and reassuring maternal presence of an Antillean childhood. The "Océan de neiges" (162)

---

[6] Charles Baudelaire, "Mœsta et Errabunda," *Œuvres complètes*, ed. M. Ruff (Paris: Seuil, 1968), 80.

of 1944, which is successively perceived as linen, feathers, dahlia, pearls, and a white rose garden, onirically joins the milky water of *Eloges* and a whole affective network of childhood memories. Snow thus becomes a mediator between two texts, two places and two eras. Instead of obliterating the past, it transports the poet back to his own "neiges d'antan" in the realm of childhood. Françoise-Renée Saint-Leger Leger links these two worlds, while at the same time measuring the distance between them.

The youthful narrator of *Eloges* proclaims his adamic power to name things and beings: "Appelant toute chose, je récitai qu'elle grande, appelant toute bête, qu'elle était belle et bonne" (24). The older, more sober voice in *Neiges* is no longer Adam but David. Like the Psalmist, he sings praise, but it is tempered by suffering and exile, by the growing weight of accumulated burdens and the larger drama of wartime France, portrayed as the "beau pays captif" (160).

Perse read and annotated the Psalms in his Crampon Bible, but several textual signs suggest that their presence in *Neiges* is mediated more specifically through the Christian liturgy. When the narrator imagines the steel mills of the Middle West as "cinglées de brèves liturgies" (158), his praise of modernity also points to the ancient rituals of religious communities chanting the liturgy at different hours around the clock. The comparison of snow to a "plain chant" (160) is an even more precise reference to the Gregorian music of these daily rituals. The poet specifically cites the "Livres d'heures de l'An Mille" (161). The Book of Hours, a kind of breviary for the faithful, is composed largely of Psalms, recited by Christians at specific intervals during the day. Such texts were present in Perse's mind at the time, as evidenced by a 1943 letter in which he praises the poet Yvan Goll, editor of *Hémisphères,* for his recent verses, worthy of belonging "sous la plus pure haleine d'un ciel de Livre d'heures."[7]

On two occasions the poet specifically locates *Neiges* at a precise moment of the day: "un peu avant la sixième heure" (157, 158), the hour of Lauds, the office of dawn. The service of Lauds begins, characteristically, by praising Yahweh, as in Psalm 147 for Thursdays "it is good to sing / in honor of our God–sweet is his praise."

---

[7] Roger Little, "Saint-John Perse à Yvan Goll: Huit lettres inédites," *Cahiers Saint-John Perse* 2, 1979, 117.

(Ps. 147:1). Then the Psalmist goes on to sing God's creation and compassion, enumerating the signs of divine power. Among them is snow:

> He gives an order;
> his word flashes to earth;
> to spread snow like a blanket
> to stew hoarfrost like ashes,
> to drop ice like breadcrumbs,
> and when the cold is unbearable,
> he sends his word to bring the thaw
> and warm wind to melt the snow.
>
> (Ps. 147:15-18)

In a biblical landscape where snow is almost as rare as in Guadeloupe, it is nevertheless present as a sign of God's power and of the force of his word. For a poet in love with language, and especially one who dreams of writing poems of praise, the Hebrew Scriptures are a supreme model.

In David's songs, praise is often mixed with lament as he evokes the tribulations caused by enemies and exile. Frequently psalms relate happy times in the past, pain in the present, and the hope of deliverance in a future that the Psalmist hopes might arrive at dawn. This same structure recurs in *Neiges,* where Perse incorporates praise and lament in a modern context of war and banishment. By entering into conversation with the Psalmists, through the intermediary of the breviary, he gives universal resonance to his own plight and that of his country. He assimilates a contemporary occupation and exile into the paradigmatic captivity of the Hebrews and echoes their demands for restitution of their land and help against foreign invaders.

The presence of the Psalms expands Perse's capacity to communicate pain and suffering and gives legitimacy to a rhetoric of supplication and lament that is muted in *Neiges* but present through ancient voices beneath the text. While the adamic song of Genesis was appropriate to the childhood of *Eloges,* the double register of the Psalms is more suitable to the complexity of *Neiges* and the narrator's trajectory from one to the other. Rewriting *Eloges* in another key, Perse conveys the pain he has endured between his lost Guadeloupe and a wartime France.

The mythological Hercules suffered burns when he donned the tunic that Nessus had poisoned. The poet seeks to assuage such pain by weaving a "linge plus frais pour la brûlure des vivants" (163). Poetry, in his eyes, can thus share in the healing powers of God, evoked in Psalm 147 of Lauds:

> Yahweh, Restorer of Jerusalem!
> He brought back Israel's exiles,
> healing their broken hearts,
> and binding up their wounds
>
> (Ps. 147:2-3)

Perse offers solace in *Neiges* by placing his mother's plight and that of all French people in a biblical context. Drawing upon the liturgical Book of Hours, he joins a long tradition of exiles and sufferers. At the same time, he initiates a parallel conversation with the New Testament, notably the angel's greeting to Mary at the time of the Annunciation.

Centuries earlier, François Villon listened to the Angelus on the bells of the Sorbonne, "Qui toujours a neuf heures sonne / Le Salut que l'ange predit." [8] This same angel is ushered into *Neiges* through a refrain where the Latin word *Ave* twice enters the text, "Comme un grand *Ave* de grace sur nos pas" (160, 161). Mary, the *Mater beata* of the Annunciation, is destined to be the *Mater dolorosa* of the Crucifixion. She is a model for all mothers, especially in time of war, when women await their sons "à l'ombre de [la] croix" (160). By comparing Madame Leger and all French mothers to Mary, Perse places their plight in an eternal context.

The contrast between the suffering woman of *Neiges* and the young mother of *Eloges* is one measure of the distance she and her son have traveled in the intervening years. On the map of rewriting that leads from one poem to the other, distance can also be charted by comparing two specific verses. The narrator of *Eloges* sings the hours in his own fashion as he praises morning, noon and evening. When he finds himself, once again, in morning, he concludes:

> Et la journée est entamée, le monde
> n'est pas si vieux que soudain il n'ait ri . . . (50)

---

[8] François Villon, *op. cit.*, 40.

Thirty years later, the narrator of *Neiges* observes:

> Et la tristesse est dans les hommes, mais cette force aussi qui n'a
> de nom, et cette grâce, par instants, dont il faut bien qu'ils aient
> souri (161)[9]

Between the laugh of *Eloges* and the smile of *Neiges* lies the wind-
ing path from child to adult.

All poets, Perse once claimed, are born "pour le plus grand
loisir, et pour le très grand luxe d'une enfance, chez l'adulte, à jamais irrévolue" (528). Returning to the past means regaining a time
when everything still lies ahead. As a time of perpetual beginnings
and the nexus of a thousand possible autobiographies, it is a privileged period to preserve forever. But to do so requires stopping
time and capturing Villon's snows of yesteryear. Impossible in Manhattan, as in Pointe-à-Pitre, this can only be done on a textual map,
where time and weather (merged in the French word *temps*) have
their own laws. The true climate of *Neiges* is esthetic. It is inscribed
on the whiteness of paper or canvas, in a place woven on looms of
dream and reality. Within its boundaries, the past is sheltered from
oblivion. If "Nos années sont terres de mouvance dont nul ne tient
le fief" (161), works of art offer at least the illusion of a haven.

In a landscape of written pages, skyscrapers forget their weight
and "une flore nouvelle, en lieu plus libre, nous absout de la fleur et
du fruit" (163). Exempted from the laws that govern time, this textual country is freed from the generative cycle that leads inexorably
from flower to fruit to disintegration and death. Art suspends the
cycle and offers perpetual flowering. By existing outside normal
generation, it arises from a kind of immaculate conception, like the
one announced in the "Ave de grâce" of the poem's refrain. But this
means that the work dedicated to the poet's mother ends, paradoxically, with a hymn to the one kind of lineage that can forgo maternity. The poem praises spiritual and artistic creation above biological
maternity and hence the son rather than the mother. In *Neiges,* a
poet-weaver takes possession of the shuttle that is used by women
in their domestic tasks, the "navette d'os" (163) and the "amande

---

[9] In a 1940 letter, Perse encourages Lilita Abreu to adopt a similar philosophy:
"Si tu pouvais mesurer tout ce que je te dois en ce moment, à tous les points de vue,
peut-être trouverais-tu un instant la force de sourire au milieu de notre souffrance."
Lettres à l'Etrangère, ed. M. Berne (Paris: Gallimard, 1987), 56.

d'ivoire" (163) of weavers. With these instruments, he creates a new kind of work that does not need women.

When praising his Guadeloupean childhood in *Eloges,* a young poet already exiled from his island, poses a series of questions: "Sinon l'enfance, qu'y avait-il qu'il n'y a plus?" (25). Or, again: "Enfance, mon amour, n'était-ce que cela?" (37). While the questions remain suspended in *Eloges,* they find some tentative answers in *Neiges,* or so we might expect from the narrator's exclamation: "ô toutes choses à renaître, ô vous toute réponse" (158). But how are we to interpret this parallel between rebirth and response?

François Villon asked many questions in his "Ballade des Dames du temps jadis," while refusing any other reply beyond the refrain itself. The poem proposes itself as the only answer:

> Prince, n'enquerez de semaine
> Où elles sont, ni de cet an
> Qu'à ce refrain ne vous ramène:
> Mais où sont les neiges d'antan?

For Villon every effort to capture the past leads back to the question itself. For his modern descendant this idea is amplified to suggest that the only way to capture the past is through art itself.

In *Neiges* Perse travels backward in time, to a distant era located at the origins of poetry, language and "locutions inouïes" (162), as well as to a more recent personal past. Dedicating *Neiges* to his mother, he affirms his identity as son and travels with her to the snows of yesteryear, to a time when she was young and everything was possible. He writes in homage, but at the same time he forges a filiation far more ancient. In this poem the "pur lignage" (160) of mother and son has repercussions well beyond the Leger family, for even as the poet acknowledges his sonship, he transforms his family tree. While inscribing his mother's presence at the entrance to the poem, Perse changes her name into an early avatar of his own poetic identity, *Saint-Leger Leger.* Giving her one of his earliest pseudonyms, he blurs the distinction between his dual genealogies as son and poet and assimilates her into the new poetic lineage of Saint-John Perse that reaches beyond François Villon to the New Testament and the Psalms.

CHAPTER 7

POEME A L'ETRANGERE: LOVE LETTER
AND GOGGLE

"J' AI eu tort de publier ce poème," wrote Saint-John Perse,
two years after composing this most personal work.[1] While
readers conjectured about the anonymous Foreign Lady and some
even claimed to know who she was, the poet expressed regret that
he hadn't, at the very least, published the poem in Argentina, where
Exil had first appeared, rather than New York. This tantalizing
poème à clef invites and even calls out for decipherment. Some of
the keys have been discovered and many doors have opened, but
there are still secrets among the conversations with "tant d'êtres invisibles" (172) who inhabit the poem.

The Fondation Saint-John Perse houses seven versions of the
manuscript, tracing its evolution as the title changed from *P Street*
to *V Street* to the *Poème à l'Etrangère*. There is also a typescript
prepared by Archibald MacLeish, Perse's friend and mentor at the
Library of Congress, along with letters indicating that the work was
composed during the hot Washington summer of 1942.[2] Arthur
Knodel has commented insightfully on all these documents, but it
was only in the 1980s that the mystery of the Foreign Lady was finally solved, by researchers working simultaneously on both sides
of the Atlantic.[3] Mauricette Berne, curator of manuscripts at the

[1] Saint-John Perse, *Lettres à l'Etrangère*, ed. M. Berne (Paris: Gallimard, 1987),
86.
[2] Letter from Archibald MacLeish, August 20, 1942: "Dear Alexis, Here is the
typescript of your poem. It is profoundly beautiful and I am grateful for the opportunity to read it." Fondation Saint-John Perse, with the manuscript of the *Poème*.
[3] Arthur J. Knodel, "V Street, Une première version du *Poème à l'Etrangère*,"
Cahiers Saint-John Perse 3, 1980, 45-70.

Bibliothèque Nationale, found her first, but a team in Washington, D.C., Jean-Louis Cluse and Sylvia Desazars de Montgailhard, soon arrived at the same realization: Perse's Foreign Lady was Rosalía ("Lilita") Abreu, Madame Adal Henraux, a beautiful Cuban woman with a magnetic personality, center of a brilliant circle of admirers that included artists, writers and political figures, Jean Giraudoux, Jacques Rivière and Léon-Paul Fargue. Edouard Vuillard immortalized her in his painting, *Madame A.S.H.*

Soon after this revelation came the stunning publication of Perse's letters to Lilita. Chronicles of love and discord, they describe the circumstances under which Lilita came to join the poet in 1941, spending two years in a small Georgetown house near his. Entries from her diary and letters to her brother provide her own commentary on the poem's meanings.

Armed with these treasures, Cluse and Desazars de Montgailhard brilliantly elucidated many of the landmarks that lie on the itinerary Perse traveled from his house at 3120 R Street to Lilita's, 3314 P Street.[4] Their discoveries made it possible to resolve many of the enigmas of the poem, to see how references to Spain, Cuba and Washington come together in a coherent pattern, and to understand specific elements of the poem, which is so deeply anchored in the shared setting and suffering of the two exiles.

The poem takes its place in a long and varied tradition of literature about cities that includes the Paris of Villon, Hugo, Balzac and Baudelaire; the London of Dickens; the Dublin of James Joyce. Perse was well aware of Joyce, who lived in Paris from 1920 to 1939 during the time when chapters of *Ulysses* were appearing in *Commerce* and *Protée*. A regular at the *Shakespeare and Co.* bookstore, Joyce was a protégé of Adrienne Monnier, who relates in her *Gazettes* how much the French public admired his account of Bloom's walks through Dublin.[5]

Joyce's Irish deambulation finds a parallel in Perse's American itinerary. On an early version of the manuscript Perse signed his poem "Washington," but he later added the reference to "George-

---

[4] Jean-Louis Cluse and Sylvia Desazars de Montgailhard, *Entre Amériques et Castilles: Lilita Abreu, l'Etrangère et Saint-John Perse*, Publications de la Fondation Saint-John Perse, Série Archives et Documents 1, Aix-en-Provence, 1987.

[5] Adrienne Monnier, *Les Gazettes d'Adrienne Monnier 1925-45* (Paris: Julliard, 1953), 215. Perse's copy of this book is dedicated "A Saint-John Perse avec ma fidèle admiration, Adrienne Monnier."

town" in an uncharacteristic movement toward specificity rather than greater universality. The result is to anchor the work in an even more precise setting and to give poetic resonance to a landscape Europeans might otherwise consider devoid of poetry. As he explained to Archibald MacLeish:

> Et ce poème, malgré mon horreur de toute poésie directe ou 'personnelle,' est malgré moi, dans sa transposition, tout impregné de ce Georgetown où je vis non loin de vous, où votre présence a pour moi tout son prix humain. [6]

Like *Pluies*, the *Poème à l'Etrangère* also belongs to a tradition of works about America. When the foreign lady evokes "tout ce bruit de grandes eaux que fait la nuit du Nouveau Monde" (171), her words recall Chateaubriand's memorable (and undoubtedly fictional) pages in the *Génie du Christianisme:*

> Un soir je m'étais égaré dans une forêt, à quelque distance de la cataracte du Niagara; bientôt je vis le jour s'éteindre autour de moi, et je goûtai, dans toute sa solitude, le beau spectacle d'une nuit dans les déserts du Nouveau Monde. [. . .] La grandeur, l'étonnante mélancolie de ce tableau ne sauraient s'exprimer dans les langues humaines; les plus belles nuits en Europe ne peuvent en donner une idée. [7]

Chateaubriand's contrast between Old and New Worlds is very much present in the architecture of Perse's poem, which is founded on the difference between the two continents and all that separates an exiled "homme de France" (169) from his native land. After referring specifically to the "Nouveau Monde" (169), the poem evokes the Old: "Et cette histoire n'est pas nouvelle que le Vieux Monde essaime à tous les siècles, comme un rouge pollen. . . ." (172). When the Foreign Lady laments that nothing in America can matter as much to her as "une clé d'Europe teinte de sang" (170), she regrets the distance between one continent and the other. The America in which she and the "homme de France" find themselves is not the idyllic landscape of Chateaubriand; their particular "nuit

---

[6] Letter dated August 19, 1942. Library of Congress.
[7] François René de Chateaubriand, *Génie du Christianisme*, I, v, 12, *Œuvres complètes* 3 (Paris: Krabbe, 1854), 89-90.

du Nouveau Monde" (169) is filled, instead, with unfamiliar sounds and languages–birds, bells and English words, unrecognizable to émigrés.

Three English words, "Alien Registration Act," stand at the entrance of the poem, announcing the protagonists' status as foreigners and the wide linguistic chasm between America and their homelands. English intrudes upon the poem in the form of a bird whose name changes from country to country, underscoring the poet's double exile from his land and his language: "cet oiseau vert-bronze, d'allure peu catholique, qu'ils appellent Starling" (170). [8]

At first glance, the American capital seems to be the antithesis of old European cities, with their layers of history and mystery. Here, in "l'Eté boisé des jeunes Capitales infestées de cigales" (167), one is less aware of tradition. In this young city, "Les sables ni les chaumes n'enchanteront le pas des siècles à venir" (167). The Foreign Lady perceives her neighborhood as devoid of history; the poet calls it a place "où fut la rue pour vous pavée d'une pierre sans mémoire" (167). But if these streets seem alienated from the past, like the "Alienne" (168) herself, Perse's achievement is to endow them with memory by inscribing them in a lineage of European writing about the New World.

By Perse's account, the work began as an amusement, but then evolved into a real poem. He called it "un goggle," referring both to face masks worn by underwater divers and to their more frivolous counterparts among multi-colored glasses. Elaborating on the definition, Lilita noted in her journal: "Des goggles sont de grandes lunettes de voyageurs sous lesquelles on peut se dissimuler et qui sont colorées en bleu, en jaunes [sic], en rose, des formes fantaisistes curieuses." [9] Just as tinted goggles color a viewer's perspective, so the lenses of the poem deform the everyday reality of P Street. Before our eyes, the landscape is transformed into a fantastic, underwater site. Like divers, Perse's protagonists wander around a submerged, silent version of Washington, feeling an exceptional weight: "Une éternité de beau temps pèse aux membranes closes du silence" (167). In the Foreign Lady's narrow, dark townhouse, days

---

[8] The starling and "les cris de martinets et toutes cloches ursulines" (169) recall T.S. Eliot's 1919 poem, "Sweeney among the Nightingales": "The nightingales are singing near / The convent of the Sacred Heart." One of the characters in Eliot's poem is a lady in a Spanish cape.

[9] Saint-John Perse, *Lettres à l'Etrangère*, 146.

are as bleak as night in a perpetual orangerie of lamps, even at noontime (171, 172).

In this poem the *sotto voce* of Chateaubriand is joined by another ancestral voice, explicit in the "sabre de Strogoff à hauteur de nos cils" (169). Jules Verne's fictional Russian hero, Michel Strogoff, was threatened by a glowing sword. It seemed inevitable that he would be blinded, but his eyesight was unexpectedly saved by the tears he wept for his mother. The presence of Strogoff in the poem is a salute to his illustrious creator. While Perse downplayed the role of books in his childhood, he did admit to reading the works of this extraordinary creator of islands and of Crusoe-like heroes. The Strogoff reference, he said, was a visual one, derived from an illustration of Verne's story. [10]

Like Perse, Jules Verne had ties in the West Indies, where his mother's family had been traders. Fascinated with the New World, he included America or its inhabitants in 23 of his 64 novels. [11] Beyond a shared Creole and American connection, the two writers also had a common friend in Aristide Briand. (The protagonist of Verne's novel *Two Years' Holiday,* whose name is spelled Briant, is said to be modeled after his homonym.) During the gestation period of *Poème à l'Etrangère,* Perse had Briand very much on his mind. As the foreign minister's closest associate, Perse was to deliver the keynote speech at a ceremony commemorating the 80th anniversary of his birth, an obligation that weighed upon him. [12]

During this period, Perse had other reasons to think about Jules Verne. Perse had long envisaged his relation to Lilita in a nautical metaphor. In one of his first letters to her, dated 1932, he wrote: "Je pense à tout ce que j'aime en vous et, qui s'éclaire parfois, à votre

---

[10] Pierre Guerre, *Portrait de Saint-John Perse,* ed. R. Little (Marseille: Sud, 1989), 188, 245. Roger Little, "Saint-John Perse à Ivan Goll: Huit lettres inédites," *Cahiers Saint-John Perse* 2, 1979, 119.

[11] Jean Chesneaux, *The Political and Social Ideas of Jules Verne,* tr. T. Wikeley (London: Thames & Hudson, 1972), 150.

[12] Perse explained his unease about the Briand speech in a letter to Lilita, dated March 15, 1942: "L'engagement que j'ai imprudemment accepté, pour la commémoration de Briand, m'oblige à être à New York le 28, un Samedi, pour prendre la parole à 2h 1/2. (L'heure la plus mauvaise pour moi, où je suis en ce moment terrassé après chaque repas et obligé de courir en hâte à mon divan, comme un sourd et un aveugle.) Je suis d'autant plus ennuyé que cette manifestation s'élargit de jour en jour, qu'on a déjà lancé une excessive publicité, et que l'on compte sur moi pour parler le premier et deux fois plus longtemps que les autres orateurs [. . .]." *Lettres à l'Etrangère,* 77-78.

insu, comme un beau fond de mer." [13] After Lilita moved to Washington, marine imagery continued, especially during the hot, humid summer. In August 1942, the poet lamented the miserable climate of the nation's capital: "aquarium vraiment trop mal réglé pour un ludion d'Europe." [14] Lilita borrowed the same image to describe her Georgetown house: "Les arbres trop penchés dispensent aux pièces silencieuses leur lumière verte d'aquarium et d'outre-tombe." [15]

In a letter to Katherine Biddle, Perse compared Washington to a fantasmagoric underwater landscape and his exile to a deep sea dive:

> Reprenant mon armure d'exilé, qui ressemble un peu trop à l'habit du scaphandrier, je crois mieux percevoir, à travers tout l'abîme du silence, la qualité des voix amicales que j'écoute encore à votre foyer. (901)

Later, in a 1948 letter to Claudel, he evoked his diplomatic career as a period of "servitude administrative, où j'ai vécu dans un scaphandre encore plus que dans une cotte de mailles" (1012).

Imagining himself a diver, the poet was a kindred spirit to Verne's protagonists in *Twenty Thousand Leagues Under the Sea,* who criss-cross seas in the Nautilus and explore the ocean floor in their underwater gear. One of the geographical oddities on the Nautilus' itinerary is the sea of milk, south of Indonesia where tiny glow worms give the appearance of a lactified ocean, like the milky summer of the *Poème à l'Etrangère,* "lourd d'opiats et d'obscures laitances" (172).

Among the many nautical sites in this Georgetown poem is the legendary Atlantis, which is twice named in the poem: first with the tramways "qui s'en furent sur rails au pays des Atlantes" (167), and then in the scent of abyss and nothingness "montant des fosses atlantides" (171). Plato described this city in the *Critias* and *Timaeus.* More recently, Verne's protagonists walk through its ruins in a memorable scene of their underwater journey. [16]

---

[13] Saint-John Perse, *Lettres à l'Etrangère*, 52.

[14] Roger Little, "Saint-John Perse à Yvan Goll: Huit lettres inédites," *Cahiers Saint-John Perse* 2, 1979, 113.

[15] Saint-John Perse, *Lettres à l'Etrangère*, 148.

[16] Jules Verne, *Twenty Thousand Leagues Under the Sea* (New York: Macmillan, 1962), 252.

After leaving Atlantis, the Nautilus becomes entangled in the almost impenetrable carpet of seaweed and plants that grow in the part of the Gulf Stream known as the Sargasso Sea. A similar fate threatens Perse's Washington trolleys on their journey toward the "ronds-points d'Observatoires envahis de sargasses" (167). As his streetcars head off "sur rails, au pays des Atlantes" (167), they intersect poetically with Verne's submarine on its way back.

Reenacting a journey toward Atlantis, Perse joins Jules Verne, sailor and literary ancestor, fellow son of the Caribbean and prodigious creator of new worlds. He also links his protagonist to Verne's larger-than-life hero, Captain Nemo. An exile *par excellence*, living under a pseudonym that means "Nobody," like his epic predecessor Ulysses who introduced himself to the Cyclops as *No One*, the magnetic Nemo is a Byronic figure, whose monogram reminded nineteenth-century readers of Napoleon.[17] The mystery of Nemo's name reverberates across Verne's novel. Such onomastic innovation was not lost on Perse, given the many poetic cryptograms of his own name and pseudonym. It is significant that the greatest mystery of the *Poème à l'Etrangère* lay precisely in the anonymity of the Foreign Lady.

In Verne's silent Nautilus, one melancholy sound is Captain Nemo playing the organ late at night to console himself. Perse's foreign lady begs a similar consolation: "un chant du soir à la mesure de mon mal" (169). The *homme de France* accedes to her wish, but in his poem the request itself becomes the heart of the song. *L'Etrangère* is thus a partner in its composition. Nemo's floating art gallery includes paintings by Velasquez, whose "hautes lances de Bréda" (172) stand guard in Perse's poem.[18] Madonnas by Raphael, Leonardo da Vinci, Veronese, and Murillo smile down from Nemo's walls. In Perse's poem these peaceful virgins are replaced by more sorrowful Spanish ones: "la Vierge du Toril" and "Votre Dame des Angoisses" (172), who serve as models of suffering. In fact, the narrator offers a panoply of predecessors in pain as a way of offering consolation to the Foreign Lady. Strogoff, who lived to

---

[17] Martin Green, *The Robinson Crusoe Story* (University Park: Penn State UP, 1990), 138.

[18] Pierre Guerre describes Count Henry Russell's cave in the Pyrénées where the young Leger found himself "dans la maison du capitaine Némo," with shelves of books in all languages. *Portrait de Saint-John Perse,* ed. R. Little (Marseille: Sud, 1989), 277.

see peace restored to his country, can give her hope, despite the glaring violence that oppresses Europe.

Another source of inspiration is Tobias, with whom the poem ends: "'Rue Gît-le-cœur . . . Rue Gît-le-cœur' chante tout bas l'Ange à Tobie, et ce sont là méprises de sa langue d'Etranger" (173). This is the biblical story of a blind father, Tobit, and his dutiful son, Tobias, who are known in French by the same name, *Tobie le Vieux* and *Tobie le Jeune*. Tobit, a Job-like figure, exiled and afflicted, yet generous to all, sends Tobias on a mission to retrieve silver coins that have been safeguarded for him in his homeland. For this long journey, he entrusts his son to the guide, Azarias, unaware that he is really the Archangel Raphael. With angelic intervention, Tobias kills a magic fish. Its potion chases the demon from his future bride, Sara, while its ointment restores Tobit's eyesight.

Perse might have remembered this episode from his biblical reading, although he did not annotate it in his Crampon Bible. But it is more likely that his memory was jogged by Paul Claudel's *Histoire de Tobie et de Sara*, published in the *Nouvelle Revue Française* in 1942, just a few months before this poem was composed. Claudel received his first copies of the *NRF* on March 21, 1942, and may have sent one specially to Washington.[19] Perse's assiduity in keeping up with Claudel's writings, as with all of the *NRF*, makes it likely that he read the play in the late spring or early summer of 1942, if not earlier in manuscript. Claudel's introduction to *L'Histoire de Tobie et de Sara*, dated September 10, 1938, suggests that the play was written several years before its publication. It was in fact a second rendition of the Tobit episode, which had already figured in Claudel's "Hymne des Saints Anges," dedicated to Gabriel Frizeau and published in 1915 in the *Corona Benignitatis Anni Dei*.

As a mentor, Claudel guided Perse's choice of a career. As a diplomat, he preceded Perse to the Orient, then to America, and specifically to Washington, where he served as Ambassador from 1928 to 1933. During that time, Claudel lived in the French Embassy at 2221 Kalorama Street, not far from the Georgetown setting of the *Poème à l'Etrangère*. Less than a decade later, Perse found himself once again in Claudel's wake. Years later when Claudel's journal was published, Perse annotated almost every page of his

---

[19] *Correspondence Paul Claudel - Darius Milhaud, 1912-1953, Cahiers Paul Claudel* 3, 1961, 246.

predecessor's activities during the years 1933-1955, including Claudel's Georgetown period. But long before reading the journal, Perse was engaged with Claudel's writing.

Textual clues serve as evidence that Claudel's retellings of the Tobias story shaped Perse's *Poème à l'Etrangère*. First there is the resemblance of genres. This poem combines the poetry of Claudel's *Hymne* with the dialogic structure of his play. Other, thematic similarities suggest that Perse engaged directly with Claudel's texts, and particularly with the more elaborated *Histoire de Tobie et de Sara*, without necessarily returning to the Old Testament.[20] Claudel transforms the biblical tale in poetic ways, elongating the time frame from three weeks to more than a year, accentuating the love story between Tobias and Sara, and elaborating the relationship between mother and son. These poetic revisions change the spare story into a dramatic play that coincides with Perse's preoccupations of the same period.

Claudel adds an underwater motif, for instance, that is not present in the Bible, and that merges with the landscape of Perse's poem. Claudel also dramatizes the love story between Tobias and his soul sister, Sara, symbol of the human spirit. This remarkable woman, haunted by demons and liberated by Tobias, bears a surprising resemblance to Lilita, as we come to know her obliquely in the *Poème à l'Etrangère* and more explicitly her correspondence. "Je suis la rose! La rose blanche et la rose rouge: Je suis la rose!,"[21] exclaims Claudel's Sara, as if she were a precursor to Rosalía Abreu, whose own name is encoded in the many roses of Perse's poem: "grandes roses d'équinoxe" (171), "rose de fer" (172), and the twice-mentioned "althaeas" (169, 171), whose other name is *roses trémières*.[22] Claudel's Sara is "le pétale extatique de la lampe qui brûle" (1255), like her counterpart in Perse's poem who lives in a dark house, "parmi le peuple de mes lampes" (169), surrounded by "un fruit de lampes à midi" (167).

Between Claudel's rose and Perse's Rosalie, there are other kinds of kinship. As Sara exclaims: "Je suis la ronce! Le paradis

---

[20] Marcel Proust also refers to this biblical episode in *Sodome et Gomorrhe* where M. de Charlus predicts that he will accompany his young friend Morel as Raphael guided Tobias. *A la Recherche du temps perdu* II (Paris: Gallimard, Bibliothèque de la Pléiade, 1954), 1073.

[21] Paul Claudel, *Théâtre* II (Paris: Gallimard, Bibliothèque de la Pléiade, 1956), 1255.

[22] Jean-Louis Cluse & Sylvia Desazars de Montgailhard, *op. cit.*, 4.

commence par la ronce. La ronce qui s'enlace à l'homme, à ses vêtements, à sa chair, et il n'y a plus moyen pour lui de bouger." [23] Perse's heroine also knows of thorns: "Peut-être aussi l'épine, sous la chair, d'une plus jeune ronce au coeur des femmes de ma race" (169).

In the biblical version of the story, Tobit is blinded by sparrow droppings that fall on his eyes as he sleeps outdoors. Claudel adds to this incident the sharpness of a scythe: "Dieu, par la faux de cette hirondelle, m'a retranché la vue" (1267). In Perse's poem a sharp instrument, reminiscent of Michel Strogoff's sword, is also responsible for "ce mal de la vue qui nous vient, à la longue, d'une trop grande fixité du glaive" (169).

One of Claudel's major additions to the biblical story is Tobias' filial piety, both to his father and his mother, Anna, whose role is expanded in the play. *Tobie* ends with a long plea on behalf of this elderly mother that recalls, or in fact anticipates, the tribute to Madame Leger that Perse would compose in *Neiges*. Another of Claudel's innovations is to enhance the role of Tobias' dog, who is present at crucial moments of the play. The dog finds his counterpart in the Georgetown poem, where the narrator's allusion to Tobias is immediately preceded by a reference to "ma chienne d'Europe qui fut blanche et, plus que moi, poète" (173). Friends of the poet understood him to be referring to his own dog, a spirited white husky left behind in France and much missed, but the evocation of the dog in this specific verse, rather than elsewhere, may have been triggered, at least in part, by the canine protagonist in Claudel's version of the Tobias' story.

One of Claudel's most poetic enhancements to the biblical story is a meditation about names that permeates *L'Histoire de Tobie et de Sara*. The Angel tests Sara by asking how Tobias should address her, so she will recognize him. Sara in turn has access to Tobias' secret name. This exchange of names finds an amusing parallel in the correspondence between Rosalía Abreu (aka Lilita, Liu) and her own Tobias who signed his letters variously as Allan-Maria, Allan, and A.

Claudel's references to names are often playful. When Anna envisages her son's departure on a perilous journey beyond the horizon, she protests: "Mais jamais, jamais, jamais, je ne laisserai partir

---

[23] Paul Claudel, *Théâtre* II (Paris: Gallimard, Bibliothèque de la Pléiade, 1956), 1255.

mon fils, mon fils unique, pour cette espèce de pays là-bas, Ragès, qu'on l'appelle, je ne sais quoi, Suze, Ecbatane, Persépolis!"[24] In fact, the dreaded Persépolis transforms Tobias by giving him a woman who will be his rose and a new name as well: "Il est parti, et le voici maintenant qui revient, et Orient est son nom!" (1259). By a poetic mimesis, Perse's trajectory mirrors that of Tobias. In his Washington-Persépolis, he finds the woman he loves and retrieves his poetic identity under the partly oriental pseudonym of Saint-John Perse.

While Tobias lies in filigrane beneath Perse's poem, another Claudel play is also perceptible in this song to the Foreign Lady. Perse's heroine may wear "souliers de bois d'or" (172), but she, or at least Lilita Abreu, could easily belong to Claudel's *Soulier de Satin*, with its global décor, poignant love, and mystical spirituality. This is how Jean-Louis Cluse and Sylvie Desazars de Montgailhard describe her:

> Non plus chaussée de satin, mais de crêpe et d'amarante, elle ne confie pas son âme à la Vierge du Pilier, mais à Celle, sanglante, du Toril, à la Vierge transpercée par sept glaives, les mêmes que l'on retrouve dans le prénom de la fille de Doña Prouhèze, Marie des Sept Epées. Elle partage avec l'héroïne de Claudel ses liens à la fois avec la France et le monde hispanique et cette vocation pour la souffrance et pour l'exil: toutes deux sont femmes de même race.[25]

Lilita's Hispanic Catholicism made her a new Doña Prouhèze, engaging with Claudel through his baroque drama set in Renaissance Spain.

In Claudel's *Soulier de Satin* the Vice-Roy declares:

> Il y a autre chose à faire d'une belle œuvre que de la copier, c'est de rivaliser avec elle. Ce n'est pas ses résultats qu'elle nous enseigne, ce sont ses moyens. Elle nous verse la joie, l'attendrissement et la colère! Elle met au cœur de l'artiste une fureur sacrée![26]

---

[24] *Ibid.*, 1234.
[25] Jean-Louis Cluse & Sylvia Desazars de Montgailhard, *op. cit.*, 15.
[26] Paul Claudel, *Théâtre* II, 734.

Claudel's stories of Tobias and Doña Prouhèze, like Jules Verne's tales of Strogoff and Nemo, play a similar role for Perse. Without copying earlier works, he converses with them in an on-going effort to expand his own world and to join a tradition that includes Verne, Claudel and others. This genealogical preoccupation is foregrounded in explicit references to lineage, as when the Foreign Lady evokes "les femmes de ma race" (169) or the narrator praises her as "grande par le cœur et par le cri de votre race!" (172). Perse's consciousness of class and race also reaches outside his poetry into letters, as when he exhorts Lilita not to "faire défaut à ta naissance et à ta race."[27]

In his correspondence with Lilita and others, the recurrent expressions "pur race" and "pur sang"[28] testify to a concern with racial purity in this Antillean who grew up surrounded by mixed races. By insisting, further, on his own kinship with Lilita, Perse also gives himself the status of *pur sang*. At the same time, by insisting on his uncanny resemblance to this soul sister, he raises the disquieting suspicion that he might be a "monstrueux semblable"[29] engaged in a relationship that seems almost incestuous: "cette étrange alliance, bien mieux, [. . .] cette étrange 'alliage,' qui nous fait incestueux."[30] Years later, in one of the last letters to Lilita, dated July 4, 1949, Perse continues to talk of "cet étrange lien secret qui est le lien d'Allan et Liu."[31]

The poignant and complicated love between "Allan" and "Liu" finds expression in their correspondence and in the most elaborate epistle of all, the *Poème* itself. Its thrice-repeated refrain is sung first by the Foreign Lady, then echoed by the church bells and finally by the angel Raphael: "Rue Gît-le-cœur" (168, 170, 173). This street is fundamental to the cartography of the poem. Impossible to locate on any Washington map, it belongs to a wider atlas of exile and love and accentuates the difference between Old and New Worlds. For the émigrés, P Street, like every other Washington thoroughfare, is paved with stones devoid of memory. By contrast, an old passageway of historic Paris typifies all the accumulated his-

---

[27] Saint-John Perse, *Lettres à l'Etrangère*, 64.
[28] *Ibid.*, 92, 118.
[29] *Ibid.*, 114.
[30] *Ibid.*, 64.
[31] *Ibid.*, 127.

tory embedded in European landscapes. The distance from P Street to the Rue Gît-le-cœur is unbridgeable in time of war, but if the poet cannot take his Lady back to Paris, he can, at least, make her sorrow resonate in a wider context. When her words are echoed by the bells and the angel Raphael, they acquire a universality that is the poet's true gift to her.

Rue Gît-le-cœur also plays a role in the *carte du tendre* of this disguised love poem, where the word "heart" makes it an apt refrain. In a letter to Lilita, dated 1940, Perse alludes to the omission of this word from their relationship and "le tabou que nous mettons l'un et l'autre sur ce mot." [32] The word *cœur* is banished from their vocabulary, but Perse cleverly reintroduces it into their discourse by making *Gît-le-cœur* the pivotal refrain of his poem. [33] This evocative street highlights the difficulties of language, for it is associated, in the poem, with misperceptions:

> 'Rue Gît-le-cœur . . . Rue Gît-le-cœur. . .' chante tout bas l'Alienne sous ses lampes, et ce sont là méprises de sa langue d'Etrangère. (168)
> 'Rue Gît-le-cœur . . . Rue Gît-le-cœur. . .' chantent tout bas les cloches en exil, et ce sont là méprises de leur langue d'étrangères. (170)
> 'Rue Gît-le-cœur . . . Rue Gît-le-cœur. . .' chante tout bas l'Ange à Tobie, et ce sont là méprises de sa langue d'Etranger. (173)

A poem built on misunderstandings and addressed to an anonymous woman naturally generates concentric circles of mystery. These are heightened by the protagonists' sibylline surroundings. The narrator goes off, "sifflant mon peuple de Sibylles" (172), while, at the heroine's door, "comme un nid de Sibylles, l'abîme enfante ses merveilles: lucioles" (171). In this atmosphere of enigmas, the poem is best approached obliquely, through intertexts that convey the unsaid and unsayable. Perse's conversations with Verne and Claudel extend the boundaries of the poem and its capacity to

---

[32] *Ibid.*, 64.
[33] The word *cœur* recurs twice in a 1942 letter, after Lilita's departure from Washington: "Je pense chaque jour à toi et mon cœur se serre, au fond de mon intolérable tramway, chaque fois que je passe devant ce malheureux P Street où tu as, si déraisonnablement, sacrifié ta santé à ton cœur." *Lettres à l'Etrangère*, 78-79.

evoke love and war, filial piety and quiet hope. The voices of these predecessors allow Perse to say more than he does: more about love than it was in his nature to say; more about hope than it was realistic to believe in 1942.

Tobias and the angel offer a lesson in optimism amid the wartime bleakness. In the biblical narrative and even more expansively in Claudel's play, exile, suffering and blindness give way to reunion, joy and sight. The jubilant homecoming of son, daughter-in-law and future grandchild brings abundant riches and restored vision. In the last verse of Perse's poem, the angel Raphael is just another misunderstood foreigner, but his presence offers hope that, having cured Tobit's blindness, he can also heal the Foreign Lady's "mal de la vue" (169). Having performed all sorts of miracles on the biblical journey to Persépolis, he can perhaps perform new marvels for a modern-day namesake, Saint-John Perse, and give him a magic balm to purvey through his poems. In retrospect, we know that the love story between the two exiles did not end blissfully, but in the pages of this "goggle" we are invited to hope that Raphael will bring about a fairy tale ending for this wartime lament, so that, like Tobias and Sara, Michel Strogoff and his beloved Nadia, the narrator and his Foreign Lady can live happily ever after.

CHAPTER 8

VENTS: AN AMERICAN EPIC OF LEAVES AND GRASS

W HEN Perse describes Pacific islands as "îles de nomencla-
teurs, de généalogistes" (238) and compares the flight of in-
sects to "des récitations de généalogistes" (208), he betrays preoccupations that underlie this as so many of his works. *Vents* is his
second longest poem and one of the longest in the French language.
Written as the war was ending, it is both universal and personal. On
an individual and autobiographical level, it reenacts the dilemmas
of an exiled protagonist trying to envisage a future back home. On
a wider plane *Vents* is a panoramic vision of the entire American
continent and beyond, a history that extends from the arrival of
early European explorers to contemporary technology.

Perse was fascinated by the conquistadors and other explorers,
three of whom, Columbus, Balboa and Drake, are named in *Vents*.
He kept annotated articles about early settlers and visitors to the
New World from the Vikings to Captain Kidd and Talleyrand.
Compared to these figures, all subsequent settlers seem like late-
comers: "les hommes tard venus de ce côté des grandes eaux"
(206). One of the most recent arrivals is the protagonist himself,
poet, traveler, exile, but a belated arrival in all three categories. His
story is haunted by specific predecessors whose voices reverberate
through the poem.

Predominant among them is Walt Whitman (1819-1892), gener-
ally considered to be America's greatest poet, author of the best
American epic and an inevitable model for any later poet undertaking an epic about the New World. Alain Bosquet's 1956 *Anthologie
de la poésie américaine* specifically links the two poets in a paragraph
Saint-John Perse underlined in his own copy of Bosquet's book:

Walt Whitman [. . .] possède un souffle large et même intem-
pérant; son vocabulaire est d'une richesse inépuisable [. . .]. Il
est sans doute le plus grand poète en vers libres du XIXᵉ siècle,
et avec Thomas Hardy, Rudyard Kipling et Emile Verhaeren,
qu'il a influencés tous trois, le plus considérable de tous avant
Claudel et Saint-John Perse.[1]

Long before Bosquet's commentary, Whitman was already prominent on Perse's bookshelf and on his mental horizon. During the
years in New York and Washington, he clipped and saved many articles about Whitman from American newspapers and magazines.[2]

Whitman came to the attention of French symbolists through
Jules Laforgue's translations in 1886. Léon Bazalgette's biography
in 1908 and translation in 1909 rendered the bard accessible to
a wider public. Displeased with this version, André Gide edited
a new volume of selected poems in 1918, with translations by
Laforgue, Larbaud and others, including himself. Although Perse
was undoubtedly familiar with Gide's edition, the one that figures
in his library is Bazalgette's two-volume translation of Whitman's
complete works. With hundreds of annotations in Perse's hand,
these are among the most penciled books in his library. He also
owned an English edition of *Leaves of Grass and Democratic Vistas*
(1919).

Coincidentally, Perse and Whitman shared a birthday, May 31.
Some other resemblances between them may not have been as accidental, given Whitman's enduring influence on the younger French
poet. Born on Long Island, New York, Whitman often evoked his
island birthplace, under its Indian name, Paumanok. His master-
piece, *Leaves of Grass,* opens with an autobiographical poem, *Starting from Paumanok* (much annotated in Perse's French edition) that
relates his origins. A love of islands linked the author of *Feuilles
d'herbe* with the French poet who claimed to have been born on the
tiny island of Saint-Leger-les-Feuilles, off the coast of Guadeloupe,
even though his birth certificate locates the event at his parents'
home in Pointe-à-Pitre (an island, still, but less romantic than the

---

[1] Alain Bosquet, *Anthologie de la poésie américaine* (Paris: Stock, 1956), 19.
Perse's annotated copy is at the Fondation Saint-John Perse.

[2] These articles, with the poet's clippings, are in folders about America, Fondation Saint-John Perse.

smaller one).[3] Given Perse's lifelong attraction to islands, it is fitting that he dated *Vents* from "Seven Hundred Acre Island (Maine), 1945."

The bard of Paumanok was a mythic figure who, like Perse, saw himself as a man of the Atlantic. At a time when most American literature looked to Europe for models, Whitman's cultural vistas were resolutely anchored in the western hemisphere. His goal was to write an epic in proportion to the size and destiny of America; his poetry is distinguished by its scope and by enumerations expansive enough to encompass the multiplicity of her people, settings, and endeavors.

One of the works Perse most annotated is Whitman's *Passage to India*, a saga about the discovery of the New World, the glories of past culture and the achievements of modern technology. It honors explorers, inventors and poets, and calls for ever-new discoveries of mind and territory. Many of Perse's annotations anticipate the kinship of subject and spirit that link this poem to *Vents*. Whitman concludes with an affirmation of movement that Perse underlined in his Bazalgette translation: "O vogue plus loin, encore plus loin, plus loin toujours."[4] This tireless forward movement is a major impetus of *Vents*, which pushes perpetually ahead: "Plus loin, plus haut, où vont les hommes minces sur leur selle; plus loin, plus haut, où sont les bouches minces, lèvres closes" (202). Similarities of language, tone, scope and goals link the two poems.

Whitman not only wrote about America, but he launched a challenge for all other writers by proclaiming the criteria for future poetry and the requisite qualifications for anyone undertaking the task:

> Are you he who would assume a place to teach or be a poet here
>   in the States?
> The place is august, the terms obdurate [. . .]
> Who are you indeed who would talk or sing to America?
> Have you studied out the land, its idioms and men?

---

[3] Mary Gallagher has suggested that Perse's claim of being born on a tiny island off the coast of Guadeloupe is a *mise en abyme* of his island birth. *La Créolité de Saint-John Perse, Cahiers Saint-John Perse* 14, 1998, 77-78.

[4] Walt Whitman, *Feuilles d'herbe*, tr. L. Bazalgette (Paris: Mercure de France, 1909), 173.

Have you learn'd the physiology, phrenology, politics, geography, pride, freedom, friendship of the land? its substratums
and objects?[5]

Whitman's terms are exacting; to know everything he stipulates
would be a daunting task. A new epic would have to be encyclopedic, encompassing all of America's landscapes and *métiers*. The
poet would need to rival (and ideally surpass) *Leaves of Grass*.
Perse takes on this challenge in *Vents* as he engages in colloquy with
his most illustrious American predecessor and attempts to compose, in French, a twentieth-century *Leaves of Grass*.

The dialogue takes place in Whitman's own language of *feuilles*
and *herbe*. *Vents* begins and ends with a tree, and leaves recur with
surprising frequency. The word *feuille(s)* figures eighteen times,
compared with ten occurrences in *Amers* and six or fewer in any
other poem. It is joined by the related words *feuillage* (1), *herbe* (6)
herbage (2), and *herbier* (1).

In *Passage to India* Perse underlined Whitman's depiction of
thought as a realm of "budding bibles," translated into French as
"Le passage vers les royaumes des bibles qui éclosent."[6] Through
this image, spiritual and intellectual activity becomes a place, a field
in which sacred texts unfold like flowers. Perse conveys a similar
but more ample vision in *Vents*. In a metaphor that parallels Whitman's, he merges the natural world with intellectual creation:
"Toute la terre aux arbres, par là-bas, sur fond de vignes noires,
comme une Bible d'ombre et de fraîcheur dans le déroulement des
plus beaux textes de ce monde" (199). Perse compares the landscape to an unfurling of texts, including the Bible. When, in the
very same stanza, Perse goes on to evoke "un très haut parfum
d'humus et de feuillages," we are compelled to wonder if these
feuillages are not, among many other things, a reminiscence of
Feuilles d'herbe, one of those "plus beaux textes de ce monde,"
which occupied such a privileged place in his library, his conception of poetry, and his own poetic creation.

There are differences, of course, between the two poets, which
Perse was careful to highlight. In 1955 he specifically thanked
Katherine Biddle for underscoring the distance between Whitman's
ample free verse and his own stricter metrics:

---

[5] Walt Whitman, "By Blue Ontario's Shore," *Complete Poetry and Selected Prose*, ed. J. Miller, Jr. (Boston: Houghton Mifflin, 1959), 247.

[6] Walt Whitman, *Feuilles d'herbe*, 169.

> Et c'est encore, m'a-t-il semblé, ce que vous avez su bien voir vous-même, mieux qu'aucun critique américain, en opposant à l'art poétique d'un Walt Whitman les exigences rythmiques 'of such a rigorous metrique: an internal metrique so exacting and precise, although kept inapparent in its enclosed order, that not one syllable of the text could be changed or displaced without serious damage . . .' (922)

While Perse saw his own meter as more demanding than Whitman's, the two poets shared numerous stylistic traits. Among Perse's many Whitmanesque procedures, Betsy Erkkila cites his abundant use of exclamations, parentheses, dashes, present participles, conjunctions, prepositions and repetitions, as well as scientific terms and specialized vocabulary. [7] *Leaves of Grass* and *Vents* are encyclopedic, enumerative poems whose celebratory tone generates a spirit of renewal, both physical and spiritual, and proclaims new vistas of human potential.

For the two poets, America represented a fresh terrain for literary creation. Whitman often described the United States as the newest home of the Muse on her westward journey from Greece and Jerusalem across Europe to the New World. In *Song of the Exposition* he charts the Muse's itinerary from Virgil to Dante, then across Germany, France, Spain and England and finally to America, where "a better, fresher, busier sphere, a wide, untried domain awaits, demands [her]." [8] Perse's own literary and personal trajectory was also linked to the western hemisphere. For a poet seeking to write a new French epic, America offered a privileged domain, unexplored by Homer, Virgil, Dante.

Saint-John Perse believed that the art of the epic had not yet been perfected and that a great French epic remained to be written, despite Victor Hugo's attempt in the *Légende des siècles,* with its monumental goal of summing up and passing on the torch of human tradition. In his 1951 homage to André Gide, Perse related a long-past conversation in which the two men distinguished between "la mauvaise gestion des Romantiques français et le Romantisme lui-même" (479)–romanticism at its best being a liberating move-

---

[7] Betsy Erkkila, *Walt Whitman Among the French* (Princeton: Princeton UP, 1980), 215-225.

[8] Walt Whitman, *Complete Poetry and Selected Prose,* ed. J. Miller, Jr., 143-145.

ment, an opening up to nature and to the subconscious. Hugo
might have been capable of bringing about a romantic revolution,
they agreed, if he had not fallen victim to other forces and betrayed
his vocation:

> Hugo, en somme, né poète, c'est-à-dire accessible malgré lui aux
> sources secrètes du subconscient, s'était aveuglément perdu, et,
> avec lui, avait perdu le Romantisme français, dans le verbalisme
> et la cécité, pour avoir sacrifié le mystère poétique à la conquête
> extérieure du succès et aux compromissions massives d'une
> grande carrière publique. (479-480)

In this same conversation, Perse proposed a new artistic revolution.
Gide's reply: "Les vraies révolutions [. . .] sont muettes, et s'accom-
plissent dans les œuvres" (480). *Vents* is an effort to accomplish the
work Hugo left undone. Like Whitman, Perse found appropriate
material in the New World, with its sagas of discovery, its vast geography and varied inhabitants. All these elements figure in the expansive scope and enumerations of his poem.

It is arguable whether either *Vents* or *Leaves of Grass* is really an
epic in the classical sense, with a hero whose exploits become the
founding myth of a people. Here, protagonists are poets rather than
warriors, and their inner conflicts are closer to drama. Yet both
works have been read as epics. William Calin believes "Saint-John
Perse is the first Frenchman, one of the first major poets in any language [. . .] to come to grips successfully with the problem of the
modern epic." [9] What gives *Vents* and *Leaves of Grass* the feel of
epic is their ambitious goal of relating the history of humankind,
from a distant past to the contemporary moment. The vast project
of embracing space and time lends an epic aura to both poems, despite their distance from the heroic tradition of Greece and Rome.

Whitman influenced the goals, themes and language of *Vents*.
But he taught another lesson, too, that had to do with France, and
was as political as it was poetic. The epic bard of American expansion was also the lyric poet of war and mourning, who composed
much of *Leaves of Grass* during or just after the Civil War. Perse
was equally familiar with this other Whitman, author of the elegies

---

[9] William Calin, *A Muse for Heroes: Nine Centuries of the Epic in France*
(Toronto: U of Toronto Press, 1983), 378.

to Abraham Lincoln–"When Lilacs Last in the Dooryard Bloom'd" and "O Captain, My Captain"–and the *Drum-Taps* poems. Perse's 1963 eulogy to President Kennedy explicitly mentions this Whitman: "Que s'éclaire l'ombre devant nous! et s'agrandisse sur la route l'histoire en cours des hommes, honorée de ses stèles! Lincoln pleuré par Walt Whitman éveille encore dans nos cœurs le très long thrène du martyr" (640). While this allusion draws a parallel between Lincoln and Kennedy, it also creates a subtle comparison between their respective eulogizers.

Whitman, the most American of poets, was also a francophile, who scattered French words and expressions across his pages. Some of his poems have French titles, while *Leaves of Grass* opens with "the word Democratic, the word en-Masse." [10] Three poems deal specifically with wartime Europe: "France: The 18th Year of these States [1793]"; "Europe: The 72nd and 73rd Years of These States [1848]"; and "O Star of France: 1870-1871." [11] Although not among his masterpieces, they are endearing transatlantic messages of solidarity. If America's greatest poet could write about a war-torn France, did not a French poet have a similar responsibility?

Evoking the ravages of the Franco-Prussian war, Whitman laments the plight of France, as a "star crucified–by traitors sold [. . .] The spear thrust in thy side." The narrator of *Vents* conjures up a similar vision as he imagines post-war France. Viewing Paris from the air, with the Eiffel Tower reflecting sunlight, he sees: "le pays tendre et clair de nos filles, un couteau d'or au cœur!" (240). Whitman also depicts the anguish of "exiled patriots' lives" and looks ahead to the time when they will be able to go home:

> Is the house shut? is the master away?
> Nevertheless, be ready, be not weary of watching,
> He will soon return, his messengers come anon.

The protagonist of *Vents* ponders these same questions and announces his own decision to return home. Perse's buoyant epic of the Americas thus ends with the narrator's more lyric determination to retrace his steps toward a country where houses have been deserted by happiness (242) and to return to the family homestead:

---

[10] Walt Whitman, *Complete Poetry and Selected Prose*, 5.
[11] *Ibid.*, 172-173; 193-194; 278-279.

> Demain, ce continent largué . . . (242)
> Que nul ne songe à déserter les hommes de sa race (240)
> Nous reprenions un soir la route des humains (234)
> Nous reviendrons un soir d'Automne (241)

Although the poet's own homecoming was delayed, like Odysseus', for many years, his poem concludes with a commitment, for which Whitman had shown the way.

While both poets recreate an epic expansion across time and space, from Europe to America and beyond, the more radical and surprising movement of their work may be the turning back. In "Passage to India," which Perse so thoroughly annotated, the dynamic movement of explorers gives way to a meditation about the healing responsibility of poets. A similar change takes place in *Vents.* After a frenetic journey the narrator asks himself: "Qu'allais-tu déserter là?" (239). He takes on the cause of the human community: ". . . Mais c'est de l'homme qu'il s'agit! Et de l'homme lui-même quand donc sera-t-il question? Quelqu'un au monde élèvera-t-il la voix?" (224).

Both Whitman and Perse attribute healing and even messianic qualities to poets. Superior to explorers, inventors and scientists, Whitman's poet is "The true son of God," [12] while Perse's is an "Homme assailli du dieu!" (213) and "gagné par l'infection divine" (230). This is a surprising declaration more characteristic of Victor Hugo than of Perse, given his longstanding reluctance to imagine divinity outside of human existence. Whether the proclamation recalls the Oriental shamans he learned about from his sinologist friend Gustave-Charles Toussaint or the American Indian sages who also fascinated him, it clearly attributes a sacred vocation to poets, especially at a crucial juncture of the twentieth century, after the atomic bomb changed human history.

Whitman also had an acute sense of his present moment. In prefaces and poems, he declared that it was time for a radically new beginning. This did not necessarily mean rejecting prior literature, but it did involve a reassessment of the past, as he suggested in "Song of the Exposition":

---

[12] *Ibid.*, 290-291.

> We do not blame thee elder World, nor really separate
> ourselves from thee,
> (Would the son separate himself from the father?)[13]

Whitman's father-son metaphor is revealing, since much of his poetry emerges from his own struggle to separate himself from Emerson, and he frequently calls on writers to rise above their forefathers. Such is the message of his important poem, "By Blue Ontario's Shore":

> The immortal poets of Asia and Europe have done their
> work and pass'd to other spheres,
> a work remains, the work of surpassing all they have done.[14]

Perse's edition of Whitman still bears a marker in this crucial page,
and we can understand how it would strike a chord in the younger
poet, whose writing both depicts and enacts an often uneasy relation to his elders.

Perse and Whitman share a common preoccupation with some
of the same "immortal poets of Asia and Europe": Homer, Virgil,
Dante, and the writers of the Bible. This may make them allies in
one sense, but it does not eliminate all tension. In "Passage to India" Perse annotated Whitman's account of two brothers reunited
at the end of long careers: "saturé d'affection, d'amour total, ayant
trouvé le Grand Frère, le Cadet se fondra en tendresse dans ses
bras."[15] The appeal of this image is understandable; to make Whitman a brother rather than a father brings him to the same generational plane. But fraternal relations are not always idyllic, as we
know from Cain and Abel (who are mentioned in *Vents*, through
the metaphor of a winter as crisp as Cain's hair [202]).

Vents is composed in kinship and rivalry with *Leaves of Grass*.
The narrator is a man of language, struggling with his muse: "Ivre
d'éthyle et de résine dans la mêlée des feuilles de tout âge–comme
au rucher de sa parole, parmi le peuple de ses mots [. . .]" (208). In-
toxicated with the leaves of all ages, and perhaps especially with the
Leaves of Grass, he seeks to live "au plus haut front / De feuilles et
de frondes!" (185). In theme, language, tone and goals, *Vents* be-

---

[13] *Ibid.*, 143, 145.
[14] *Ibid.*, 242.
[15] Walt Whitman, *Feuilles d'herbe,* 172.

longs to the lineage of *Leaves of Grass,* but its complicated relation
to the earlier work includes both homage and *fronde,* tribute and
struggle. "[. . .] la terre avec nous, et la feuille, et le glaive–et le
monde où frayait une abeille nouvelle" (249). The juxtaposition of
leaf and sword is suggestive of Perse's ambiguous relationship with
his American predecessor. Despite, or perhaps because of Whitman's honored place in Perse's life, library and writings, he is a
model to be matched or surpassed.

Taking on Whitman's challenge to write a "gigantic and generous poem about America," [16] Perse reaches beyond him in time and
space, to lands beyond the United States and to the newest inventions. Whitman stopped at locomotives and gasometers; Perse
evokes atomic energy in a resolutely modern epic that seeks to be a
"feuille magnétique" (251) and an "herbe nouvelle" (226), even
as it is permeated with a Whitmanesque vocabulary of leaves and
grass:

> Couronne-toi, jeunesse, d'une feuille plus aiguë! (195)
> Semences et barbes d'herbe nouvelle! (192-193)
> le vent à cent lieues courbant l'herbe nouvelle (226)

The word *semence(s)* recurs four times in *Vents,* suggesting the
poet's explicit aim, like Whitman's, to create a new lineage. In a
verse Perse noted in "The Sleepers," Whitman celebrates the process of generation: "Parfaits et purs sont les génitoires qui ont
préalablement projeté la semence, parfaite et pure la matrice qu'il
s'y noua." [17] In *Vents,* as in Perse's earlier poems, allusions to generation and lineage are frequent.

Inheritance is a highly charged issue, since Perse's protagonist is
a relative newcomer in the history of culture. To claim the place he
wants, he must proclaim the end of an inherited tradition. To depict
(and perhaps hasten) its demise, the poet calls upon multiple
metaphors of destruction that apply both to society at large and to
the literary heritage. The very wind of the title is one such destructive force. Bankruptcy is another image for the end of a tradition,
where the past has a "goût d'enchères, de faillites" (183). There are

---

[16] Walt Whitman, Preface to 1855 edition of *Leaves of Grass, Complete Poetry
and Selected Prose,* 412.

[17] Walt Whitman, *Feuilles d'herbe,* 187.

many others. In a single passage of section I:6 the narrator offers four different metaphors for destruction: extinction ("Basse époque [. . .] qui s'éteint là"), loss of faith ("comme un grand pan de croyance morte"), miscarriage ("membrance fausse") and shipwreck ("tout nous vient à bas–toute la mâture et tout") (192). Perhaps the most damaging metaphor is the depiction of tradition as a series of "grands désastres intellectuels" (183).

The only solution is a clean sweep. As Perse wrote to Adrienne Monnier, the poem is meant to express "l'impatience générale à l'égard de toutes choses consommées, de toutes cendres et de tous acquêts de l'habitat humain" (553). Whatever the winds don't disperse must be washed away: "grandes évacuations d'œuvres mortes" (206). Whatever remains after that can be forgotten or reduced to anonymity: "Souvenirs, souvenirs! qu'il en soit fait de vous comme des songes du songeur à la sortie des eaux nocturnes. Et que nous soient les jours vécus comme visages d'innommés" (213). The poet's role is to collaborate with these forces of wind and water in cleaning away the debris of tradition, beginning with books and libraries. In a celebrated episode he excoriates past writings:

> Ha! qu'on m'évente tout ce lœss! Ha! qu'on m'évente tout ce leurre! Sécheresse et supercherie d'autels . . . Les livres tristes, innombrables, sur leur tranche de craie pâle . . .
>
> Et qu'est-ce encore, à mon doigt d'os, que tout ce talc d'usure et de sagesse, et tout cet attouchement des poudres du savoir? comme aux fins de saison poussière et poudre de pollen [. . .] (186-187)

Given the poet's own position as a consultant at the Library of Congress during the war years, readers have rightly seen this passage as a (remarkably accurate) portrait of that august repository and of Perse's rebellion against its dusty contents. While this autobiographical dimension is surely present, the depiction also fits into a deeper and more complicated struggle with tradition. Harold Bloom has suggested that every new writer secretly harbors "the dark wish that the libraries be burned in some new Alexandrian conflagration, that the imagination might be liberated from the greatness and oppressive power of its own dead champions." [18] A

---

[18] Harold Bloom, ed., *John Keats: Modern Critical Views* (New York: Chelsea House, 1985), 1.

similarly dark wish pervades *Vents,* reaching even beyond libraries to attack all the accumulated weight of consecrated authority, all the "usure et [. . .] sécheresse au cœur des hommes investis" (179). In *Amitié du Prince* the pollen of wisdom carries a positive connotation; it suggests the solemnity of ancient texts and knowledge. But the pollen is now seen as a suffocating dust that wind must blow away, just as it topples statues and monuments honoring past eminence (184-185).

The targets are almost always male forefathers, although they do include the female figures printed on money, because of their symbolic role in bourgeois society. The narrator's demands are repeatedly and explicitly heralded as radical and non-negotiable:

> Nos revendications furent extrêmes (191)
> [. . .] ma demande n'est pas usuelle. / Car l'exigence en nous fut grande, et tout usage révoqué (204)
> Notre grief est sans accommodement, et l'échéance ne sera point reportée (240)
> Il n'y a plus pour nous d'entente avec cela qui fut (244)

It is revealing that his reclamations are couched in the juridical vocabulary of inheritance rights: "nous nous avançons, hommes vivants, pour réclamer notre bien en avance d'hoirie" (192); "Qu'on nous donne, ô vivants, la plénitude de notre dû!" (192, 204). The inheritance he claims is a broad one. While there are many autobiographical references in the poem, this particular patrimony goes beyond the individual to include all human beings. In the wake of a devastating war and the explosion of an atomic bomb, this is a call for humanity to seize life over death and to begin anew after the destruction. With this philosophy the poet gives priority to newness and creativity over past authority. Indeed, to come into his inheritance, the poet-narrator must break with the past and with predecessors. "Tout à reprendre. Tout à redire. Et la faux du regard sur tout l'avoir menée!" (186); "il est temps enfin de prendre la hache sur le pont" (192).

Across the pages of this poem, a dispossessed and angry poet-narrator tries to remove the obstacles to his inheritance. In the course of the poem, he comes to triumph, at least thematically, by imposing his authority on his listeners, like the man he describes in Section I who arrives at a ceremony, only to be invited to "'Parler en maître'" (182).

The narrator announces a new reign, directed toward the future. Through the rhetoric of the poem, he suggests that predecessors have been left behind, replaced by people who have drunk the new wine of the future:

> Ceux qui songeaient les songes dans les chambres se sont couchés hier soir de l'autre côté du Siècle, face aux lunes adverses.
> D'autres ont bu le vin nouveau dans les fontaines peintes au minium. Et de ceux-là nous fûmes. (190)

Old genealogies will be supplanted by "sang nouveau" (181) and an "essence future!" (222). By transforming the dialectic early/late into old/new, the narrator valorizes the new and becomes the beginning of a new lineage. He creates a new chronology of marriage and birth:

> la terre vendangée pour de nouvelles épousailles (249)
> Et par là-bas mûrissent en Ouest les purs ferments d'une ombre prénatale (196)
> Et c'est naissance encore de prodiges sur la terre des hommes (200)

Henceforth, all creation will be future-oriented, in the wake of "aubes nouvelles" (222), "l'An neuf" (203, 247), "l'An nouveau" (246) and "un nouvel âge de la terre" (213). Having disposed of the past, everything is new: "Enchantement du jour à sa naissance . . ." (229); "Un monde à naître sous vos pas! hors de coutume et de saison!" (247).

By stressing birth, the poet makes all previous time look like gestation and waiting. In a similar maneuver, he posits a cyclical renewal, where dead seasons are followed by "fêtes du Printemps vert" (186) and by "murmure et chant d'hommes vivants, non ce murmure de sécheresse dont nous avons déjà parlé" (183-184). Even more radically, he declares an evolution in literary works, with forward progress: "les écritures aussi évolueront. –Lieu du propos: toutes grèves de ce monde." (229). Earlier steps in the evolution can be left behind.

Each of these metaphors–seasons, evolution and birth, new blood and new wine–is a way of jettisoning the past. The poet-narrator reduces forefathers to dust and anonymity and transforms himself metaphorically from one of the "hommes tard venus" (206) into a spokesperson and judge: "Que le poète se fasse entendre, et qu'il dirige le jugement!" (226). With this declaration he proclaims his supremacy above earlier voices. Last in the tradition of writers, he becomes the beginning of a new line. Last among westward travelers he becomes the first of the conquistadors of the spirit.

In the long enumeration of section III:4, the poet-protagonist emerges as the leader of a vast and varied people: ". . . Avec son peuple de servants, avec son peuple de suivants, et tout son train de hardes dans le vent" (226). He will take possession of a new land and occupy the central place: "Et sur le cercle immense de la terre, apaisement au cœur du Novateur. . ." (193). Through a succession of metaphors, Perse transforms the narrator from last to first and peripheral to central.

An onomastic transformation also occurs in this poem. The protagonist is nameless: "Homme de peu de nom. Qui était-il, qui n'était-il pas?" (186). All of *Vents* revolves around this question, suggesting but never revealing his identity. As the poem opens, the narrator associates himself with those he calls "hommes de paille, En l'an de paille" (179). A straw man, like these, he hears an inner voice, calling into question his weight as a poet: "Je t'ai pesé, poète, et t'ai trouvé de peu de poids" (195).

Although these phrases denote lightness, they carry the weight of T.S. Eliot, the eminent American poet who translated *Anabase* in 1930. A few years earlier Perse had done his own adaptation/translation of Eliot's *Hollow Men.* The epigraph of that poem, "A penny for the Old Guy," he translated as "Aumône aux hommes de peu de poids" (465). What is, in the original, a reference to Guy Fawkes' Day becomes, in Perse's version, a multitude of human beings defined by their lightness on the scales of social importance. [19] Eliot calls them "the hollow men / The stuffed men"; for Perse they are "les hommes sans substance [...] les hommes faits de paille." The same phrases *hommes de paille* and *peu de poids* return in *Vents,* initiating a conversation with Eliot, whom Perse admired throughout his life, despite temperamental differences that once prompted him to observe: "Il a trop peur de la vie pour me comprendre pleinement." [20] Realizing the prestige of Eliot's *Anabase*

---

[19] I am indebted to Arthur J. Knodel for this clarification.

[20] Perse made this observation in a conversation related to me by Arthur Knodel.

translation, Perse repeatedly tried to entice him to tackle later poems: "Je ne puis espérer, dans cette génération nouvelle, rencontrer
jamais le miracle d'un nouvel Eliot, assez hautement Eliot pour se
permettre l'élégance envers l'œuvre d'un autre." [21] Perse's wish went
unfulfilled, but the correspondence continued, and in 1958 Perse
looked back on their long relationship as a "compagnonnage littéraire qui m'a été si cher" (1040).

Incorporating Eliot's verses into *Vents*, Perse pays tribute to an
eminent colleague and fellow descendent of Whitman. But his tribute carries a reprimand and a correction, for Eliot's poem, like his
mock-heroic *Waste Land*, is about sterility, death and endings. *The
Hollow Men* closes with the memorable verses (which Perse did not
translate): "This is the way the world ends / Not with a bang but a
whimper." *Vents* proposes an antithetical message, replacing Eliot's
"dead land" of "dry grass" with a promise of planting and harvest.
The pessimistic vision of an American in England is revised by the
new-found (and often precarious) optimism of a Frenchman in
America.

At the beginning of *Vents,* the weightless people are specifically
the poets: "Je t'ai pesé, poète, et t'ai trouvé de peu de poids" (195).
But if a poet is light *(leger)* at the beginning, he acquires weight and
stature during the epic voyage of the poem. The narrator entreats
mathematicians and scientists not to weigh poets: "ne pesez pas les
hommes de ma race" (241), but he goes on to endow them with a
particular gravity, thanks to "la lourde phrase humaine" (241). The
narrator begins as an "Homme de peu de nom" (186), and even in-
dulges in a seeming pun on the poet's given name: "Notre stance est
légère sur le charroi des ans!" (188), but through the poetic activity
of *Vents*, he acquires weight, as does the poem. Claudel acknowledged this in his own pun when he wrote of *Vents*: "je me sens devant votre œuvre comme devant quelque chose d'important et que
l'on n'aborde pas, comme c'est le cas de le dire, à la légère." [22]

Perse considered *Vents* his most important and most unjustly
neglected poem, delineating a philosophy of history and of poets'
own role within it. It sweeps across time with broad stokes while at

---

[21] Correspondence Perse - Eliot, letter 11, May 7, 1953, Fondation Saint-John
Perse.
[22] Correspondance Claudel - Saint-John Perse 1917-1949, June 24, 1949. All
references are to letters at the Fondation Saint-John Perse.

the same time obliquely relating a personal story. Alexis Leger, Secretary General of Foreign Affairs, exiled in America, bears a surprising resemblance to a character in his poem:

> Ainsi quand l'Enchanteur, par les chemins et par les rues,
> Va chez les hommes de son temps en habit du commun,
> Et qu'il a dépouillé toute charge publique,
> Homme très libre et de loisir, dans le sourire et la bonne grâce,
> Le ciel pour lui tient son écart et sa version des choses [...]
> (189)
> Qu'on nous cherche aux confins les hommes de grand pou-
> voir, réduits par l'inaction au métier d'Enchanteurs (189-190)

A public official, stripped of his diplomatic role, acquires an even
greater power: the capacity to enchant. This vignette, with its parallels to Leger's own trajectory, suggests that he too might be an Enchanter, comparable to the most famous one of the literary tradition,
François René de Chateaubriand, whose nickname, *l'Enchanteur,*
coined by Sainte-Beuve, has stuck.[23]

Another French writer-diplomat played a role in the history of
Vents. Four years after the poem appeared, Paul Claudel acqui-
esced to Perse's desire for an article about it. He accepted the task
with reluctance, daunted, perhaps, by the length and complexity of
the poem but more likely disappointed by Perse's philosophy with
its emphasis on human existence rather than divinity. In July 1949
Claudel confided to his journal (published in 1969, while Perse was
still alive to read it): "Le 14, commence à m'occuper de l'article
promis à Alexis Leger, ce q[ui] m'ennuie énormément." In a subsequent entry, ostensibly from July 26, he noted: "Terminé mon étude
sur *Vents* de S[aint] J[ohn] P[erse]."[24] The themes of Claudel's article, as he saw them, were that *Vents* is an epic poem and that Perse
is a pagan, or pre-Christian poet, for whom the present is more important than the afterlife.

The fate of this article offers a revealing and even amusing window onto Perse's relations both with his predecessors and with posterity. When published in the November 1949 *Revue de Paris,*
Claudel's piece garnered warm thanks from the poet, who immedi-

---

[23] *Le Nouveau Dictionnaire Robert de la Langue Française* (1994) proposes, as an
example of the word *enchanteur,* "Chateaubriand fut surnommé 'l'Enchanteur.'"

[24] Paul Claudel, *Journal* I (Paris: Gallimard, Bibliothèque de la Pléiade, 1969),
629.

ately sent a telegram expressing gratitude for the "magnifique article dont élévation de ton noblesse et générosité m'émeuvent." In a
subsequent letter, Perse praised the "très belle chose que cette
étude de grand style que vous avez voulu me consacrer: pénétrante
à l'extrême dans sa 'compréhension' et généreuse toujours dans son
interprétation. [. . .] J'ai tout aimé d'un tel écrit, jusqu'à ses digres-
sions et ses échappées personnelles" (1019). Despite this praise, the
poet nevertheless edited the article drastically for the 1950 collective volume, *Honneur à Saint-John Perse*. The meticulous revisions,
recorded on his personal copy of the *Revue de Paris*, are illuminating, since they highlight the areas of greatest sensitivity. Claudel,
who was an octogenarian at the time, observed that *Vents* was not
the work of an unknown, adventurous twenty-year-old, but of "un
vieil homme, déjà, de soixante ans." [25] (Perhaps this was Claudel's
revenge for Perse's reference, a year earlier, to "la magnifique
frondaison de votre large maturité. C'est la vieillesse splendide de
Sophocle" (1013).) Claudel's *vieil homme* obviously did not please
the subject, who blacked out *vieil*.

Claudel struck another sensitive chord when calling the poet "à
peu près inconnu" (4). Perse buried this observation in black ink.
Nor did he appreciate Claudel's formulation: "Mais Dieu est un
mot que Saint John Perse évite, dirai-je religieusement? et que pour
un empire–n'est-ce pas Léger? [sic]–il ne laisserait pas sortir de ses
lèvres" (15). Perse eliminated *n'est-ce pas* and *Léger* from the question which is now well known in its edited form.

One of the passages Perse most assiduously revised deals with
literary kinships. Claudel attributed to Perse a long list of ancestors.
The author of *Vents* kept some of the comparisons, but omitted
others. He was willing to be compared to Hawthorne, Poe, Cald-
well and Faulkner; Chateaubriand and Novalis; Ezekiel and ancient
Greek and Hindu poets; Lao-Tzu, Lucretius, and even Christopher
Columbus. But he excluded Robert Louis Stevenson, Nikolaus
Lenau, Jean-Paul Richter, Romain Gary, Julien Green and Jean
Moréas. He also erased Claudel's exclamation, "Nous sommes loin
de Marcel Proust!" (12), although he later restored it in a footnote
to the Pléiade edition of his works (1301).

---

[25] Paul Claudel, "Un Poème de Saint-John Perse," *Revue de Paris*, 56, novembre 1949, 13. Perse's annotated version is at the Fondation Saint-John Perse. Subsequent references to this article are indicated in parentheses.

Claudel's varied list of perceived ancestors suggests the wide range of voices one can hear beneath this long, complex poem. Claudel is right to cite Chateaubriand, whose depictions of America were a backdrop for Perse's own travels and writing. The reference to Faulkner points to a whole literature of the American south that could have nourished *Vents* II:3-5, although Faulkner does not figure in Perse's personal library. The list does not take into account some of Perse's more immediate sources, notably his own trips in America and the travel brochures and magazine articles he collected and annotated.[26]

One element of Claudel's article that Perse does not contest is the portrayal of *Vents* as an epic that captures the electricity of America. While Claudel does not mention Walt Whitman, electricity brings us back to this bard of America, author of "I Sing the Body Electric," whose presence underlies the poem.

A twentieth-century traveler to the United States inevitably records his reflections against a background of earlier pages. After years of reading and annotating Whitman, Perse conversed with him across the pages of his own poem. *Vents* may be a meditation about wind, but it is also about leaves and branches and about the "très grand arbre du langage" (180).

Two trees frame the poem and highlight the poet's ongoing preoccupation with generations and ancestors. The tree in the first canto is a beggar who has "fripé son patrimoine" (180), while its counterpart, in the last, is noble, "de haut rang" (251); the first is sterile, "à sec de feuilles" (251), while the other rises up with "Sa feuille magnétique et son chargement de fruits nouveaux" (251). These two trees serve as bookends for *Vents*. In the space between them, the poet cultivates a special kind of tree that will not wither. He merges botany and geology into an image of leaves that are as permanent as rock: "Les écritures nouvelles encloses dans les grands schistes à venir . . ." (185); "Là nous prenons nos écritures nouvelles, aux feuilles jointes des grands schistes . . ." (214). In the pages of *Vents* he seeks to forge a new species of leaf, "une feuille plus aiguë!" (194), that will allow the poet of Saint-Leger-les-Feuilles to join the bard of *Leaves of Grass* in the lineage of epic writings about America.

---

[26] Margaret Mitchell's *Gone with the Wind* and the famous 1939 film version may also have contributed to Perse's evocation of the white-columned homes and the "Belles" (208, 209) who once inhabited them.

CHAPTER 9

THE TEXTUAL SEAS OF *AMERS*

T HE narrator of *Amers* is not alone when he relates that "il y avait un si long temps que j'avais goût de ce poème" (263). Perse also nurtured the poem across many years, publishing it in segments from 1948 to 1957. In a letter to Lilita Abreu in 1947, he revealed an ambitious poem in progress, maybe even too ambitious, he felt, yet a work for which he had high hopes.[1] The plan, as he explained a few months later, was to create "une œuvre d'assez longue haleine où je sois sûr de n'accueillir jamais rien d'amer, ni de triste, ni même de nostalgique."[2] One of the curiosities of *Amers* is how the poet, who intended to exclude everything bitter or *amer* from his poem, ultimately chose that very word for its title.

Rich in connotations, *Amers* denotes the seamarks or guideposts that stand along the shore as objects of mediation between land and sea, whether natural ones like peaks or constructed ones like lighthouses. In this polyvalent word there is also *mer*, the sea. But when the word occurs in the poem, three times, it is as the adjective bitter, beginning on the first page when the narrator asks: "Amères, nos lèvres de vivants le furent-elles jamais?" (259). Perse's hero had at times resented his plight and wished for a different one. His frustration led him to exclaim in *Vents:* "N'est-il rien que d'humain?" (233). But in *Amers* he is no longer bitter. While earlier works are haunted by the past, this one looks to the future and to the momentary epiphanies that are our closest intimations of eternity.

---

[1] Saint-John Perse, *Lettres à l'Etrangère,* ed. M. Berne (Paris: Gallimard, 1987), 108.
[2] *Ibid.*, 120.

Forty years after the *Récitation à l'éloge d'une reine,* this is a self-proclaimed "récitation en l'honneur de la Mer" (261), in which the Sea is not only a Queen but, in the poet's words, a reservoir of eternal forces (570). Located "au confluent de toutes mers et de toutes naissances" (376), it is the mirror and symbolic destination of all human quests, temporal and eternal

The scope of the poem is vast, although it is not, by usual definitions, an epic. Indeed, *Amers* defies classification into any single genre, since it combines odes and hymns, drama, philosophy, liturgy and literary theory. The French critic, Jean Paulhan called it an epic that changes into a hymn (1131). Poet W.H. Auden compared *Amers* to Pindaric odes and psalms of praise (1132). Across the work protagonists address the sea in registers Perse himself defined as interrogation, adjuration, imprecation, initiation, appeal and celebration (571).

The poet returns here to his earliest impulse of praise, but in a different timbre from *Eloges.* After the exuberance of the earliest poems, *Amers,* like the sea it extolls, has the tone of a "récitatif sacré" (371). Structured like a religious processional and echoing both Homer and Pindar, it seeks to recreate the solemnity of a ritual ceremony. After the resolutely modern setting of *Vents, Amers* returns to a distant past when the choral poet was still a prophet and inspired interpreter.

Amers is unique in Perse's poetry for its multiplicity of narrators, many of whom are women. Speakers range from the anonymous voices of the invocation, Strophe and chorus, to an array of more specific ones: the Master of Stars and Navigation, Tragediennes, Patrician women, a poetess, the girl prophet, the city daughters, the foreign traveler, and, at greatest length, two lovers. Individually and collectively they offer a hymn to all of the promises and potentialities symbolized by the sea. This multi-voiced choral poem, written by a poet in his sixties, is a work of healing and union after the dislocations and ruptures of exile. Perse's longest poem, it is both a metaphysical and a metatextual exploration. Reconciling himself with the past, he meditates about life and death and about the forces that might be strong enough to endure death. One is love, and the poem is a hymn to the "souveraineté d'aimer" (350). Another is art, and *Amers* is the poet's affirmative answer to the question posed by his narrator: "Et contre la mort n'est-il que de créer?" (366).

The ocean is an appropriate backdrop for this ambitious poem, given Perse's life-long fascination with the sea. His very first autobiographical entry in the Pléiade edition announces a maritime childhood: "formé très tôt à l'équitation et à la vie sur mer" (x). Subsequent passages chronicle voyages around the globe by a poet-sailor who once claimed his veins were filled with salt-water (883). *Amers* was written in part on islands and one segment of the manuscript bears the signature "St. John Island, avril 1951, Monhegan Island, septembre 1951." From a lifetime of sailing, the poet brought to his writing a first-hand acquaintance with salt and brine.

But the sea of *Amers* is more than this; it belongs to a long history of conquests and adventures, real and literary. It is a multiple and contradictory site of literature and lore, the "Mer légendaire de nos pères" (289), rich with the heritage of Homer, Virgil and the great sea writers down to Conrad. [3] When speakers describe their desire to inhabit "la mer qui change de dialecte à toutes portes des Empires" (302), their words evoke the sea that is Greek for Homer, Latin for Virgil, Italian for Dante, and French for the poetic heirs of those creators.

Given Perse's oft-proclaimed alienation from the Mediterranean, especially before settling on the presqu'île de Giens, and his equally energetic self-definition as a man of the Atlantic, we are amply forewarned that the longitude and latitude of *Amers* are unlikely to be confined to an ordinary atlas and can best be charted on special textual and intertextual maps of the "mer antique" (371), the "mer de Jason" (350).

As the "Table des Grands" (366), the "Site des Grands" (366), "Contrée [et] heure des Grands" (372), the sea has a tradition of heroes. At the same time, it is also a text:

> O Mer vivante du plus grand texte (290)
> Mer exemplaire du plus grand texte (293)
>   Textuelle, la Mer s'ouvre nouvelle sur ses grands livres de pierre (295)
>   la Mer elle-même, sur sa page (371) [. . .] sur ses grands livres ouverts (376)

---

[3] An admirer of Conrad, Perse had underlined in *Some Reminiscences* the phrase "he had the rating of a second-class able seaman (matelot léger)." London: Nash, 1912, 226. Fondation Saint-John Perse.

Even better, this textual sea is a Mallarmean blank page, "inallusive et pure de tout chiffre" (267), awaiting the creation of a new work. All these references to a textual sea suggest that *Amers* must also be read as a meditation on books and literature and as an *ars poetica*. Indeed the very first words of the poem denote reading: "Et vous, Mer, qui lisiez dans de plus vastes songes" (259). Early on, a young woman asks: "Et cette mer encore est-elle mer, qui creuse en nous ses grands bas-fonds de sable, et qui nous parle d'autres sables?" (309). Her question conveys well the sense of other seas, other shores, other texts whose presence can be felt.

The abundant references to earlier stories stand in apparent contradiction of Perse's oft-proclaimed hostility to books. A complex love-hate relationship is evident all across his life and poetry. It has been quipped that during his five years at the Library of Congress he never borrowed a book (1336), while one of the greatest compliments he could pay Léon-Paul Fargue was to declare: "Rien de livresque dans son art, qui naît de source vive et n'élève point de perles de culture" (492). Perse's supposed hostility to culture erupts most violently in *Vents*, in the famous diatribe against libraries. Later in that poem, the narrator undergoes a kind of conversion, pledging to return home and embrace human concerns after many kinds of exile, but he still has a score to settle with libraries and literature. He, and through him Saint-John Perse, work through that conflict in *Amers*.

Perse believed that tension lies at the heart of all poetry. Commenting on a work by Fargue, he discerned "cette discorde latente qui règne au cœur de tout poème–ce nœud de poulpe des contraires qu'assemble toute rive poétique" (530). A similar knot of contradictory forces involves the sea of *Amers* which is "Multiple et contraire" (372). At the heart of the poem lies a tension between past literature and future poetic creation; on the one hand a long cultural tradition, on the other, the empty space for potential works. *Amers* is permeated by the awareness of an inheritance coming from afar: "Au très grand large loin de nous fut imprimé jadis ce souffle" (326). The juxtaposition of *souffle* and *imprimé* yokes in an uneasy pairing two traditionally antagonistic forces: spontaneous inspiration and a written text. The conflict between them is reenacted in the title, themes, scope and design of the poem, each of which expresses and eventually seeks to resolve the duality between past and future.

In a single, monumental sentence, the poet-narrator of *Vents* enumerated all the objects he would like the wind to sweep away:

> Balises et corps morts, bornes militaires et stèles votives, les casemates aux frontières, et les lanternes aux récifs; les casemates aux frontières, basses comme des porcheries, et les douanes plus basses au penchant de la terre; les batteries désuètes sous les palmes, aux îles de corail blanc avilies de volaille; les édicules sur les caps et les croix aux carrefours; tripodes et postes de vigie [. . .]
> (184)

The list continues, for the poet would topple all monuments, just as he would discard all of past literature and the seemingly dead weight of culture, destroying lifeless works to make way for the new. Curiously, many of the monuments he seeks to disperse–beacons, buoys, stelae, turrets, and look-out posts–are examples of seamarks or *amers* along the coast. The narrator of *Vents* would eliminate these landmarks and abolish our cultural reference points, but in a dramatic reversal the poet of *Amers* ushers them back, proclaiming them in his very title. The new fate of these seamarks is a measure of the transformation from the previous poem to this one.

On the long list of monuments, one of the most familiar ones is suspiciously missing: lighthouses or *phares*. Their absence from a quasi-exhaustive list and from a whole poem about the sea is revealing, perhaps even more so because this is the edifice immortalized in Baudelaire's famous and widely anthologized poem, *Les Phares*, which Perse had annotated in his sister's copy of Baudelaire's works. Later, in Henri Peyre's anthology, *Pensées de Baudelaire* (Corti, 1951), he again annotated the poem. *Les Phares* is not really about the sea, of course, and its lighthouses are not buildings but great artists: Rubens, Leonardo, Rembrandt, Michelangelo, and fellow creators. Baudelaire pays tribute to art and to the geniuses who make it.

Whether or not Perse had this poem in mind during his American years, there is a strong sense in *Vents* and earlier poems that the poet would prefer to sweep away markers and monuments, including the masterpieces of past artists, in order to begin anew. By the time of *Amers* a change has taken place. Although certain voices continue the call to forget and erase the literary past–the Tragédiennes, in particular, express their "écœurement [. . .] de toute l'œuvre célébrée" (290) and talk about setting aside "toute mémoire" (291)–the poet does not attempt to do so. Instead, he welcomes back the monuments, *phares/amers* on the cultural horizon. His self-proclaimed and longstanding aversion to books is tempered, although never entirely overcome. There is a poetic justice in linking Baudelaire to Perse's reconciliation with culture, since the poet often attributed his hostility to books to the primal literary scene of watching his father's library arrive in France after its ill-fated journey from Guadeloupe, with only one salvageable page, specifically from Baudelaire's *Fleurs du mal.*

Half a century later, Perse assimilates into *Amers* a vast heritage that goes back to Homer and the Bible. But its presence is not always peaceful. At noontime, on the surface of the sea "luit soudain la majesté terrible de l'Ancêtre" (301). This majestic and terrible Ancestor could be any one of the predecessors whose voices relay the ancient tradition into French. The poet's unease with this lineage can still be felt. Sometimes the family tree feels like the ones the chorus decries: "trop de grands arbres à l'entrave, ivres de gravitation, s'immobilisent encore à ton orient de mer, comme des bêtes que l'on trait" (374). The chorus warns against the burden of such a lineage: "Et du pénate ni du lare que nul ne songe à se charger; ni de l'aïeul aveugle, fondateur de la caste" (374). But despite this caveat, blind forebears are not banished from *Amers*–neither Anchises, father of Aeneas, nor the blind bard Homer. Instead, the modern poet renews the attempt to define his own place in a literary genealogy.

It is significant that among many epithets the sea is also called the "mère du puîné" (380). Every modern writer is a *puîné* or younger offspring in relation to the tradition, like the star that is evoked in the poem: "dernière venue et tard sevrée" (344). *Amers* continues the effort to overcome this position. Yet, unlike *Exil*, where the narrator claimed to seek a "grand poème né de rien, un grand poème fait de rien" (124), *Amers* comes closer to acknowledging that it is a *grand poème fait de tout.* The poet described it to his Swedish translator as a "Reprise de la grande phrase humaine" (571), and it indeed encompasses, in encyclopedic fashion, the cultural heritage of western civilization.

Allusions to history, geography, literature and mythology play varied roles in the poem, ranging from passing references that heighten local color to more sustained and substantive networks of sound and meaning. In the famous enumeration of personages from the cultural tradition, Princes, Pirates, Merchants, exiled nomads, Usurpers of thrones. . . (265), their very anonymity makes them surrogates for all the other characters who people history, literature and myth. Although they are nameless in the poem, they call to mind their countless avatars in history and literature and give the poem an aura of universality and timelessness.

Some references are anchored in specific places, like the Barbary pirates (357) who plied the North African coast until the nineteenth century. But most allusions point to a distant past of kings and empires. With the Erythrean virgin (339) and the Nubian women (344) Perse creates an atmosphere that is simultaneously oriental, exotic and ancient. The biblical world also intervenes through Baal, three times evoked (365, 371, 380), Mammon and Dagon (365), Istar (340) and Lot's wife (374). These allusions reinforce the sense of a "récitatif sacré" and give an impression of religious weight to the poem. Another abundant set of allusions points even further back in time toward the Sibyl of Cumae and her compatriots in the eternal world of myth.

When young girls in the poem compare their mothers to the Roman goddesses of destiny, "aux seins des Parques" (315), they elevate their own childhood to a divine plane and endow their words with a wider resonance. When the woman lover speaks of "un nom plus frais qu'Anchise" (343), her allusion to this mortal suitor of the divine Aphrodite opens the possibility of seeing Perse's own heroine as a modern-day Aphrodite. At the same time, the reference to Aeneas' father brings us directly into the world of Virgil's epic. Cybele, the fertility goddess, evoked at the end of the lovers' dialogue, also lends mythological stature to the protagonists and their story.

Jason and Medea, Circe and Calypso are among the inhabitants of *Amers*. With these and fellow heroes Perse constitutes his own *Commedia*, synthesizing history, literature and mythology into a summa of ancient culture. Above all, he creates a continuum with the founding narratives at the origins of western literature and with the legendary place of origin, which is Troy. The sky of *Amers* is dotted with allusions but one constellation dominates. This is, of course, the repeated reference to Troy, which is incorporated into the sound and rhythm of the poem as well as to its major themes.

We expect coastal cities to play an important role in a poem whose title denotes seacoast structures and an "Architecture fron-

talière" (274). The first strophe is entitled "Des Villes hautes s'é-
clairent sur tout leur front de mer . . . ," and the word *ville(s)* returns twenty-three times, yet virtually the only city to be named is
Troy, which is prominently linked to the line that serves as a refrain:
"Une même vague par le monde, une même vague depuis Troie." [4]
This verse recurs nine times, with slight permutations, and generates a special geography around Troy and the Mediterranean. It reinforces the impression of a story of origins, in the epic tradition of
Homer and Virgil, and makes of Troy a prototype, a kind of Ur-city,
from which the rest of human history emerges.

Built, so legend says, by Poseidon and protected by Athena,
Troy/Ilion stood at the crossroads of Europe and Asia. Its names
seem to have designated a sacred or magically encircled city. [5] Site of
the war immortalized in the *Iliad*, this is the city that perished for
Helen's sake and came to be associated with both war and literature. [6] As early as *Anabase,* Troy was present on Perse's horizon with
"les vaisseaux plus hauts qu'Ilion sous le paon blanc du ciel" (98).
This early poem about the founding of a city is one of Perse's first
efforts to create a modern epic. The endeavor continues in *Vents* on
the scale of a continent. In *Amers,* Troy occupies a pivotal place as a
city of archaeology, history, myth, and tragedy, departure point of
Odysseus and Aeneas and of the classical tradition. (Years later,
when Perse traveled through the Mediterranean on a friend's yacht,
he jotted in his notebook: "La mer Ilion.") [7]

In *Amers*, Troy is not only a place of origin but a nexus of
sounds and meanings. Manuscripts of this as of other of Perse's poems reveal elaborate networks of echoes, rhymes and rhythms at
the heart of his creative process. [8] The word *Troie* belongs to such a
configuration. It reverberates through words like *sois là, bois, foi,
voie, voix, lois, noix, Rois, poix, bois*. At the same time, it rhymes

---

[4] The refrain appears in slightly different forms on pp. 326, 330, 334-335, 336, 337, 339-340, 352, 356, 358, 360.

[5] Jack Lindsay, *Helen of Troy* (Totowas, NJ: Rowman and Littlefield, 1974), 108.

[6] Homer probably never saw Troy, since it was already a legend for minstrels in his day. According to Heinrich Schliemann, the real Troy was only a twentieth as large as Homer claimed, but that still made it as large as Athens. *Troy and its Remains,* tr. and ed. P. Smith (London: John Murray, 1875), 345.

[7] Saint-John Perse, "Croisière aux Iles Eoliennes," *Cahiers Saint-John Perse* 8-9, 1987, 265.

[8] Roger Little, *Saint-John Perse* (London: Athlone, 1973), 112.

with *proie, baudroie, droits, détroits* and the key word *Etroits*, title of the longest episode and seventeen times repeated. Another nexus of meaning centers around *Etroits* itself and forms a second refrain, repeated three times with minor transformations: "Etroits sont les vaisseaux, étroite notre couche" (326, 350, 337). The two networks intersect in the rhyming of *Troie* and *Etroits*. In their convergence, they unite two of the poem's major goals: to encompass the cultural heritage back to Troy and to overcome the narrowness of traditional verse, to find "un plus large mètre" (293) and "un plus large souffle" (293). As Perse retraces his steps across ancient civilizations, allusions are not enough to carry the poem back to a heroic time. A parallel journey unfolds in the sounds and rhythms of the poem, connecting it with that "même souffle depuis Troie."

An important part of this enterprise is respiration in its most fundamental, physiological sense. "Respirer avec le monde" (455): this, for Perse, is the poet's principal task. In his view, Dante succeeded in capturing, in a new language, the rhythm and respiration, the *souffle*, of earlier masterpieces. In French literature, Perse credited Claudel with breathing new life into poetry, opening up its meter and its possibilities, thanks to "la grande houle de [son] œuvre" (1016). It was France's good fortune, he wrote, that "aux heures où sa mesure semble la plus étroite, un apport démesuré et comme extérieur vienne élever sa crue" (1016). In these metaphors, art is a kind of ocean wave, *la grande houle,* coming to widen the narrowness, the *mesure étroite,* of poetry in need of breadth and breath. [9] Perse congratulated Claudel on being the wave that enlarged French versification, especially in the early poems (the ones he most admired), *Connaissance de l'Est* and the *Cinq Grandes Odes:* "Il étendit à de plus larges bords la mesure française" (483). Perse saw the poems as emerging from "un très lointain mouvement" (484) and believed that after Claudel, "le lieu n'est plus le même" (484). These statements suggest that Perse's admiration for Claudel's work was closely linked to how his predecessor expanded the possibilities of French poetry.

We now know that while Perse was writing *Amers* in the early 1950s he was also re-reading Claudel's early works, borrowing im-

---

[9] Claudel's role is considerable in *Amers,* where May Chehab has traced the links back to *Connaissance de l'Est* and the *Cinq Grandes Odes.* "Le Thème de la mer chez Claudel et Saint-John Perse," *Souffle de Perse* 5-6, 1995, 65-78.

ages from them and trying in his own way to enlarge the rhythm of French poetry.[10] In keeping with his theory that a poem should merge with its subject and become the thing it expresses (566), Perse was particularly concerned about making his verses mirror their object. He wished them to advance "largement et longuement, s'il s'agit de la mer ou du vent; étroitement et promptement s'il s'agit de l'éclair" (566).

To understand this goal, it is revealing to look at a specific verse of *Amers*. The male lover, contemplating the woman beside him, reflects:

> Libre mon souffle sur ta gorge, et la montée, de toutes parts, des nappes du désir, comme aux marées de lune proche, lorsque la terre femelle s'ouvre à la mer salace et souple, ornée de bulles, jusqu'en ses mares, ses maremmes, et la mer haute dans l'herbage fait son bruit de noria, la nuit est pleine d'éclosions . . . (328-9)

In this prodigious sentence-long verse, the narrator's thought process engenders movement in its image. His *souffle* not only spans sixty-one words but it rises in tandem with *la montée* of desire, like the tide it evokes. Just as the man is compared to *la mer salace et souple*, so the verse itself has a suppleness that carries it to its final explosion/*éclosion,* before it trails off in suspension marks. Its provisional halt preserves the illusion that the *souffle* might resume and continue forever. In the sound and pace of words and phrases, the poet merges meaning and form in an effort to recreate an epic breadth and breath.

The nexus of *Troie* and *Etroits*, which is incorporated into the sounds of the poem, also inflects its themes. The dramatic "Etroits sont les vaisseaux" episode plays out a dialectic of narrowness and breadth that mirrors other tensions between intimacy and independence, immobility and movement, woman's wish for alliance and man's desire for liberty. In the course of the poem, these dualities find a temporary synthesis in the image of woman as vessel (329), combining the intimacy of a cabin with the expanse of the ocean, the narrowness of a boat and the freedom to navigate.[11]

---

[10] May Chehab, "Le Thème de la Mer chez Claudel et Saint-John Perse," *Souffle de Perse* 5-6, 1995, 65-78.

[11] Perse specifically commented on the dual symbolism of the vessel as "vase et nef." *Saint-John Perse: Correspondance avec Dag Hammarskjöld,* ed. M.-N. Little, *Cahiers Saint-John Perse* 11, 1993, 112.

In *Amers* narrowness applies to love and to literature. The vessel is both woman and poem, sailing through time and space, propelled by the *souffle* of the poem's other refrain, the "même souffle depuis Troie." In this love poem, often compared to the biblical *Song of Songs*, sexual love and poetic creation are linked: "Etroite la mesure, étroite la césure qui rompt en son milieu le corps de femme comme le mètre antique" (335). The ancient meter in this verse highlights a final dimension of *Amers* as a metatextual reflection on language and art. The words *image, strophe, Chœur, Ode* and *récitation* (371) coexist in close proximity.

Perse often referred to the French language in spatial metaphors, calling it a "lieu géometrique," an "asile" and, for him, "la seule patrie imaginable" (551). In *Amers* language is called the "Terre de ma seigneurie" (268) and seen as a land that must be conquered. When the poet-narrator undertakes his hymn to the sea, he explains that the native land, the patrimony of the French language, must be recaptured through his song: "Le beau pays natal est à reconquérir, le beau pays du Roi qu'il n'a revu depuis l'enfance, et sa défense est dans mon chant" (268). The word *défense* underscores *Amers*' mission to be an *art poétique*, a twentieth-century *Défense et illustration de la langue française,* defining for modern literature what Joachim du Bellay charted in the Renaissance: a blueprint for future poems. In *Amers* they are described as "de très grandes œuvres à venir dans leur pulsation nouvelle et leur incitation d'ailleurs [. . .]. Très grandes œuvres et telles, sur l'arène, qu'on n'en sache plus l'espèce ni la race" (292, 293). Vast in scope, rhythm and resonance, the ideal works of the future are defined in words of breadth: a "plus large mètre," a "plus grand mètre," a "grand style" (293). Significantly, they are meant to elude genealogy.

The narrator is explicit about the effect he seeks to produce on listeners: "Je vous ferai pleurer [. . .] Pleurer de grâce, non de peine" (260). Moreover, the audience is to rejoice in his song and take heart, deriving from it "la grâce du sourire" (262). In a more ambitious declaration, he likens his song to the almost mystical encounter with "la chose sainte," leading to awe: "Aâh [. . .] ce cri de l'homme à la limite de l'humain" (266).

While describing such effects, *Amers* seeks to produce them in its own readers. Predicting vast works linked to an epic *souffle,* *Amers* also attempts to be one. The *défense* of poetry becomes, in the writing, an *illustration* of such poetry. When the Tragédiennes

call for "le ton du plus grand art" (293), the word tone is important, since much of *Amers* is an effort to recreate in French a tone
of ancient ritual through processional structure, echoes of Pindaric
odes, allusions to Troy, and expansive verses that seek consciously
to participate in a "même souffle depuis Troie." The singer of the
Invocation promises to tell his story "comme il convient qu'elle soit
dite" (260). Even more boldly, he proposes a new work, unlike any
previous one: "un chant de mer comme il n'en fut jamais chanté"
(261), but his song emerges from, and reacts to much that has gone
before.

Across the pages of *Amers* multiple voices play out the tension
between past and future. Two themes in particular communicate
and attempt to resolve the conflict. One has to do with forgetting.
Various narrators proclaim the need to forget and thereby abolish
the past. They seek a place to discard tradition: "où l'on verse à
l'oubli tout le bris de l'histoire et la vaisselle peinte des âges morts"
(358). Echoing the anti-library diatribe of *Vents,* they excoriate our
cultural cargo of books and artifacts. Persistent in proclaiming their
frustration with "tout l'appareil caduc du drame et de la fable"
(292), the Tragédiennes willingly surrender their cultural baggage in
order to be more receptive to inspiration (291).

A second, related theme is that of erasing. The sea is described
as a "face lavée d'oubli dans l'effacement des signes, pierre af-
franchie pour nous de son relief et de son grain" (267). From this
maritime surface, all traces of civilization appear to be absent, such
that the present generation can create its own wake: "Derrière nous
tout ce sillage qui s'accroît et qui s'allaite encore à notre poupe, mémoire en fuite et voie sacrée" (358). But if many voices in *Amers*
call for rupture with human culture, they are ultimately surpassed
in and by the poem. *Amers* is not an attempt to abolish culture, but,
rather, to reconcile past and present. Appeals to erase and forget
are balanced by recurrent instances of inscribing and remembering.
The same sea that is "immémoriale" is also "mémorable" (372).

Remembrance is perhaps most dramatically enacted in the dialogue between the two lovers. While the man seeks, above all, to set
out unfettered on uncharted seas, woman plays the role of memory
and tradition: "La nuit t'ouvre une femme," she says to him, "son
corps, ses havres, son rivage; et sa nuit antérieure où gît toute mémoire" (331). In the process of resolving the tensions between male
and female, forgetting and remembering, effacing and inscribing,

Amers works toward a reconciliation of tradition and creation. Ultimately these contradictory forces reach a temporary harmony in the final verses of "Etroits," where the couple joins a long lineage of lovers across time. In this scene, remembrance prevails: "Et longue mémoire sur la mer au peuple en armes des Amants" (358).

Assembling multiple strands of classical and biblical civilization, Perse continues his ongoing conversation with unnamed interlocutors. But in *Amers* a new set of voices joins the dialogue. While earlier works were dominated by the voices of ancestors, Perse now finds himself an "elder" in his own right, addressing a younger generation of writers (notably Jean-Paul Sartre) to whom he offers an explicit and defiant reply. In a post-war era where he perceives fragmentation, skepticism, abdication and even nihilism, Perse champions the wholeness of the human vocation and the possibility of seeking meanings. He knew his ideas were a direct challenge to contemporary and existentialist philosophy. As he explained to Lilita: "C'est évidemment une gageure! Et de l'esprit de contradiction en pareille époque." [12] Later, in a letter to Dag Hammarskjöld, he elaborated:

> J'ai voulu exalter, dans toute son ardeur et sa fierté, le drame de cette condition humaine, ou plutôt de cette *marche* humaine, que l'on se plaît aujourd'hui à ravaler et diminuer jusqu'à vouloir le priver de toute signification, de tout rattachement suprême aux grandes forces qui nous créent, qui nous empruntent et qui nous lient. C'est l'intégrité même de l'homme–et de l'homme de tout temps, physique et moral, sous sa vocation de puissance et son goût du divin–que j'ai voulu dresser [. . .] (569-570)

By the poet's account, *Amers* arises from the urgency of defining and proclaiming the spiritual dimensions of human life. At first glance, this is a surprising mission for a poet whom Claudel chided for his reluctance to talk about the divine. *Amers* indeed marks a transformation in Perse's outlook and perhaps most especially in his view of the past.

When the chorus presents its final wish to the sea, the hope is for a landscape of summits:

---

[12] Saint-John Perse, *Lettres à l'Etrangère,* 120.

[. . .] nous avions pour toi ce rêve d'une plus haute instance:
L'assemblée, à longs plis, des plus hautes cimes de la terre,
comme une amphictyonie sacrée des plus grands Sages institués
–toute la terre, en silence, et dans ses robes collégiales, qui prend
séance et siège à l'hémicyle de pierre blanche . . . (366)

This dreamed geography of mountain peaks arrayed like a sacred assembly of wise people resembles the beacons in Baudelaire's "Phares," giants of the cultural tradition. In the referential and textual sea of *Amers*, and its dual meditation about literature and human destiny, past culture and future creation come together in the new and permanent seamarks, or *amers,* that remain as markers along the shore. The poem closes with "l'homme de vigie, là-haut" (385), like a human lighthouse on top of a promontory, hoping perhaps to join the august assembly of summits that stretches back across Baudelaire to Virgil, Pindar, Solomon and Homer.

CHAPTER 10

CHRONIQUE AND THE STAIRCASE OF ELDERS

A poet removes his mask in the final verse of *Amers*. Immediately afterward, in 1959, a new poem begins with "nos fronts mis à nu pour de plus vastes cirques" (389). Yet we know better than to believe in the divestment of a poet who chooses a mask rather than a photograph for the cover of the Pléiade edition of his works. And we know enough to be wary of a narrator who says "nous voici" (389). He sings about human experience in a voice that is both individual and multiple:

> Grand âge, nous venons de toutes rives de la terre. Notre race est antique, notre face est sans nom. Et le temps en sait long sur tous les hommes que nous fûmes (393)

Actor and ventriloquist, this narrator is everyman and one man, the voice of history and the autobiographical voice of a poet confronting old age and beyond. His recollections embrace both individual and collective odysseys.

Written when Saint-John Perse was in his seventies, *Chronique* is suffused with the urgency and poignancy that accompany the retrospective summation of a long life. Situated in a precise locale, "Ici, ce soir" (399), it is one of his most personal poems, with allusions to his own trajectory from the Antilles to China, America, and finally to Giens in southern France, where the poem is located. Those who have watched the sun set from Perse's home in Provence attest to the accuracy of the portrayal. Perse himself, in a letter to Mina Curtiss, described it as the kind of sky one normally associates with the tropics. [1] But *Chronique* rises above its Mediterranean setting and the poet's personal journey to join a long lineage of meditations about time, aging and immortality. Cicero's *De Senectute* is one classic in a genre that includes writings by Seneca, Plutarch, Montaigne, Hugo and innumerable others. In addressing the *Grand âge*, Perse evokes predecessors who are explicitly present in the poem as "grands Aînés" (392). The portrait of these elders is unflattering indeed:

> Nous en avions assez du doigt de craie sous l'équation sans maître . . . Et vous, nos grands Aînés, dans vos robes rigides, qui descendez les rampes immortelles avec vos grands livres de pierre, nous n'avons vu remuer vos lèvres dans la clarté du soir: vous n'avez dit le mot qui lève ni nous suive (392)

In these verses, figures of the past are compared to silent stone giants descending the immortal staircase of history. What is the word they have not been able to say, the "word that would live and be with us" as Robert Fitzgerald translates it? [2] And what is the poem's brief with the Elders and their books of stone?

One dispute is with the portrayal of aging that the Elders have bequeathed to us. In the eighth decade of his life, Perse is resolutely unwilling to accept the idea that time inevitably brings diminution. This refusal is central to the poem. As he explained in a famous letter to Dag Hammarskjöld, the title comes from the Greek word *Chronos*: "Sous son titre, *Chronique*, à prendre au sens étymologique, c'est un poème à la terre, et à l'homme, et au temps, confondus tous trois pour moi dans la même notion intemporelle d'éternité" (1133). [3] All of these elements–time, earth, and humankind–are present in the poem, but time is the focus.

By most reckonings, the western literary tradition dates its origin from the ancestor whom legend portrays as the blind and aged Homer. In the *Iliad,* Priam laments to his son Hector the misfortunes of old age (22:68-70): "Pity me too!–still in my senses, true,

---

[1] Manuscript of letter to Mina Curtiss, dated June 25 [1957]. Pierpont Morgan Library, New York.
[2] St.-John Perse, *Chronique,* trans. R. Fitzgerald, *Collected Poems* (Princeton: Princeton UP, Bollingen LXXXVII, 1983), 582.
[3] The original letter figures in *Alexis Leger - Dag Hammarsjköld: Correspondance 1955-1961,* ed. M.-N. Little, *Cahiers Saint-John Perse* 11, 1993, 164.

but a harrowed, broken man, marked out by doom–past the threshold of old age."[4] At the beginnings of literature, old age is already
lamented, but Perse re-writes Homer and the subsequent tradition
to contradict classical depictions of aging.

Plato played an important role in fixing the *topoi* of old age. His
Republic begins with the aged Cephalus telling Socrates what it is
like: "The majority of us bemoan their age: they miss the pleasures
which were theirs in youth; they recall the pleasures of sex, drink,
and feasts, and some other things that go with them, and they are
angry as if they were deprived of important things . . ."[5] Cephalus
himself has a more sanguine view: if one's life is moderate, then old
age is only "moderately burdensome."[6] The essence, he concludes, is
to lead a just life. This opening conversation, whose primary role is to
set the scene for the *Republic*, actually had a great influence on later
writers, since it was among the earliest formulations of the standard
complaints of old age and the exhortation toward moderation. Aristotle, Cicero, Seneca and Plutarch all contributed to the rather
gloomy classical portrait of old age as a time of reason, virtue and
peace (at best), but also of diminution, resignation and waiting.

At the end of the Renaissance Montaigne added his voice to this
ongoing meditation. Steeped in classical authors, he depicted aging
in their manner. In the essay "Of Age" (I,57) he remarks how Han-
nibal and Scipio and almost all the great people of ancient times
had accomplished their deeds by the age of thirty. After that, "vivacity, quickness, firmness and other qualities much more our own,
more important and essential, wither and languish."[7] Montaigne ac-
cords the last word of his essays to old age, ending with a quotation
(in Latin) from Horace's prayer to Apollo:

> Grant me but health, Latona's son,
> And to enjoy the wealth I've won,
> And honored age, with mind entire
> And not unsolaced by the lyre.[8]

---

[4] Homer, *The Iliad*, tr. R. Fagles (New York: Penguin Classics, 1990), 543.
[5] Plato, *Republic*, tr. G.M.A. Grube (Indianapolis: Hackett, 1974), 3.
[6] *Ibid.*, 4.
[7] Michel de Montaigne, "Of Age," *Complete Essays*, tr. D. Frame (Stanford: Stanford UP, 1976), 238.
[8] Michel de Montaigne, "Of Experience," *Complete Essays,* 857.

When Saint-John Perse takes up his own lyre in *Chronique,* it is to protest the image of senescence as decline inherited from Montaigne and antiquity. He has another conception, different from the ancestral wisdom. This vision, elaborated in the poem, ultimately takes on mythological proportions, but it begins by protesting against his recent and familiar forebear, Victor Hugo.

The presence of a weighty ancestor is not surprising in a poem that is placed under the sign Chronos. The title refers, most immediately, to time, but it also suggests its homonym, the god Kronos, son of Earth and father of Zeus. Although the two words have separate origins, they became associated as early as Aristotle, who wrote in *De Mundo:* "God being one yet has many names, called after all the various conditions which he himself inaugurates. We call him Zen and Zeus [. . .] He is called the son of Kronos and of Time, for he endures from eternal age to age." [9] Kronos, god of the old order, was defeated by his son and relegated to the darkness of Tartarus so that Zeus might dominate sky and earth. At the threshold of *Chronique,* the implicit presence of Kronos sets the stage for another father-son drama, this one between a modern writer and at least one of his "grands Aînés" (392). In contesting the inherited depiction of old age, Perse rebuts the vision of an ancestor.

Chronique can be read, at least in part, as a conversation with a specific Elder around a specific poem, one of Hugo's best known and most widely anthologized works, *Tristesse d'Olympio.* [10] Literary historians link the poem to Hugo's October 1837 pilgrimage to the village of Les Metz, where he had spent some idyllic time with Juliette Drouet. Hugo composed the poem while he was in his thirties. He relates the story of a man revisiting sites of a past love, but tells it through the prism of a desolate old age. His tone is doleful; all traces of the narrator and his beloved have vanished from the surroundings:

> De tout ce qui fut nous presque rien n'est vivant;
> Et, comme un tas de cendre éteinte et refroidie,
> L'amas des souvenirs se disperse à tout vent! (st. 15)

---

[9] Aristotle, *De Mundo,* tr. E.S. Forster (Oxford: Clarendon, 1914), 401a15.

[10] "Tristesse d'Olympio," composed in 1837, appeared in *Les Rayons et les ombres* (1840). References to the poem, with stanza numbers in parentheses, are drawn from Hugo, *Poésies* II (Paris: Imprimerie Nationale, "Lettres françaises," 1984), 287-293.

In his romantic despair, the narrator experiences his mental state as old age, although there is no indication of his actual years. Like any authentic romantic sufferer, he is old before his time and conveys bleak images of his loss of power:

> Toutes les passions s'éloignent avec l'âge,
> L'une emportant son masque et l'autre son couteau,
> Comme un essaim chantant d'histrions en voyage
> Dont le groupe décroit derrière le coteau. (st. 33)

This depiction formulated by a young Hugo is refuted, virtually point by point, by the narrator of *Chronique*. Reversing the chronology, Perse becomes the Elder who, at age 72, can teach the young Hugo what age is really like.

The protagonist of *Tristesse* wanders all day and then, at dusk, begins a thirty-stanza lament. His counterpart in *Chronique* also speaks at nightfall, but his is a call to action: "Lève la tête, homme du soir" (389). The protagonist of *Tristesse* is compared to a "paria" (st. 8) contemplating the scenery as an outsider. By contrast, the observer in *Chronique*, looking out on a vast geography reddened by the sunset, dominates the scene. He is king of the site and of the moment: "Notre royaume est d'avant-soir, ce grand éclat d'un siècle vers sa cime" (392).

In Hugo's poem senescence is darkness; what remains of existence is "un tas de cendre éteinte et refroidie" (st. 15). *Chronique* denies these ashes: "Grand âge, vous mentiez: route de braise et non de cendres." (391); "Ceux qui furent aux choses n'en disent point l'usure ni la cendre, mais ce haut vivre en marche sur la terre des morts" (399). Perse's insistence on *braise* or glowing embers in place of Hugo's *cendre* or cold ashes signals the radical difference between his vision and his predecessor's.

In *Tristesse d'Olympio* we learn that nature has been instructed to erase us from places we have inhabited:

> [Dieu] dit à la vallée, où s'imprima notre âme,
> D'effacer notre trace et d'oublier nos noms (st. 30)

Traces of the lovers are swept from the setting and even their names are forgotten. In *Chronique* Perse takes up this same dialectics of naming and anonymity, but in a way that turns the tables on Hugo.

"Eponyme, l'ancêtre, et sa gloire, sans trace" (395). The ancestor in this verse remains anonymous and, even worse, leaves behind no vestige of his accomplishments, even though he is supposed to have given his name to a place. Like the other "grands Aînés" of the poem, Hugo has the come-uppance of remaining unnamed.

In Hugo's final stanzas, he paints a terrifying portrait of old age:

> Où l'homme, sans projets, sans but, sans visions,
> Sent qu'il n'est déjà plus qu'une tombe en ruine
> Où gisent ses vertus et ses illusions; (st. 35)

The saga of this tomb-like man ends in a dark place, devoid even of starlight: "dans cette nuit qu'aucun rayon n'étoile" (st. 38). By contrast, Perse revalorizes darkness, making it an exalted quality: "cette part en nous divine qui fut notre part de ténèbres" (394). In response to Hugo's protagonist who turns his attention backward: "N'existons-nous donc plus? Avons-nous eu notre heure?" (st. 16), Perse's narrator looks ahead: "Nous sommes pâtres du futur" (401). The narrator of *Tristesse* laments to his beloved that all signs of their passage are gone: "De tout ce qui fut nous presque rien n'est vivant" (st. 15). In *Chronique* "tous les hommes que nous fûmes" (393) live on in some mysterious way, for Perse takes the drama of old age and enlarges it to a universal scale, with time extending both backward and forward. He assimilates one lifetime into a geological time frame stretching back to the early period of earth formation, to a "nuit dévonienne" (401). In the other direction, *Chronique* looks ahead, "car notre route tend plus loin" (391).

If *Chronique* begins as a disagreement with the "grands Aînés" and their traditional portrayals of old age, it enlarges this conversation into a broader meditation about life and poetics. It seeks to go beyond the limits that dominate *Tristesse d'Olympio*: the metrical limits of measured verses and quatrains; the narrative limits of one romantic protagonist; the chronological limits of one lifetime. This effort takes Perse out of ordinary time: "Le temps que l'an mesure n'est point mesure de nos jours" [. . .] Et ceci reste à dire: nous vivons d'outre-mort, et de mort même vivrons-nous" (391).

Certainly, the stakes are higher for Perse than for a "thirtysomething" Hugo, whose narrative lament owes more to romantic posturing than to a confrontation with mortality. In *Chronique* Perse seeks the words he did not find in the ancestors. In response to their "équation sans maître" (392), he attempts a "chant du Maître" (404). This means gaining mastery through the power of language. To do so, he invokes the earth goddess, to whom the poem is addressed: "O face insigne de la Terre, qu'un cri pour toi se fasse entendre, dernière venue dans nos louanges" (402). The poet does not call the earth by her Greek name, Gaia, but introduces her under another of her appellations: "Et la grenade de Cybèle teint encore de son sang la bouche de nos femmes" (391).

Under Cybele's gaze, the poet-narrator assumes successive guises that link him to the mythological lineage of Gaia and Kronos, Hercules, Mercury and Zeus. Through these avatars, Perse elevates his drama to another plane; he transcends Hugo and other Elders to join a family of heroes who are larger than life and impervious to time. One of the episodes he singles out is the famous tunic of Hercules. When this god of the twelve labors, descendant of Perseus, Kronos and Zeus, has the misfortune of angering Nessus, the outraged victim takes revenge by poisoning Hercules' tunic in order to burn his body. Seeking to learn more about human suffering, Perse's narrator asks fate to tell him "quelle main nous vêt de cette tunique ardente de la fable [. . .]?" (394). A few years later, Perse repeats the same image in relation to Léon-Paul Fargue: "Le nervosisme moderne de Fargue lui tisse, à fleur de chair, une soyeuse tunique de Nessus" (516). Donning the tunic in *Chronique* is a way of identifying with Hercules, both in his suffering and his divine destiny.

Finding no remedy for his pain, Hercules builds a huge fire, like the "très haut seuil en flamme" (389) that illuminates *Chronique*. He ends his life in the flames, but with Zeus' reassurance that only his human component will burn; the eternal part will endure. For Hercules, as for the narrator of *Chronique,* the "lit de braise" (390) is actually a "route de braise" (391), leading beyond. Zeus guides Hercules to Mount Olympus and grants him eternity in an apotheosis that serves as a model for the perpetuation of "cette part en nous divine" (394) that the narrator of *Chronique* is confident will survive the fire of death.

Another son of Zeus is the multi-talented Hermes. Ambassador and messenger of Olympus, famed for his precocity, Hermes climbs out of his cradle as a baby and threads strings across a turtle shell to invent the lyre. Curiously, the narrator of *Chronique* singles out a tortoise shell among his favorite childhood objects, "l'écale de tortue géante encore malodorante" (395). From what we know of Perse's creative process, this reference undoubtedly evokes a real, smelly, sea-turtle shell from his Guadeloupean past, but given the multiplicity of allusions that reverberate from his words and ideas, it is likely that this same tortoise shell also points beyond autobiography to other, symbolic realms. The mythological resonances of the shell are one of the poet's many links with Hermes, inventor of song and thus a particularly appropriate mentor for Perse's own effort to write a "chant du Maître" (404). It is said that Apollo was so enchanted by Hermes' instrument that he traded his staff to have it. This is the famous caduceus, another symbol of Hermes, which figures in *Chronique*: "Le caducé du ciel descend marquer la terre de son chiffre. L'alliance est fondée" (403). Given Hermes' role as a go-between, a celestial diplomat and patron of treaties, he is all the more present in this caduceus of alliance that links sky and earth.

As the god of shepherds and travelers, Hermes often disguises himself in a cape, akin to the "cape de laine" (394) and the "vaste bure" (401) that figure in the wardrobe of *Chronique*, along with the "ample cape du berger jusqu'au menton nouée" (401). As a guide for travelers, Hermes leads souls on their ultimate journey to the afterlife. This role gives him special credence in a poem that specifically addresses the messenger of death: "O Mort parée d'un gantelet d'ivoire" (391). What guide could be more attuned to the poet-narrator that this polyvalent god, inventor of the alphabet and of astronomy, patron of orators and musicians, and as crafty as the multi-masked narrator of Perse's poetry. But if this clever god navigates throughout the poem, it is ultimately his father who presides.

As the supreme lawgiver and guardian of order, Zeus is the model for the narrator's dominion: "Nous étendons à tout l'avoir notre usage et nos lois" (398). One of Zeus' signatures is the recurring lightning that illuminates the poem. It figures as a kind of refrain in a verse that appears twice, with slight variations:

Nos œuvres vivent loin de nous dans leurs vergers d'éclairs (395)
Et nos actes s'éloignent dans leurs vergers d'éclairs (403)

Perse's autobiography chronicles his life-long fascination with lightning. He believed that all true poets, including himself, are person-

ally invested by it.[11] Dante's soul, for example, was "comme griffe
d'éclair" (457), while René Char needed no other "signe d'élection
que cet éclair au front" (542). In Perse's much-annotated copy of
Walter F. Otto's *Dionysos: le Mythe et le Culte* (1969), he specifically noted passages about lightning, including the dramatic conflagration in which Semele was consumed by Zeus' bolts while
conceiving Dionysus. Another frequently-underlined book in his
library, William Howitt's *History of the Supernatural* (1863), explains how electricity, magnetism and light are interrelated phe-
nomena; human souls, "exiled into this earthly life and animal
body,"[12] are destined to become citizens of the world of spirits. In
Chronique lightning creates a mythological aura and a sense of an-
ticipation: "Demain, les grands orages maraudeurs, et l'éclair au
travail" (403).

Before then, in a precarious present moment, *Chronique* is criss-
crossed four times by eagles, another privileged symbol of Zeus.
One of them emerges from stone: "La voix de l'homme est sur la
terre, la main de l'homme est dans la pierre et tire un aigle de sa
nuit. Mais Dieu se tait dans le quantième [. . .]" (391). This enigmatic eagle may symbolize the quasi-divine, or perhaps ungodly,
power of nuclear energy, discovered a decade earlier in uranium
and possessed by a new race of Protheans who lack divine guid-
ance about its use. A second, more accessible eagle is the one that
serves as a model for the native American ritual dance: "Jadis les
hommes de haut site, la face peinte d'ocre rouge sur leurs mesas
d'argile, nous ont dansé sans gestes danse immobile de l'aigle"
(399). The Indian eagle dance, which the poet himself visualized
from first-hand accounts by Francis and Katherine Biddle, becomes
in these pages a symbol of art. For a privileged moment, dancers
are immobile with arms extended, in the form of a cross or a scale,
while time seems to stand still. In this "danse immobile de l'âge sur
l'envergure de son aile" (399), participants live the seeming contradiction of intense action and apparent motionlessness. Similarly, in
a work of art, the poet suggests, one can capture the intensity of life
and the permanence of eternity.

---

[11] Mireille Sacotte, *Saint-John Perse* (Paris: Belfond, 1991), 35.
[12] William Howitt, *The History of the Supernatural* I (Philadelphia: Lippincott,
1863), 57. Fondation Saint-John Perse.

Chronique closes with one final bird and a liturgical gesture of summation:

> Nous élevons à bout de bras, sur le plat de nos mains, comme couvée d'ailes naissantes, ce cœur enténébree de l'homme où fut l'avide, et fut l'ardent, et tant d'amour irrévélé . . . (404).

This "hatching of nascent wings," [13] in Fitzgerald's translation, signals the imminent birth of yet another bird in this story of rebirth and regeneration: "Car maintes fois sommes-nous nés, dans l'étendue sans fin du jour" (394). In one sense, the plural *we* refers to all human beings, but it can also be read as progressive maskings and unmaskings of the narrator, and ultimately of the poet himself, who speaks more autobiographically than usual in the verses of *Chronique.* In this poem of literal and figurative sunset, he surveys the geography of his lifetime and meditates on what lies ahead. Having declined early offers to follow Chateaubriand's example and write his memoirs, he composes them now in his own fashion, obliquely and in poetry, but with the same vast perspective over a lifetime.

Perse's reflections raise more questions than they can answer, however, for it is not clear what lies ahead, or who is listening, or who will receive the offering: "L'offrande, ô nuit, où la porter? et la louange, la fier? (404). He begins *Chronique* by reproaching his Elders for failing to provide words to live by. At the end he realizes that he, too, may fail to provide such words, or at least all of the needed ones: "la chose est dite et n'est point dite" (397).

Appropriating the age-old metaphor of life as a day, Perse reflects on the brilliant lateday sun, illuminating a tree: "L'arbre illustre sa feuille dans la clarté du soir" (399). That is no ordinary tree, but a specific one from his past: "le grand arbre Saman qui berce encore notre enfance; ou cet autre, en forêt, qui s'ouvrait à la nuit" (399). On one level, these exceptional trees, remembered from Guadeloupe, seem to confirm the oniric richness of our earliest family memories. But if Perse's looks back in *Chronique* to roots and trees of childhood, he also looks beyond them to a different kind of genealogy, one where he can forge an artistic lineage, distinct from normal procreation: "Nous passons et, de nul engendrés,

---

[13] St.-John Perse, *Chronique,* tr. R. Fitzgerald, 603.

connaît-on bien l'espèce où nous nous avançons?" (394). At this point in his life, he is interested in a new kind of birth, the one that leads to immortality: "il est d'autre naissances à quoi porter vos lampes!" (392). In *Chronique* Perse elevates his genealogical meditation to a cosmic level as he strolls through the mythological world of Kronos and Gaia, and dons the successive masks and robes of their descendants, Hercules, Hermes and Zeus, to plumb the mysteries of time and eternity. *Amers* closed with a temporary immortality: "Nous qui mourrons peut-être un jour disons l'homme immortel au foyer de l'instant" (385). *Chronique,* by contrast, bathes in the quiet realization that death will come, even as the poet meditates about time and the many ways to capture it. In the course of the meditation, Perse's poem about old age becomes an Ovidian hymn to rebirth in all its different manifestations and to the forces capable of rising above ordinary time to the one kind of eternity most compelling to the poet: immortality.

CHAPTER 11

OISEAUX: FROM AUDUBON TO BRAQUE
AND BEYOND

S AINT-JOHN Perse looked at birds with the eye of a poet and the expertise of a naturalist. Ushered into his writing in 1907 with *Pour fêter des oiseaux* (which later became *Cohorte)*, birds remained there forever, soaring to the place of honor in *Oiseaux.* "Le thème de l'Oiseau semble avoir hanté toute sa vie Saint-John Perse" (1134), notes the poet in the third-person autobiographic chronology of the Pléiade volume. Indeed, birds abound in Perse's poetry –some 106 references to 55 families or species, according to Maurice Rieuneau–and have been the focus of excellent critical studies. [1] This passion was more than purely literary. The Pléiade chronology offers numerous references to bird-watching expeditions, sightings of rare birds, and Perse's admiration for ornithologists. The entry for 1905 is the first mention of a close encounter with a bird:

> Rencontre, en haute montagne désertique, d'un oiseau solitaire qu'il ne devrait plus jamais revoir, mais dont le souvenir ne pourra s'effacer de sa mémoire: le 'tichodrome échelette' ou *Tichodroma Muraria* de Linné, plus connu des alpinistes sous le nom de *Rose-des-Alpes* (xiii)

---

[1] See Maurice Rieuneau, "Sur Saint-John Perse et les oiseaux d'Audubon," and Jean Dorst, "*Oiseaux* vus par un ornithologue" *Espaces de Saint-John Perse* 1-2, 1979; Marie-Noëlle Little, "L'Aile, motif et réseaux des poèmes d'Amérique," and Jennifer Weir, "Catalogues américains d'oiseaux 'montés' par Saint-John Perse," *Espaces de Saint-John Perse* 3, 1980; Pierre van Rutten, *Le langage poétique de Saint-John Perse* (The Hague, Paris: Mouton, 1975); Christian Doumet, *Les Thèmes aériens dans l'œuvre de Saint-John Perse* (Paris: Minard, 1976).

More than half a century later, one of the final entries, dated 1969, records Perse's pleasure about progress on a law "pour la protection des derniers grands rapaces de France (loi promulguée seulement en 1972)" (xlii). The parenthetical update makes this the final event in the autobiography, which otherwise ends with 1971.

Perse's personal library contains dossiers of newspaper clippings and more than fifty books about birds. Over thirty of them are annotated. A typical example is his copy of Henry David Thoreau's classic *Maine Woods*. Using as a checklist Thoreau's "List of Birds which I saw in Maine between July 24 and August 3, 1857," Perse noted how many of Thoreau's birds he himself had observed. Given the poet's admiration for Edward Lear's *Nonsense* books, it is likely that he also knew the ornithological drawings of this versatile nineteenth-century creator who illustrated John Gould's *Birds of Europe*.

If Perse wrote both as naturalist and as poet, if his birds are both real and figurative, they take on yet another dimension in *Oiseaux* where the protagonists of the title are, at least in part, the painted birds of another work of art. To enter into Perse's last major work, we must first situate this "oiseau peint" (411) and let it guide us to the central issues of the poem.

Georges Braque fills much of the horizon of *Oiseaux,* at least on first reading. His twelve extraordinary lithographs, entitled *L'Ordre des oiseaux,* seem, as the narrator suggests, to be its subject. But this may not in fact be true, for while *Oiseaux* is ostensibly about Braque's birds, it is unlikely that Braque was its initial inspiration or subject. Perse in fact took pains to affirm that the collaboration with Braque occurred very late in the process of creation and that the text was "conçu en toute indépendance, les références à l'Oiseau de Braque y étant ajoutées après coup" (1030). Among Perse's papers there is a detailed, typewritten account in which he explains to an unspecified reader, who may simply be posterity:

> Je crois bon de vous éclairer sur les conditions dans lesquelles cette œuvre a été écrite . . . En fait, le texte d'OISEAUX n'a pas été écrit pour illustrer ou commenter la suite lithographique de Braque, et ne s'y réfère point directement, non plus qu'à aucune œuvre particulière du peintre. L'œuvre écrite et l'œuvre peinte étaient indépendantes l'une de l'autre. Encore moins pouvait-il y avoir subordination de l'une à l'autre, la première étant antérieure à la seconde.

A l'heure (1961) où Braque se mettait au travail pour la préparation du grand album d'Oiseaux à publier à l'occasion de son 80ème anniversaire (1962), on avait su, à Paris, que j'achevais moi-même ici une œuvre poétique sur le thème de l'oiseau. On m'a demandé, pour faire plaisir à Braque, avec qui je partageais une réelle affection, de réserver la publication originale de mon texte pour une présentation simultanée des deux œuvres dans une même grande édition de luxe et sous un titre commun de circonstance. Je m'y suis prêté de grand cœur, et l'émotion qu'en a manifestée Braque m'a profondément touché. La communication de mon manuscrit l'a amené à réclamer plusieurs ajournements du projet en cours, pour lui permettre d'ajouter quatre planches nouvelles s'inspirant directement de quelques pages de mon œuvre poétique (et dans une conception beaucoup moins statique que celle qui lui était coutumière). (Braque était déjà familier avec mes œuvres antérieures, et plus particulièrement avec AMERS.) J'ai eu à cœur, de mon côté, d'ajouter à mon texte poétique quelques pages de méditation esthétique se reférant incidemment à la vision métamorphique du peintre et à l'Oiseau de Braque en général. [2]

Perse insists here that his work is not an illustration of Braque's lithographs, and indeed that it pre-dates their collaboration, except for some minor additions. His clarification serves, in the first instance, to warn that *Oiseaux* is not a mere accompaniment to Braque's art. At the same time, this elaborately-detailed chronology raises the essential question about what the poem was conceived to be *before* its last-minute association with Braque. If the references to Braque were added "après coup," what was the poem about before this belated association? Who were the birds in its original conception?

Braque's bird, we are told by the narrator of *Oiseaux*, is not a simple motif: "Il n'est point filigrane dans la feuille du jour, ni même empreinte de main fraîche dans l'argile des murs" (416). If Braque's protagonists do not function like watermarks on Perse's page, certain other figures do. Appearing as a kind of filigree or as

---

[2] *Oiseaux* dossier, Fondation Saint-John Perse. Perse made the same point in a 1962 letter to Jean Paulhan, saying the poem was "conçu en toute indépendance, les références à l'Oiseau de Braque y étant ajoutées après coup." *Correspondance Saint-John Perse - Jean Paulhan*, ed. J. Gardes Tamine, *Cahiers Saint-John Perse* 10, 1991, 245.

fresh handprints, they illuminate the meaning of the poem and point toward some of its deepest mechanisms.

As a poem about a work of art, *Oiseaux* fits into an illustrious tradition of ekphrasis, descriptions of real or imagined art works, a tradition that dates back to Homer's depiction of Achilles' shield in the *Iliad*. Virgil tried his hand at ekphrasis with Aeneas' shield, and Perse himself experimented with it early on, in his unpublished poem about a Gauguin painting. He returns to this mode in *Oiseaux*, as he continues his meditation about fusing past with future, inheritance with originality. Although the poem seems at first reading very different from Perse's other work, it is really a sequel in which he renews his colloquy with French ancestors in the New World and follows in the footsteps of a most colorful precursor who is never mentioned in the poem, but who plays a major role in our understanding of it. This is Jean-Jacques Audubon, who chose to be called John James Audubon, premier ornithologist in the American imagination, whose name is virtually synonymous with birds.

It seems clear that Audubon's birds play a more compelling role in the poem than Braque's, and that *Oiseaux* most likely began as a meditation about the ornithologist, only to be transformed en route, with minor revisions, into a tribute to Braque when the artist invited Perse to join in a collaborative work. On close observation, many of the supposed descriptions of Braque's birds actually apply more accurately to Audubon's.

Saint-John Perse was captivated by Audubon, which is not difficult to understand, given the magnetism of this most exotic French settler. Born in the Caribbean a century before Perse, of a Creole mother and a French father, Audubon spent nine years in the Antilles before moving to France. Legends surround him. One myth, which he encouraged in order to camouflage his illegitimate birth, claimed that he was the Dauphin, son of Louis XVI and Marie-Antoinette, rescued by a French naval officer and taken to the West Indies. Another probably apocryphal story has him studying art in Paris with the painter David. It has been said that Audubon was a man "congenitally incapable of telling merely the unvarnished, unembellished truth. Seldom could he resist the temptation to make a good story better. And some details of his own biography he made out of whole cloth."[3]

---

[3] Frank Levering, "The Enchanted Forest," *The Bicentennial of John James Audubon*, ed. A. Lindsey (Bloomington: Indiana UP, 1985), 82.

At age eighteen, Jean-Jacques was sent to America to engage in commerce, but showed little interest in anything but ornithology. His grand idea was to draw a complete collection of American birds in their natural habitat, accompanied by commentaries. The project was immensely ambitious, since life-size depictions meant that the pages had to be almost 40 by 30 inches large, in a format known as double elephant folio. When the set was finished, it contained 435 plates and sold for $1000–a fortune at the time. In 1826 Audubon set off for Europe to sell subscriptions. Playing into the European fascination for Sir Walter Scott, Washington Irving, James Fenimore Cooper, Davy Crockett and Daniel Boone, he received a hero's welcome in England and an introduction from Cuvier to the French Royal Academy, but he garnered only 49 subscriptions to *The Birds of America.*

During his lifetime Audubon published over 500 "bird biographies," based on his observations of birds' habits, settings and characteristics. Perse owned and annotated a copy of *The Bird Biographies of John James Audubon,* selected and edited by Alice Ford. He collected various other Auduboniana, including two prints, a postcard of the ornithologist, and at least one newspaper clipping about him. Perse's acquaintance began early. Although the ornithologist is not specifically cited in the 1907 *Cohorte,* he is probably one source of its detailed information about specific birds. In 1913 Perse mentioned to Claudel the "marcassin de Guyane [. . .] pour lequel Audubon cherchait ses plus jolis mots de Yankee louisianais" (726). The bird expert earned a cameo appearance in *Vents:* "Et ce n'est pas assez de toutes vos bêtes peintes, Audubon! qu'il ne m'y faille encore mêler quelques espèces disparues: le Ramier migrateur, le Courlis boréal et le Grand Auk . . ." (200).[4] Audubon also figures in two letters to Roger Caillois where Perse describes the Anhinga bird.[5]

---

[4] See Maurice Rieuneau's commentary on this verse, *op. cit.,* 342. Audubon's Water Turkey appears a second time in *Vents* as "la dinde d'eau des fables, dont l'existence n'est pas fable" (207). His drawing seems to be present as the narrator asks: "A quelle page encore de prodiges, sur quelles tables d'eaux rousses et de rosettes blanches, aux chambres d'or des grands sauriens, apposera-t-il ce soir l'absurde paraphe de son col?" (207).

[5] "L'Oiseau 'Anhinga' *(Vents,* II,4), à mon très grand regret, existe bien scientifiquement sous ce nom (Anhinga Anhinga), illustré depuis longtemps par Audubon. Son nom populaire est 'Water-Turkey' ou 'Snake-Bird'" (561). In a subsequent letter Perse elaborates that the bird has been "Vulgarisé par les illustrations d'Audubon *(The Birds of America, 1827-30)* sous la présentation suivante: 'Black-bellied Darter, Poltus Anhinga, Linn'" (965).

In these references, the poet cites Audubon as a naturalist and illustrator, but other evocations are more personal. The Pléiade chronology lists for the year 1951: "Découvre aussi le portrait, au crayon gras, d'un Audubon vieilli et barbu, fait par lui-même à Londres avec cette inscription de sa main: 'Almost happy!'" (xxvi). This same bearded man returns elsewhere in the Pléiade volume, in a letter Perse claimed to send to his friend and benefactor, Mina Curtiss, after taking possession of the Mediterranean villa she purchased for him. In the published version of the letter, the poet compares his own sentiments to those of the celebrated bird watcher: "'Almost happy!' ai-je lu un jour, à la Nouvelle-Orléans, au bas d'un autoportrait, au crayon gras, d'Audubon (daté je crois de Londres, vers la fin de sa vie)–un Audubon âgé, barbu et grave, grisonnant, mais toujours aussi beau sous l'étendue de son immense regard créole" (1058). What is astonishing about this mention is that it does not figure in the real letter, which is now at the Pierpont Morgan Library. Rather, it was added a decade later while Perse was assembling, revising and rewriting letters for his collected works. This affectionate homage to Audubon carries all the more weight for being inserted belatedly in a reinvented correspondence.[6] (Mina Curtiss, aware of the revisions in the published versions, is said to have commented that Perse wrote wonderful letters–especially those she never received!)[7]

Perse had the same kind of "immense regard créole" he attributed to Audubon, and shared with him a kinship forged from similar backgrounds and parallel itineraries. Both were "hommes d'Atlantique" (xl), as Perse liked to call himself, natives of the Antilles, transplanted back to France and then to America. Each had a naturalist's eye for detail, a predilection for precise nomenclature and a determination to study the world in its specificity. Finally, each possessed an artist's capacity to transform reality into works of imagination. Their trajectories, from the Caribbean to France and America, a century apart, hold many similarities, including an anecdotal incident that figured prominently in both lives. For Audubon it was among the worst moments of his career:

---

[6] On Perse's revisions to his correspondence with Mina Curtiss, see Renée Ventresque, *Le Songe antillais de Saint-John Perse* (Paris: L'Harmattan, 1995), 205-211.

[7] Cited by Mireille Sacotte, *Alexis Leger-Saint-John Perse* (Paris: L'Harmattan, 1997), 46.

> Once, before proceeding to Philadelphia on business, I looked
> to the welfare of all my drawings, placed them carefully in a
> wooden box and left them to the care of a relative for several
> months. On my return I asked for my box and what I was
> pleased to call my treasure. It was produced and opened. But
> reader, feel for me. . ., a pair of Norway Rats had taken posses-
> sion, and reared a young family among the gnawed bits of paper
> which, a few months before, had represented nearly a thousand
> inhabitants of the air![8]

This nightmare of opening a container to find all the pages destroyed calls to mind that memorable (and possibly apocryphal)
episode in Perse's own autobiography when his father's books were
destroyed en route to France.[9]

In 1842 Audubon was given United States citizenship by President Tyler. A parallel gesture figures in Perse's chronology for 1949:
"Loi spéciale prise en Congrès pour l'admission d'Alexis Leger,
comme citoyen français, au statut de résidence permanente aux
Etats-Unis" (xxv). When the narrator of *Oiseaux* cites "Les vieux
naturalistes, dans leur langue très sûre et très révérencieuse" (410),
he alludes to a whole tradition of ornithologists, from Linnaeus forward. But he is also referring, surely, to that other old French naturalist, the "Almost happy" Audubon of the New Orleans drawing.
And when he evokes "l'oiseau peint de Braque" (411), the prints he
describes bear a much closer resemblance to the *Birds of America*
than to modern lithographs.

The "gauchissement de l'aile" (420), the "tension dardée de
tout le corps, ou cet allongement sinueux des anses du col" (422)
are all familiar attributes of Audubon's birds. Similarly, the process
of stalking, capturing and studying a bird was hardly as characteristic of Braque as it was of the naturalist-painter, who first hunted
and wired his subjects before painting them. This precedure is particularly well portrayed in *Oiseaux* IV where Perse enumerates the
various phases of the process: "La fulguration du peintre, ravisseur
et ravi, n'est pas moins verticale à son premier assaut, avant qu'il
n'établisse, de plain-pied, et comme latéralement, ou mieux circu-
lairement, son insistante et longue sollicitation" (413). One can eas-

---

[8] Alice Ford, ed., *Audubon, by Himself* (Garden City: Natural History Press,
1969), 72.
[9] See Chapters 1 and 9 of this book and page xi in the Pléiade chronology.

ily imagine Audubon entertaining this kind of circular acquaintance with the bird he has captured, passing from the ravisher to the one who is ravished, sitting in rapt attention before his guest.

From birdwatcher and hunter to painter: such was the continual passage of Audubon with each new subject. The captured bird would begin its evolution from drawing or painting to an engraving, which would then be colored: "L'oiseau, hors de sa migration, précipité sur la planche du peintre, a commencé de vivre le cycle de ses mutations. Il habite la métamorphose. Suite sérielle et dialectique. C'est une succession d'épreuves et d'états, en voie toujours de progression vers une confession plénière . . ." (413). The narrator credits Braque with a long and patient knowledge of birds, but his depiction more accurately reflects Audubon's hours of study and contemplation. During the time the naturalist devoted to a painting, his attitude could be summed up by the words of *Oiseaux:* "Vivre en intelligence avec son hôte devient alors sa chance et sa rétribution. Conjuration du peintre et de l'oiseau" (413).

Audubon's goal was to capture each bird in the vigor of its movements, the precision of its details and the essence of its natural setting. His drawing would thus be like the one described in *Oiseaux:* "chose vive, en tout cas, et prise au vif de son tissu natal" (411). Audubon seized the entire milieu of his subjects, like the Mogol conqueror of the poem, who journeyed home with a bird, a nest, a song, and "tout l'arbre natal lui-même, pris à son lieu, avec son peuple de racines, sa motte de terre et sa marge de terroir, tout son lambeau de 'territoire' foncier évocateur de friche, de province, de contrée et d'empire . . ." (412). Audubon's elephant-size pages offered 1200 square inches of space, but even this sometimes cramped larger birds who had to be hunched over prey to fit on the page. As a result, observes natural historian Michael Harwood, the larger birds "seem to be about to burst from the margins of his paintings; they convey a marvelous sense of unrestrained life and energy [. . .] There are often two or more birds in a composition, usually *doing* something–fighting, courting, feeding young, defending the nest." [10]

Bent over, sometimes awkwardly, to fit on their page, and always threatening to break out of their confines, Audubon's birds in-

---

[10] Michael Harwood, "A Watershed for Ornithology," *The Bicentennial of John James Audubon,* ed. A. Lindsey (Bloomington: Indiana UP, 1985), 43.

deed have the kind of "gauchissement de l'aile" (420) that is evoked in *Oiseaux*. The awkwardness of their form on the page is part of the process of capturing their movement. In Audubon's colored birds the activity is palpable, as in the paintings depicted in *Oiseaux:* "Rien là d'inerte ni de passif. Dans cette fixité du vol qui n'est que laconisme, l'activité demeure combustion. Tout à l'actif du vol, et virements de compte à cet actif!" (416). Here, as in other descriptions, the birds of *Oiseaux* call to mind the shape and feel of Audubon's drawings. At other times, Perse's avian protagonists remind us as well of Audubon's language, since words and images come together in the work of this artist-naturalist-writer.

If Braque's birds are, in the narrator's eyes, "inallusifs et purs de toute mémoire" (425), Perse's birds, by contrast, are eloquent with allusion and memory. The poem opens with an epigraph from Persius: ". . . *Quantum non milvus oberret* (Plus que ne couvre le vol d'un milan.)" [11] This Kite bird, which is a kind of hawk, merits three separate prints in Audubon's *Birds of America*, illustrating three different varieties. The Mississippi Kite, in particular, has a silhouette strikingly like that of a Braque lithograph. It would not have been difficult for the poet to take words that were originally composed about Audubon's Kite bird and apply them to Braque's lithographs. Equally striking are linguistic echoes that link Audubon's birds to the protagonists of *Oiseaux*.

In the first stanza, one of Perse's birds is identified by his call: "Et son cri dans la nuit est cri de l'aube elle-même: cri de guerre sainte à l'arme blanche" (409). In an earlier version of this verse, the poet explicitly mentioned the Crusades: it was a "cri de [croisade et de] guerre sainte." Perse later eliminated the reference, but his verse still conveys the idea of a holy war. At the same time it recalls one of Audubon's most celebrated and reproduced prints: the Man o' War Bird, *Fregata Magnificens*. The Man o' War seems to have been one of Audubon's favorite birds, and perhaps Perse's as well, to judge from the annotations in his copy of *Audubon's Bird Biographies*. The Man o' War is noted for his speed. In Audubon's words: "The power of flight of this bird I conceive superior to that perhaps of any other." [12] His vision is so acute and his movement so rapid that he

---

[11] Nicholas Castin has pointed out an error in Perse's epigraph. The verb in Persius' poem is *errat*. "Saint-John Perse et les Poètes Latins: Epigraphes et métrique interne," *Souffle de Perse* 5-6, juin 1995, 11.

[12] *The Bird Biographies of John James Audubon,* ed. A. Ford (New York: Macmillan, 1957), 24.

"gains on his prey like a meteor." [13] This makes him a kindred spirit to the hero of *Oiseaux* who descends "dans une vibration de faux, se confondre à l'objet de sa prise" (413) and who is also placed under the sign of war: "Son aventure est aventure de guerre" (416), with "lances levées à toutes frontières de l'homme!" (426).

Another striking model for *Oiseaux* is Audubon's Washington Sea-Eagle, *Falco Washingtoniensis*, one of the naturalist's most memorable profiles. Audubon mistakenly believed he had discovered a new species (in fact, it was a Washington Sea-Eagle, an immature bald eagle). What connects this exceptional episode to *Oiseaux* is the dimension of naming. Audubon describes with poignancy and excitement his emotion on sighting this eagle: "It was in the month of February, 1814, that I obtained the first sight of this noble bird, and never shall I forget the delight it gave me. Not even Herschel, when he discovered the planet which bears his name, could have experienced more rapturous feelings." [14] Herschel's planet does not, in fact, bear his name. He originally called his discovery *Georgium Sidus*, in honor of King George, but a long-standing tradition of mythological names prevailed and the planet came to be called Uranus.

Audubon could have baptized the bird with his own name, but he had another plan instead:

> The name which I have chosen for this new species of Eagle, the 'Bird of Washington,' may be considered by some as preposterous and unfit. But as it is indisputably the noblest bird of its genus that has yet been discovered in the United States, I trust I shall be allowed to honor it with the name of one yet nobler, who was the saviour of his country, and whose name will ever be dear to it. To those who may be curious to know my reasons, I can only say that as the New World gave me birth and liberty, the great man who insured its independence is next to my heart. He had a nobility of mind and a generosity of soul such as are seldom possessed. He was brave, so is the Eagle. Like it, too, he was the terror of his foes, and his fame, from pole to pole, resembles the majestic soarings of the mightiest of the feathered tribe. If America has reason to be proud of her Washington, so has she to be proud of her great Eagle. [15]

---

[13] *Ibid.*, 25.
[14] *Ibid.*, 101.
[15] *Ibid.*, 103.

Audubon plays a double role in this episode, first as a naturalist discovering a new species, and then as a poet attributing a name to his discovery. In this dual process he resembles his twentieth-century descendant, preoccupied with names and with what he deemed the "plus haute vocation, qui toujours fut celle de nommer" (683). In naming the Washington Eagle, Audubon paid tribute to the New World, which gave him "birth and liberty," and to the father of the American nation. By a curious coincidence, another adopted Frenchman ends his bird work with the same name, although as a geographical referent, since *Oiseaux* is signed "Washington, mars 1962."

In the early days of American ornithology, Audubon often had the privilege of naming unknown birds. Perse appropriates this privilege in *Oiseaux* when he invents for Braque's birds the new name of *Bracchus Avis Avis* (424). This formulation, which naturalists use to signify the type that becomes an archetype, calls to mind the poet's own early pseudonym, Saint-Leger Leger, which he forged by doubling his patronym, as if also to become an archetype. Throughout his life, he would revise and remotivate his names.

Alexis Leger began life with a name that had inevitable linguistic connotations: *léger*, light, as in the expression *light as a feather*. Research by Claude Thiébaut indicates that it was the poet's father who initially removed the accent from the family name Léger, but this did not suffice to remove its connotation of lightness. Alexis Leger gave greater resonance to the name by expanding it to Saint-Leger Leger, but even this did not eliminate the possibility of puns on lightness, including Jacques Prévert's, when he humorously inscribed a copy of his *Paroles* to "Saint-Lourd Lourd." The best way to exchange Leger for a name with more weight, more mystery, and a grander genealogy was to select a radically new pseudonym.

Both components, Saint-John and Perse, are associated with eagles. The biblical Saint John, sometimes called the eagle of Patmos, is linked to the bird of the Apocalypse, while the mythical Perseus soars in the air like an eagle, thanks to winged shoes provided by Hermes. In both allusions the bird is not *léger;* he is imposing, monumental, and awesome. It is as if, by an alchemy of language, the poet could replace one proverbial analogy, *light as a feather*, with another one, that suggests vision and genius: *eagle eyed*. The substitution, first performed in the 1920s when Perse created his pen name, and later renewed in *Pluies,* is reenacted in *Oiseaux* where he plays once again with the resonances of that name. And what more privileged site for remotivating a *nom de plume* than a poem where the lightness of ordinary birds is replaced by the nobility and perspicacity of eagles?

During the period when Perse was composing *Oiseaux,* he was also writing the autobiographical chronology for the Pléiade edition of his works. Both texts share a concern with names and ancestors. In the biography, a detailed and sometimes fanciful genealogy links Alexis Leger to a long tradition of illustrious ancestors. While Audubon nurtured the myth that he was the Dauphin, Louis XVII, Leger proclaimed himself a descendent of Gaston de Foix, the fourteenth-century chevalier and patron of the arts (xxi).

The birds of *Oiseaux,* whether Audubon's or Braque's, are likened to the "rassemblement d'une famille entière d'ailes" (422). Perse's own work is a similar effort to constitute a family, not so much of wings as of *plumes*–pens–and to create a family tree that assembles forebears with whom he feels and seeks an affinity. The word *affinité* appears four times in *Oiseaux,* and in no other poem, although it figures twice in the prose texts of the Pléiade edition. These occurrences, in a homage to André Gide (1951) and a commentary on Léon-Paul Fargue (1963), help us understand why its fourfold repetition in *Oiseaux* is significant.

In the first instance, Perse praises Gide for having created a "libre réseau d'affinités littéraires où se retrouveraient un jour, en 1909, et comme à leur insu, les éléments divers et très épars d'une singulière Pléiade: sans liens réels, sans engagement ni charte ni manifeste–pour une 'Défense' encore 'et Illustration de la Langue française'" (476). One of the members of that illustrious 1909 group was Leger himself, whose *Images à Crusoé* had just been published in the *Nouvelle Revue Française.* Through Gide, Leger entered this twentieth-century Pléiade and inherited the mission to create a new Renaissance, following in the footsteps of Joachim du Bellay's *Defense.*

The second occurrence of the word *affinité,* in the tribute to Léon-Paul Fargue, dates from the same period as *Oiseaux.* Here Perse seeks to define Fargue's place in the French tradition and portrays him as a "poète de pure naissance [qui] garde sa prérogative auprès des mieux situés de ses aînés" (510). After evoking Fargue's purity–the ultimate compliment–and his independence from his elders, Perse goes on to depict Fargue's love of words, "les mots portés à leur inclination première et leurs affinités secrètes, par leur aînesse et leur jeunesse et leur élan vital" (525). The affinities among words (as among writers) gravitate around metaphors of youth and age, lineage and inheritance, in this passage where the poet seeks to show how Fargue, and perhaps he himself, are worthy of figuring in the genealogy of their elders.

The same thematic network underlies *Oiseaux*, with its search for affinity and filiation. The narrator insists that Braque's birds do not emerge from literature or legend. They do not descend from Noah's dove or Poe's raven, from Pindar, La Fontaine, Lautréamont, Baudelaire or Coleridge. But they do have a special genealogy because they are simultaneously (and like Fargue) of a "caste nouvelle et d'antique lignage" (424). This is the crucial tension Perse himself had to resolve: how to take his place at the end of an old and illustrious French *lignage* while at the same time initiating a *caste nouvelle*; how to be both a successor to French and classical forebears and a brand new voice with his own legacy to bequeath.

A preoccupation with engendering underlies much of the poem, beginning with the blood relatives, "consanguins" (409), of the first verse and prolonged through a semantic field that includes seeds and sowing, race and caste, types and archetypes. This constellation of words, and other related ones, is a road map to Perse's genealogical thinking at the time. In the very first entry of his Pléiade biography the author describes himself as the "seul garçon d'une famille de cinq enfants" (ix). As the only son, without progeny, he could not transmit the family name. But as a poet he could perpetuate that of Saint-John Perse through poems that would act as seeds. This idea recurs six times in *Oiseaux* in the sequence of *semence/ semences/semés/ensemencent/ensemencez* (419, 423). The narrator says of Braque: "vous ensemencez d'espèces saintes l'espace occidental" (423). Just as the artist fecundates the future with his works, the poet also aspires to "ensemence[r] à long terme nos sites et nos jours" (423), even if the haunting presence of sowing, seed and fertility belies a profound fear of sterility, both poetic and physical.

In the poem, Perse weaves a heroic genealogy. By evoking Persius' Kite bird on the threshold of *Oiseaux*, he links his work to the classical tradition and unites his heroes with the eagles of a heroic past. In the course of its creation, a poem which began as a work *about* birds, becomes a kind of poetic Phoenix. In the mythical genealogy of birds, the Phoenix is a pre-eminent ancestor. Although there is no female in the species, the male ensures progeny by setting fire to a nest of aromatic plants and magical herbs. From the ashes a new bird is born, making the Phoenix the symbol of immortality. At its deepest level, *Oiseaux* is a meditation about immortality and about the legacy to leave to posterity. It is a poem about wings and flight and how to conquer time.

In his autobiography, Perse describes his grandmother, Augusta de Caille, "qui avait été admirée jeune fille par Lamartine et lui gardait toute sa ferveur" (xiv). *Oiseaux* can be read as an elaborate echo of the famous verse from Lamartine's own poem, *Le Lac:* "O temps, suspends ton vol!" Perse's weapon against the flight of time is the permanence of art, works like Braque's and Audubon's (and, ideally, his own) which capture time and motion and render them eternal: "ils éternisent au point fixe le mouvement même du vol" (415); "effusion faite permanence" (420).

If the poem is a symbol of eternity, the poet, too, transforms himself through language into a sort of Phoenix, capable of self-engenderment without need of a female. He looks back on a long line of forebears (all of whom, significantly, seem to be forefathers) and forward to the transmission of his poems and his name to future generations. *Oiseaux* is both an *art poétique* and a work of art by which the poet forges a poetic genealogy in hopes of immortalizing the name of Saint-John Perse.

CHAPTER 12

PRECARIOUS ETERNITY: *CHANT POUR UN EQUINOXE*

A T the end of his life, Saint-John Perse gathered four short poems into a collection entitled *Chant pour un équinoxe*. The
timing of its publication–in the year of his death–creates the aura of
a culmination and a testament. But such a reading is misleading, for
these poems are less a conclusion than a cluster of pieces that sometimes seem like fragments of earlier writings, assembled in the
poet's waning years. When narrators refer to "œuvres parcellaires"
(1398) and "œuvres [. . .] éparses" (1395), they capture the feel of
the poems themselves. Perse himself saw them as elements of a
vaster, unfinished project. When he sent the short equinox poem to
Le Monde in 1972, he stipulated that Gallimard would retain all
rights to "l'œuvre intégrale en cours dont ce fragment est détaché."[1] This longer project was a poem in honor of Gaia, the
Greek goddess of the earth. After the poet's death, his widow carried out his request to destroy the unfinished drafts, leaving only
these four published segments of a partial mosaic. Albert Henry believes they constitute an artificial collection, without real unity.[2]

Perse for his part considered the last poems to be a new and
perhaps even surprising initiative, and warned: "Mes prochains
poèmes surprendront ceux qui croient que je vais rester toujours le

---

[1] Fondation Saint-John Perse, Dossier "Chant pour un équinoxe." Perse entitled this folder "Projet annulé du publication au MONDE." The poem was accepted
for publication and Perse received proofs, but for unspecified reasons, it was not
published.

[2] Albert Henry, ed., *Saint-John Perse, Nocturne* (Paris: Gallimard, Publications
de la Fondation Saint-John Perse, 1985), 42.

même."[3] His prediction is both accurate and erroneous. These poems, the most intertextual of his works, echo words, themes and passages from his earlier works and thus generate less surprise than a sense of *déjà lu*. But if the language is familiar, the tenor of the poems assumes an unexpected and poignant urgency. True to his prediction, the poet indeed reserves some surprises for readers.

Perse's last poems are colored by images that shaped previous ones: kings and lineage, race and rank, sources and sowings. But this time the seed is divine: "la semence de Dieu s'en va rejoindre en mer les nappes mauves du plancton" (437). Three decades after Claudel's famous remark that God is a word Saint-John Perse religiously avoids (1130), we find *Dieu*, capitalized, fourteen times in one brief group of poems, compared with only eight occurrences in the hundreds of previous pages. Other gods (*dieu/dieux*) also figure four times. Together they hint at a new step in the poet's ongoing conversation with culture.

These final poems are both troubled and troubling, told by multiple narrators, male and female. The men's voices range from confident and almost hopeful to resigned, disheartened and bitter. During the years when Perse was composing these poems, he was also, and above all, editing the Pléiade edition of his complete works, looking back over his life and composing the literary monument that would survive him. Some of the emotions inherent in that colossal project—retrospection, anxiety, frustration, pride and disappointment—spill over into the poems. In voices that are charged with immediacy, narrators undertake a dialogue with destiny that differs from Perse's previous conversations with elders. His preoccupation is less with the inherited tradition than with a legacy to bequeath, less with others than with himself. Most of the voices that accompanied earlier poems are silenced. Now the most urgent colloquy is with posterity. The principal interlocutors, with one notable exception, are himself, his own work and forces beyond human scope.

The four poems of this collection appeared separately over a span of six years, in the chronological order of their signatures:

---

[3] Jean Bernard, *Mon beau navire* (Paris: Buchet/Chastel, 1980), 161, quoted in Steven Winspur, *Saint-John Perse and the Imaginary Reader* (Geneva: Droz, 1988), 158.

Chanté par Celle qui fut là, 1968
Chant pour un équinoxe, 1971
Nocturne, 1972
Sécheresse, 1974

When Perse assembled them into a single volume, he explicitly altered the chronological order, exchanging the first and last poems. The series thus opens with the longest, *Sécheresse,* and closes with *Chanté par Celle qui fut là,* in a sequence that transforms the cumulative effect of the poems.

At the threshold of the collection, *Sécheresse* prophesies drought. In a tone drawn from wisdom literature and reminiscent of *Amitié du Prince* and *Anabase,* a narrator extols the benefits of spiritual thirst. Dryness is a time of ascesis and creativity, like the "soirs de grande sécheresse" that served as a refrain for *Amitié du Prince* (65, 69). Despite apparent barrenness, it is "un temps de croître et de créer" (678), followed in the normal cycle of seasons by a rebirth of life. The prophecy of *Sécheresse* is couched in a biblical language of exodus, transgression and heresy, of called and chosen people; it ends by invoking a "temps de Dieu" and a "terre de Dieu" (1400). But the narrator's prayer for divine favor is unrequited, here as in *Chant pour un équinoxe,* where heaven's only response is thunder, "qui fut brève, et ne fut que fracas" (437).

The second poem is a dialogue between man and woman in the spirit of *Etroits sont les vaisseaux.* Its concluding invocation to the earth, "O Terre, notre Mère" (438), links it to *Chronique* which the poet also intended, at least in part, as a hymn to earth (1133). Once again he adopts a cosmic scale. Placing this poem, and ultimately the whole collection, under the sign of the equinox, he seeks once again, as in *Amers* and *Oiseaux,* to arrest time.

In *Chronique* Perse proclaimed that his journey would not stop with death: "notre route tend plus loin" (391). In the third poem of this collection, *Nocturne,* he charts the itinerary anew, anticipating future works and imagining the "fruits d'une autre rive" (1395). Finally, in *Chanté par Celle qui fut là,* he entrusts the summation to a narrator who is both woman and *anima,* an earthly companion and an incarnation of the eternal feminine. Her name, "Celle qui fut là," echoes the lover's blessing from *Amers:* "Grâce pour celle qui fut là" (338), but this time it is the woman who gives the blessing. As *anima,* she rises above the present to guarantee the kind of permanence inscribed in the sea of *Amers:* "Celle toujours qui nous fut là et qui toujours nous sera là" (372).[4] Like the sea, this woman links past and future. She is depicted as a "demeure ouverte à l'éternel" (431) and a "cœur ouvert à l'éternel" (433). Her last word, and that of the collection, is *mémoire.* Entrusted with preserving the poet's memory, she is an example proposed to future readers. The poet leaves nothing to chance; rather, he composes and dictates the very words of remembrance, placing his script in the mouth of the one who is to remember. (The poem's original title, *Récité par celle qui fut là,* gives an even better idea of how the narrator is meant to transmit words entrusted to her by another.)

In the equinox collection Perse looks to the future even as he assembles diverse fragments and echoes of earlier works. The Pléiade edition is a parallel initiative where the poet unites disparate documents, events, friendships and encounters of a lifetime into a single vessel for immortality that Mireille Sacotte compares to Noah's Ark.[5] In both endeavors, he converses with his own past and, even more urgently, with destiny. The tenor of his conversation is perhaps best revealed in Perse's reordering of chronology. By changing the sequence of the poems, he specifically reroutes our path through them, from a different starting point to a new destination. He guides us from prophecy toward eternal remembrance. Entering the collection through *Sécheresse,* we encounter a protagonist in the lineage of earlier Persean heroes. Belonging to an "élite" (1396, 1399) and a cohort of "élus" (1396, 1399), he is an "Appelé" (1396), called to realize every potential. Given his vocation, nothing seems impossible: "Je tiens pour consonance de base ce cri lointain de ma naissance" (1396). Born to a larger-than-life existence, he invokes gods of the mythological family. Maia, "Mère de tous songes" (1397) is also the mother of Hermes, patron of poets, messenger of the gods and a favorite figure for Perse. In his Egyptian guise, as Anubis, he is a kind of talisman for Perse.[6] This god of obstetrics

---

[4] The reference recalls another *Amers* passage: "Sois avec nous Celle du dernier soir, qui nous fait / honte de nos œuvres, et de nos hontes aussi nous fera grâce [. . .]" (378). The presence of this woman of the "last evening" is appropriate in a poem about the end of life. Perse used a similar expression in a 1948 letter to Lilita: "Merci, Liu, d'être là, d'avoir toujours été là." *Lettres à l'Etrangère,* ed. M. Berne (Paris: Gallimard, 1987), 125.

[5] Mireille Sacotte, "Le Rire de Saint-John Perse," *Europe* 799-800, Nov.-Dec. 1995, 135.

[6] Anubis was also a talisman in Perse's friendship with United Nations Secre-

was the patron of new ideas and new creation. In another more solemn role, Anubis-Hermes serves as usher to the afterworld, an appropriate role in a poem of old age, published in Perse's eighty-seventh year.

Across *Sécheresse*, a growing prophetic furor leads to ever more exalted promises that are meant to be fulfilled in the "heures démentielles" (686) of some future time. The poem announces wonders to come, when the messenger of the gods will come to call. The protagonist of *Amitié du Prince* wore a crest of feathers on his helmet as a sign of spiritual favor. He was designated the "Prince sous la huppe, comme l'oiseau chantant le signe de sa naissance" (65). In *Sécheresse,* the hoopoe bird returns as a divine messenger: "la Huppe messagère cherchera encore sur terre l'épaule princière où se poser" (680). The protagonist expects to receive this message. He prays to be touched by "l'amorce fulgurante" (686) of genius and divinity, like his predecessor in *Vents,* "crêté de foudres et d'aigrettes sous le délice de l'éclair, et lui-même tout éclair dans sa fulguration" (223). He aspires to be tapped by divine inspiration and even somehow to become divine: "que l'homme en Dieu s'entête" (1400). The wish is vain; his Faustian urge is doomed to failure. No such fate is reserved for humankind: the poet's realization of this truth underlies the poem's final, enigmatic verse: "Singe de Dieu, trêve à tes ruses" (1400).

Given Perse's particular fascination for monkeys, the presence of this one in his last verse is fraught with meaning. In an early manuscript the poem ended with: "Singe de Dieu, trêve à tes ruses! et face au sol." The disappearance of the last four words only heightens the mystery of the exclamation. Journalist André Brincourt, relating Perse's penchant for stories, noted with a certain exasperation that he was "incontrôlable sur les singes," despite attempts to steer conversations to more literary topics.[7] In a dossier entitled "Faune terrestre" the poet kept a *National Geographic* magazine feature about monkeys, including Hanuman, the Monkey

---

tary-General Dag Hammarskjöld. Each man had a small Egyptian statuette of the jackal-headed god; Perse's was a gift from Hammarskjöld. Almost half the letters in their fascinating and moving correspondence allude to the mysterious smile and multiple roles of Anubis. See Marie-Noëlle Little's discussion in *Alexis Leger-Dag Hammarskjöld: Correspondance 1955-61,* ed. M.-N. Little, *Cahiers Saint-John Perse* 11, 1993, 68-81.

    [7] André Brincourt, *Messagers de la nuit* (Paris: Grasset, 1995), 104.

God of India. Perse's own *singe de Dieu* calls upon myriad connotations reaching from the natural world to literature, philosophy and mythology.

Because of their talent for mimicry, monkeys are often linked to the notion of doubles, an idea that pursued the poet. Writing about his civic and poetic identities, in a 1941 letter to Archibald MacLeish, Perse recounted a Malaysian aboriginal belief that human beings have doubles, representing our creative selves, who accomplish marvelous feats as we sleep (549). He related to André Gide a slightly different version of the tale in which repressed desires circulate at night in the form of monkeys, doing what is not permissible by day (480). The idea even colored Perse's relationship with Lilita Abreu. Imagining she had a double who stayed with him when she herself was away, he once signed a letter "De tout cœur, avec mon Macaque." [8] Human doubles can be mischievous or benevolent, but a monkey of God is much more problematic. As the last verse of the poem, the exclamation has a special and even portentious tone.

There is a long tradition of human beings aping attributes of god. Perse's early and voracious reading of Nietzsche could have uncovered the philosopher's speculation that "If God created the world, he created man to be his ape, as a perpetual source of amusement in the midst of his rather tedious eternities." [9] One of God's most tantalizing attributes to imitate is, of course, immortality. The legendary Monkey King, from the 16th-century Chinese classic, *Journey of the West*, stole the peaches of immortality in an ill-fated attempt to outwit mortality. In Shakespeare's *Measure for Measure*, a trickster monkey illustrates misguided, pretentious human behavior:

> . . . man, proud man
> Drest in a little brief authority
> Most ignorant of what he's most assur'd,

---

[8] Saint-John Perse, *Lettres à l'Etrangère*, ed. M. Berne (Paris: Gallimard, 1987), 80. Charles Dolamore also cites the story in "A propos de Sécheresse," *Cahiers du 20e siècle* 7, 1976, 125.

[9] Friedrich Nietzsche, *The Wanderer and his Shadow, Complete Works* 7, ed. O. Levy, tr. P. Cohn (New York: Russell, 1964), #13, p. 193. Colette Camelin identified this reference in *L'Eclat des contraires: La poétique de Saint-John Perse* (Paris: CNRS Editions, 1999), 283.

> His glassy essence, like an angry ape,
> Plays such fantastic tricks before high heaven
> As would make angels weep; (II:2, 117-122)

Efforts to mimic God are simply ruses, tricks designed to imitate what we cannot be. If Perse's verse is a rebuke to the over-reaching protagonist, it may also be a self-critique by the poet himself, suggesting that he too is a trickster, like Hermes, and must at the end of his life cease playing tricks. However exalted his role, he cannot rise above the human plane, or, as one of his favorite philosophers, Heraclitus, observed: "In the matter of wisdom, beauty and every other thing, in contrast with God, the wisest of mankind will appear an ape." [10] Perse's modern "Singe de Dieu" draws upon myriad connotations of monkeys and tricksters, as the poet wistfully renounces his quests for omniscience and immortality and calls a halt to the very ruses he has so long and deftly plied. This poignant observation gives all the more weight to the poet's tribute to Georges Braque: "franc de tout masque, qui ne rusait jamais" (537).

If the *Equinoxe* collection had ended with this poem, and this verse, it would have conveyed a profound doubt about the power of poetry and the limits of human inquiry. It would have concluded with skepticism about the possibility of rising above the human condition, of communicating with a spiritual realm, or achieving immortality through art. But Perse chose not to close with this anguished questioning. Instead, he arranged the poems in such a way that the last three address, and perhaps assuage, the doubts of the first. In the revised order, the sequence retraces the trajectory of *Pluies, Vents,* and other poems whose narrators grapple with similar existential questions. After a frenzied flight toward some divine realm, the traveler of *Vents* comes to a standstill: "Mais quoi! n'est-il rien d'autre, n'est-il rien d'autre que d'humain?" (234). In this same realization, he understands the force of love and resolves to renew human relationships: "Où êtes-vous qui étiez là, silencieux arome de nos nuits, ô chastes libérant sous vos chevelures im-

---

[10] Heraclitus, *Fragments*, tr. T.M. Robinson (Toronto: U of Toronto Press, 1987), Fragment 83, p. 51. It was later cited in Plato's *Greater Hippias*, 289b. Serge Canadas sees the monkey of God as the harbinger of reason. "Passage de l'équinoxe," *Cahiers Saint-John Perse 2*, 1979, 29. For Nicholas Castin, the transformation from *songe* to *singe* changes the creator into a creature. "La Stratégie de la négation: *Sécheresse*," *Souffle de Perse 3*, janvier 1993, 89.

pudiques une chaleureuse histoire de vivantes?" (234). The women of *Vents*, "qui étiez là," are precursors of "celle qui fut là," the woman of the equinox collection who guides him, once again, to human love.

In Perse's last poems, woman is a positive force of reconciliation. In an inverse trajectory from Dante's Beatrice, this heroine leads the poet back toward the human realm, the only possible site for encountering the divine. The frenzied ecstasy of *Sécheresse* gives way in *Chant pour un équinoxe* to a more peaceful sense that epiphanies occur in unexpected places and forms. God does not, will not, engage in direct conversation with the poet, but he may show himself in other ways, through the multiplicity of nature: "Dieu l'épars nous rejoint dans la diversité" (437).

Chant pour un équinoxe opens in the present, "L'autre soir il tonnait" (437), but it reaches back in time and space to encompass mythological, biblical and historical traditions, from Chi Huang-ti, the legendary Chinese patron of thunder, and Seth, the Egyptian storm god, to Cheops, patron of the largest pyramid at Gizeh, and Saul, the first king of Israel. In Perse's manuscript, three other candidates vied for Saul's place. One is the Indian emperor Asoka, whom Perse had underlined in his *Nouveau Petit Larousse Illustré* as "un des plus grands souverains de l'Inde," from the third century B.C. The other candidates were the Persian king Sapor and Johannes Kepler, whose claim for inclusion may have been his role as a founding father of cosmology. Although Kepler did not remain on the roster of giants, his presence in an early draft signals Perse's continuing meditation about the transmission of greatness. While regal dynasties are bequeathed through family lines, genius is governed by a different lineage. In the poem there is a child "dont nul ne sait la race ni le rang" (437). Such is the ideal genealogy of intellectual and artistic creation.

The evocation of dynasties and creativity gives a peaceful exhilaration to *Chant pour un équinoxe*. A more sober tone follows in *Nocturne*, where a narrator looks back upon his life, surveying the fruits of his labor. In the broadest sense, these are the accumulated deeds and relationships of a lifetime, but they are also, more specifically, works of art. The presence in a short poem of *œuvres, thème* and *aveu* suggests a link to Perse's own work. Poems are his offspring, "de notre sang nourris" (1395), and his verdict is harsh: "Nous n'y trouvons point notre gré" (1395).

If past accomplishments are disappointing, new fruits are ripening before his eyes: "Les voici mûrissants, ces fruits d'une autre rive" (1395). A forward momentum is inscribed in the grammar of the poem, in a future perfect tense that projects the protagonist's journey forward: "Et ceux qui l'auront vu passer diront: qui fut cet homme, et quelle, sa demeure?" (1395). This question stages both the protagonist's departure and others' reactions to it. Posterity is meant to ask who he was; the answer lies partly in the poem and partly in the full Pléiade volume. In both creations, Perse anticipates and shapes posterity's response to his life and works. He continues this effort in the fourth poem where *celle qui fut là* speaks in words the poet scripts for her and in part for us.

In this collection, Perse's preoccupation with present and future mutes many, but not all, voices of the past. One important interlocutor can still be heard. This is Paul Valéry, whose footsteps Perse traced, quite literally, in the Provençal setting of his last decades, at the tip of the Giens peninsula. Perse's home, "Les Vigneaux," was built on a site named "La Polynésie," where Valéry used to stay in the 1920s and 1930s as a guest of the Countess of Béhague. It was here that Valéry wrote *La Cantate de Narcisse* in 1938.

Arriving in Giens exactly two decades later, Perse made a point of highlighting the geographic overlap with his illustrious predecessor, as in the interview where he explained: "Autrefois, Valéry habitait la presqu'île de Giens. Il n'y avait que deux maisons, la sienne et celle que j'ai acquise il y a quatre ans." [11] In the Pléiade edition of Valéry's works, Perse annotated the biographical entry for 1925: "Va se reposer chez la Comtesse de Béhague, dans sa propriété de Polynésie, à l'extrémité de la presqu'île de Giens, dont les décors–îles, rochers, arbres–servent de thèmes à ses gravures." [12] Pierre Guerre, Perse's longtime friend, describes a walk on which the new resident pointed out Valéry's lodgings (1341). Apparently this was a regular routine for visitors to "La Polynésie." When Perse invited T.S. Eliot, he noted that "Notre ami Valéry passait sur cette presqu'île de Giens ses vacances, auprès de Mme de Béhague, dans une maison voisine de la mienne" (1040).

---

[11] Christian Gali, "Quatre heures avec Saint-John Perse," undated, unidentified clipping in the Sylvia Beach archive, Princeton University Library.

[12] A. Rouart-Valéry, "Introduction biographique," in Paul Valéry, *Œuvres* I, ed. J. Hytier (Paris: Gallimard, Bibliothèque de la Pléiade, 1957), 48. Perse also noted a visit in 1932, p. 56.

"Les Vigneaux" was chosen and purchased for Perse by his American benefactor, Mina Curtiss, to whom he wrote many grateful letters. [13] A comparison of the originals with the Pléiade versions reveals just how much Perse rewrote them for publication. The two most important letters seem to have been entirely invented. [14] In one, dated September 9, 1958, he cites Valéry three times, in contexts ranging from gastronomy to philosophy, even though the writer did not figure in original letters of that period. Perse inserted the allusions a dozen years later, when he was simultaneously composing the equinoxe poems and editing the Pléiade volume. The references are thus all the more significant for having been added for posterity. One mention, on the lighter side, evokes a local vintner "chez qui Valéry, en bon Méridional, aimait parfois flairer la cuisine provençale" (1061). On a more serious note, the poet describes his intellectual interaction with the poet of Sète and reflects upon "cette lumière latine où se perdit, je crois, tant de savoir et tant de connaissance," adding parenthetically, "(j'en disputais jadis, amicalement, avec Paul Valéry!)" (1059). The debate between the two poets is mentioned again when Perse enumerates (in the Pléiade, but not in the original letter) the many literary figures who preceded him in the region: "Stevenson et Conrad, et le cher Edward Lear; Bourget, Vogüé, Edith Wharton; Lamartine et Michelet, Tolstoï lui-même, qui l'eût cru? et Valéry enfin, que j'aimerais tant pouvoir encore taquiner, en lui rappelant ici que la lumière méditerranéenne nous frappe de cécité et clôt pour nous le seuil métaphysique" (1062). In this list of predecessors, the last-but-not-least "Valéry enfin" is crucial. Perse regrets that he can no longer tease the late Valéry about sun, light and metaphysics. But the poems of Giens are, in their own way, a sparring in which Perse prolongs what he called the "amicable dispute" with his predecessor and crosses that metaphysical threshold the Mediterranean sun seemed to close.

---

[13] Perse's correspondence with Mina Curtiss is now at the Pierpont Morgan Library in New York.

[14] Renée Ventresque discusses Perse's rewriting of the Curtiss letters in *Le Songe antillais de Saint-John Perse* (Paris: L'Harmattan, 1995), 205-211. Valéry figures once in the correspondence at the Pierpont Morgan Library, in a letter dated September 17, ostensibly from the mid-1960s, where Perse announces that the tourists have left and he and his wife "pouvons jouir, à peu près seuls, de la plage de Valéry, et nous nous en donnons à cœur joie."

While Perse was composing the *Chant pour un équinoxe,* he was also rereading Valéry with pencil in hand, leaving abundant marks in the margins of prose and poetry. Perse's annotations signal the specific passages that caught his attention and offer a privileged glimpse into the dialogue between the two poets. One such place is Valéry's observation that "Le meilleur ouvrage est celui qui garde son secret le plus longtemps. Pendant longtemps on ne se doute même pas qu'il a son secret." [15] Valéry's remark could be applied to Perse's own enigmatic poems, which envelop a multiplicity of secrets, many of them destined (and even designed) to remain elusive. Only occasionally is it possible to elucidate them through conversations that inform the texts. Echoes in Perse's last poems hint at the hidden presence of Valéry as an unnamed interlocutor and suggest that the equinox collection was written in company with, and partly in response to this predecessor in Giens and on the terrain of French letters.

Paul Valéry, born in 1871 and Perse's senior by sixteen years, was indeed an elder. The younger poet explicitly deemed him that in a 1933 letter where he named the "trois Aînés qui signent cette requête: Henri de Régnier, Marcel Prévost et Paul Valéry" (1140). As early as 1909, Perse confided to Gustave-Adolphe Monod that Valéry was "une des seules 'figures' qui m'intéressent encore" (658).

The friendship began early. According to Valéry's diary, the young man called on him in 1912, declaring: "Edgar Poe et vous, les deux hommes que j'ai le plus souhaité connaître." [16] In Perse's telling, their meeting inaugurated an "amitié nouée avec Paul Valéry, en dehors de tout milieu littéraire" (xvi). Under the rubric 1914-1916, he mentions another "longue conversation avec Valéry, qui lui avoue les raisons d'ordre humain (il attend un enfant) l'incitant à reprendre la plume et à se faire une place dans la littérature (indications fournies, à cette occasion, sur l'évolution de *La Jeune Parque*" (xvii).

Linked by a shared admiration for Edgar Allan Poe and Robinson Crusoe, the two writers inhabited overlapping circles in their contemporary literary and intellectual milieux. Names cited in Valéry's

---

[15] Paul Valéry, "Littérature," *Tel Quel* in *Œuvres II,* ed. J. Hytier (Paris: Gallimard, Bibliothèque de la Pléiade, 1960), 168. This and other annotated volumes are at the Fondation Saint-John Perse.

[16] A. Rouart-Valéry, "Introduction biographique," in Paul Valéry, *Œuvres I,* ed. J. Hytier (Paris: Gallimard, Bibliothèque de la Pléiade, 1957), 35.

Pléiade biography and underlined in Perse's copy of the volume also figure in his own life: Anna de Noailles, Princess Bassiano, André Gide, Joseph Conrad, T.S. Eliot, Rainer-Maria Rilke, Rabindranath Tagore, Aristide Briand, Niels Bohr, Albert Einstein.

The Pléiade edition of Perse's work includes a long letter to Valéry from China, dated 1917, that alludes to an earlier "émouvante conversation" (823) in Paris. The original letter is not in the archives and cannot be verified, but even if it was remembered or created specially for the purpose, its authenticity matters less than the place the poet gives it, so many years later, in the Pléiade volume.

Soon after Perse's return from China in 1921, social gatherings brought the two men together. In February, 1922, Valéry was entrusted with an invitation:

> Cher Monsieur,
>
> Marie Laurencin vous prie à déjeuner, ce mardi (quoique gras) a midi 1/2. Elle me charge de vous l'écrire, ce que je fais bien volontiers dans l'espoir de me rencontrer chez elle avec vous. Tous mes souvenirs. Paul Valéry.

Half a century later, living in a Mediterranean geography inhabited by the ghost of Valéry, Perse was once again drawn into dialogue with his predecessor. In 1967, passing the island of Palmarolla, he jotted in his notebook: "Le vrai 'cimetière marin.'" [17] Later, within sight of the Italian coast, he observed "Gênes laissé à [son fond] comme Valéry." [18]

One of the best-known events in Paul Valéry's life is the famous "nuit de Gênes" of 1892, a dramatic spiritual event, recorded in his notebooks: "Nuit effroyable–passé sur mon lit–orage partout–ma chambre éblouissante par chaque éclair.–Et tout mon sort se jouait dans ma tête. Je suis entre moi et moi." [19] This crisis prompted the young Valéry to abandon poetry for more than a decade and to focus solely on his intellect. Perse's last poems might be read as his own "nuits de Giens," during which he debates with himself about past and future.

---

[17] Saint-John Perse, *Croisière aux Iles Eoliennes, Cahiers Saint-John Perse* 8-9, 1987, 157.

[18] *Ibid.*, 251.

[19] Agathe Rouart-Valéry, *op. cit.*, 20.

Given the contrasting temperaments and trajectories of the two writers, it is not surprising that Perse was often critical of Valéry. Michel Philippon has dubbed the two men Monsieur Teste and "Monsieur Thorax," [20] referring to Valery's ratiocinations and Perse's preoccupation with respiration. In Perse's view, Valéry saw poetry as a feast for the intellect, music for the mind; he emphasized the cerebral while Perse embraced all human ways of knowing and perceiving. This may not have been a totally accurate reading, and certainly does not account for the sensuality of Valéry's poems, but it allowed Perse to envisage a distinct contrast between Valéry's intellectualism and his own desire to connect fully to life, through mind and body, including the very process of respiration. [21]

Perse also reproached Valéry for the disparateness of his writing and for an *œuvre* that he described to Jean Paulhan as a "dispersion fortuite, comme anecdotique, où Valéry s'est laissé dissiper, par manque de maîtrise et d'esprit de suite, par manque aussi d'exigence de vivant" (1032). On another occasion Perse remarked to André Brincourt: "Valéry? Moins un grand poète qu'un grand écrivain; il refusait la part d'insaisissable. Du reste, il n'y a pas de grands poètes méditerranéens. Valéry aurait dû être l'exception à cette règle." [22] If Valéry was not a great poet of the Mediterranean region, in Perse's eyes, then the position remained open for him. *Sécheresse* is his unfinished effort to write a great poem, situated in southern France and connecting with the mysterious spiritual realm he felt eluded the earlier visitor to Giens.

Despite all these reservations, Perse admired Valéry, and reminisced to Gide about "toute cette tranche géologique française, aujourd'hui bien raréfiée, où m'intégraient nos amitiés communes: Valéry, Fargue, Larbaud, Rivière" (1001). In the same vein, he told Adrienne Monnier how "Valéry, Fargue, Larbaud étaient part vivante, entre nous, d'une même trame amicale" (998). Perse grieved Valéry's death, as he explained to Gide: "L'absence de Valéry me peinera grandement. Ses dernières lettres (peu avant sa mort) étaient empreintes, humainement, d'une singulière et émouvante

---

[20] Michel Philippon, "Discours de la rééducation volontaire: la lettre à Frizeau de mars 1907," *Saint-John Perse: Les Années de formation,* ed. J. Corzani (Paris: L'Harmattan, 1996), 195-204, 201.

[21] Arthur Knodel, *Saint-John Perse: A Study of his Poetry* (Edinburgh: UP, 1966), 87.

[22] André Brincourt, *op. cit.*, 104.

franchise. A vous, je rapporterai un jour deux de ses confessions in-
tellectuelles les plus inattendues" (1011). Whether the poet ultimately communicated these unexpected avowals to Gide may never
be known, but he did pursue his reflections on Valéry. In 1968
Perse honored E.M. Cioran by calling him "l'un des plus grands
écrivains dont puisse s'honorer notre langue française depuis la mort
de Paul Valéry" (541).

The two poets were linked in ways Perse revealed, perhaps un-
wittingly, when paying homage to Léon-Paul Fargue in 1963. In a
tribute that is characteristically expressive of his own deepest traits
and qualities, he located Fargue in the French tradition, "[a]près
Claudel et Valéry, à son rang de puîné tenant sa part du chant"
(509). Perse himself was a sibling in this same family, a latecomer
following Claudel and Valéry and seeking his place between the two
giants. "Entre la masse basaltique d'un Claudel et les pures cristalli-
sations d'un Valéry" (509): this portrait of Fargue is equally apt for
Perse, whose destiny was also to steer between the Rodin-like concreteness of Claudel and the ethereal cogitations of Valéry.

A parallel dialectic is apparent even in Perse's musical preferences. In his early music reviews, published in the *Pau-Gazette* under the signature A.L., Daniel Aranjo finds an admiration that alter-
nates between the intellectual and the sensual, between the cerebral
music of a Vincent d'Indy, on the one hand, and what Perse perceived as the more organic rhythms of a Stravinsky on the other.
With Valéry on the d'Indy side and Claudel on the other, Aranjo
concludes: "il y aura toujours un côté Valéry et Vincent d'Indy pour
équilibrer et corriger, filtrer, un côté Claudel et Stravinsky." [23]

Valéry and Claudel form the Scylla and Charybdis between
whom Perse had to navigate, feeling the pull of each. On one side
was Valéry's rigorous formalism of language; on the other, Claudel's
overriding presence as an incarnate being and religious believer.
Perse had good reasons to avoid both. In the 1940s he confided to
Allen Tate his sense that Valéry had exhausted the limits of form
and that French poetry needed a greater sensitivity and new, more
varied rhythms (1295). In Perse's poems of that period, Claudel

---

[23] Daniel Aranjo, "La Jeunesse Musicale d'Alexis Leger," *Saint-John Perse: Les
Années de formation,* ed. J. Corzani (Paris: L'Harmattan, 1996), 205-215, 208. See
also Aranjo's complete study, *Saint-John Perse et la musique* (Pau: J&D Editions,
1988).

looms large, like the banyan tree at the threshold of *Pluies*: "Le banyan de la pluie prend ses assises sur la Ville" (141). But three decades later, in *Sécheresse,* the same verb announces an opposing climate, closer to Valéry: "la sécheresse sur la terre aura pris ses assises" (1396). This new landscape favors drought over rain, and the "grandes offensives de l'esprit" (1396), traditionally associated with the poet of Sète.

In assembling his collected works in the 1960s, Perse placed first among the homages a 1922 letter praising the *Introduction à la Méthode de Léonard de Vinci* and Valéry's "exigence spirituelle conduite aux limites de la rigueur intellectuelle" (463). Although Perse came to doubt this intellectual project, Valéry's prominent place in the volume signals his continued importance, more than half a century after their initial encounter. In notes to the volume, Perse specifically cites his efforts on Valéry's behalf. Referring to himself in the third person, he describes how, as Secretary General of the Ministry of Foreign Affairs, "il s'efforcera toujours d'aider de son mieux Paul Valéry, en le faisant charger, par le 'Service des Œuvres,' de conférences littéraires ou de missions culturelles dans les villes d'Europe; en lui ménageant aussi l'accès à des organismes internationaux comme la 'Coopération intellectuelle'" (1139). In the 1920s Perse "fit assurer à Paul Valéry" a position as director of the literary journal, *Commerce* (1139), and in 1935 nominated him (unsuccessfully) for the Nobel Prize in Literature.

Perse's personal library is further evidence of his lifelong engagement with this man who had been voted the greatest living French poet (a distinction he underlined).[24] Among his books are some 25 volumes of Valéry's works. Many are inscribed by the author and at least four are annotated by Perse. In a 1926 edition of *Charmes*, he made abundant marks on *Le Cimetière marin,* a poem that was surely present in his mind as he wrote *Amers*. He also underlined these verses from *La Pythie:*

> Une sombre carcasse d'âne
> Eût bien servi de ruche aux dieux!

When the chorus of *Amers* depicts the sea as a "ruche des dieux" (367), Valéry's shadow is not far behind. Perse even inserted

---

[24] Agathe Rouart-Valéry, *op. cit.,* 44.

Valéry's picture in the front page of *Amers*. When rereading the poet of Sète, Perse gave particular attention to the *Album de vers anciens, La Jeune Parque,* and Valéry's biographical chronology from the Pléiade edition, perhaps seeking a model for his own chronology.

Having admired (and critiqued) Valéry for most of the century, Perse pays him tribute, albeit anonymously, in these last poems by engaging him on his own terrain, both literally and figuratively.

This kind of interaction between writers and predecessors was well-known to Valéry. In a letter to Henri de Régnier, he commented: "Puisqu'il faut avouer que l'existence littéraire est à demi faite de gigantesques combats contre le passé, je ne vois pas de manière plus élégante que la vôtre de confondre ces bizarres adversaires antérieurs. Alors ce ne sont plus que des prophètes." [25] It is not surprising that Perse annotated this passage about gigantic combats, and we can understand why he would have appreciated Valéry's clever transformation of predecessors into precursors.

For the poet of Sète, great works can be measured by their resonance in other art, both earlier and later. This thought seems to have struck a chord with Perse, who annotated it in his copy of *Tel Quel:* "Une œuvre d'art (ou généralement de l'esprit) est importante quand son existence détermine, appelle, supprime, l'existence d'autres œuvres déjà faites ou non." [26] Works of the past offer a challenge and a handicap for later writers. As Valéry himself noted in another (also annotated) letter: "Le problème capital de la littérature depuis 1840 jusqu'en 1890, n'est-il pas: Comment faire autre chose que Hugo? Comment être visible malgré Hugo? Comment se pencher sur les cimes de Hugo?" [27] Valéry is overly optimistic when he claims that the Hugo "problem" ended in 1890, since more than half a century later Saint-John Perse was still debating with his ancestor. By Valéry's reckoning, such engagement

---

[25] Paul Valéry, *Lettres à Quelques'uns*, 66. Fondation Saint-John Perse.

[26] Paul Valéry, "Littérature," *Tel Quel II,* in *Œuvres II,* ed. J. Hytier (Paris: Gallimard, Bibliothèque de la Pléiade, 1960), 178.

[27] Paul Valéry, *Lettres à Quelques'uns*, 149. Fondation Saint-John Perse. Elsewhere Valéry did realize the longevity of Hugo's influence, as he noted in "Victor Hugo: Créateur par la forme": "On prétend que Victor Hugo est mort, et qu'il l'est depuis cinquante ans . . . mais un observateur impartial en douterait. Hier encore, on s'attaquait à lui comme à un simple vivant. On essayait de l'exterminer. C'est là une grande preuve d'existence." *Œuvres* I, ed. J. Hytier, 583.

could give retroactive importance to the poet of Jersey. By the same calculation, Valéry's own works are enhanced Perse's poetic responses to them.

When Perse reread Valéry, and particularly *Le Cimetière marin,* in his later years, he felt a kinship that might not have existed earlier. Living in southern France, especially in the dry season, Perse found new connections to Valéry's poem where noon is evoked three times: "Midi le juste" (st. 1), "Midi là-haut" and "Midi sans mouvement" (st. 13). [28] The same moment of temporary immobility presides over *Sécheresse*: "Midi l'aveugle nous éclaire" (1399); "Midi l'Aboyeur cherche ses morts dans les tranchées comblées d'insectes migrateurs" (1400). [29] Drought favors austerity over abundance, rigor over excess, spirit over body. It renders visible the concision of human intelligence and "l'homme à son plus vif: au plus lucide, au plus bref de lui-même" (1398). In this geography where inhabitants are "rongés de lucidité" (1400), Perse engages with his predecessor in a meditation about human consciousness. He borrows metaphors from *Le Cimetière marin*, only to reverse their valence.

Valéry's narrator contemplates the sea from a promontory above it, enchanted by the smooth, shimmering surface which reminds him of eternity. His meditation shuttles between life and death, movement and stasis, speech and silence, light and shadow, until he sees intimations of his own death: "Je hume ici ma future fumée" (st. 5). Privileged times are noontime and the solstice, temporary, cosmic moments of equilibrium that give the impression of permanence. The lure of stasis is great, with its illusion of eternity, but the narrator ultimately shakes off the temptation. Midday passes; the sea becomes ruffled; a breeze rustles the pages of his book. The meditation is over. Valéry's famous verse, "Le vent se lève!. . . Il faut tenter de vivre" announces a resolution to reconnect with life and action in the imperfect human world of change and mortality. [30]

---

[28] Paul Valéry, "Le Cimetière marin," *Œuvres I*, ed. J. Hytier, 147. References to the poem are drawn from this edition and identified by stanza number in parentheses.

[29] The word *Aboyeur* occurs only one other time in Perse's poetry, also capitalized and in a similar context of death: "comme l'Aboyeur des morts au bord des fosses funéraires" (*Amers,* 373).

[30] See Suzanne Nash's insightful study of Valéry's rewriting of Hugo, "Valéry traducteur de Victor Hugo, *Génétique et Traduction*, ed. S. Bourjea (Paris: L'Harmattan, 1995), 107-120.

The epigraph of the *Cimetière* is drawn from Pindar's *Pythian Odes*: "O my soul, strive not for immortal life, but exhaust the domain of the possible." For most of Perse's life, he too subscribed, even more vigorously than Valéry, to that philosophy. His poems sing of change and dynamism. All except for the Equinox collection, that is, where a curious change occurs. Haunted by the inexorable movement of time, Perse seems at the end of his life to opt for the other pole of Valéry's dialectic. The narrator of *Chanté par Celle qui fut là* knows that "toutes choses courent à leurs fins" (431); so does the protagonist of *Sécheresse*, when he declares: "Brève la vie, brève la course, et la mort nous rançonne" (1399). But Perse, haunted by the limited time that remains before him, seeks to slow and even stop its movement. In this endeavor, he returns to Valéry's privileged moments, noon and the equinox, when time appears to stand still. The effort is precarious; noon passes quickly; the equinox is scarcely longer: "équinoxe d'une heure entre la Terre et l'homme" (438). But these hours offer a symbolic respite on the path to an "autre rive" (1395). Transforming the imagery of the *Cimetière marin*, Perse gives a new and positive meaning to stasis and creates a hymn to immobility.

In this poem's setting which Albert Henry describes as "un lieu de fin de vie," [31] Perse rewrites the work of Valéry's youth from the vantage point of old age and brings a personal urgency to their common meditation about life, death and human consciousness. His final poems are an attempt to capture life as it advances "au pas de l'espadrille" (1397). In *Amers* Perse had already described a temporary eternity, "l'homme immortel au foyer de l'instant" (385). In *Oiseaux* immortality seemed most attainable in the "haut suspens" (423) of art. Now, in this last collection, placed under the sign of the equinox, Saint-John Perse prolongs forever a time of equilibrium between day and night. As early as 1963, in a tribute to the *Cahiers du Sud*, he expressed his affinity to this particular moment of fullness: "l'heure vous dit sa plénitude à l'équinoxe de Septembre" (534). There is surely a poetic justice in the timing of the poet's death, just three days short of an autumnal equinox, in September 1975.

---

[31] Saint-John Perse, *Nocturne*, ed. A. Henry (Paris: Gallimard, Publications de la Fondation Saint-John Perse, 1985), 41.

CHAPTER 13

GENEALOGICAL REVERIES: SAINT-JOHN PERSE'S
AUTOBIOGRAPHY

It seems, as one becomes older,
That the past has another pattern,
and ceases to be a mere sequence–
T.S. Eliot, "The Dry Salvages,"
Four Quartets

SAINT-JOHN Perse's autobiography is perhaps best read as a poem, revealing not only for what it tells us but for all that is unsaid. His chronology stands at the threshold of the Pléiade edition, like another *Ecrit sur la porte,* half a century after the original one in *Eloges.* Although placed at the beginning of the volume, the autobiography was composed at the end, to retrace the poet's life and works. Beginning with the word "Naissance," it relates the genesis and evolution of an individual and an *œuvre.* More than just an introduction, this is a complete text with its own internal structure –a work of art in its own right, combining welcome and epitaph, fact and fiction, myth and reality, or, as Philip Roth once wrote "the kind of stories that people turn life into, the kind of lives that people turn stories into." [1]

Readers approach a Pléiade volume with a particular horizon of expectations, shaped in part by what Gérard Genette calls the paratext: the format, binding, paper, title page, and the serious critical apparatus that characterizes this prestigious series. This particular volume offers both less and much more than we anticipate. While Perse is not the only poet to be honored by a Pléiade edition in his

---

[1] Philip Roth, *The Facts: A Novelist's Autobiography* (New York: Farrar, Straus and Giroux, 1988), epigraph.

lifetime, he is the first to have composed his own book. The absence of an editor from the title page points to an invisible and omnipresent narrator who has shaped all facets of the volume, writing his autobiography in the third person, establishing the notes, revising the correspondence, and sometimes even composing letters retroactively. The poet's dual role as subject and editor makes every detail both suspect and significant. Even the paratextual elements, normally assumed to be objective and scholarly, are literary creations.[2] Under the guise of traditional scholarship, this volume is an autobiographical monument in which letters, biographical entries, and notes all serve as ateliers for self-fashioning.

The poet assumes an objective tone to portray his life, with amusing results at times, as when he stipulates that *Exil* is "Daté par Saint-John Perse de 1941" (1109), or that the translator Denis Devlin "fut amicalement aidé dans sa tâche par l'auteur" (1112). Knowing who wrote the notes gives a particular edge to the observation: "On sait l'attrait qu'a toujours exercé pour Saint-John Perse le sel, dans son principe et sa substance" (1098). And we can only wonder what lies behind the statement that Perse's adaptation of T.S. Eliot's *Hollow Men* "est la seule traduction que l'on connaisse de lui" (1141).

This is not, of course, the first autobiography to be composed in the third person. Perse owned and annotated several works in the genre, including Henry Adams' *Education* and Charles de Gaulle's *Memoirs*. What distinguishes this one is its explicit (mis)labeling as a biography, which thus subverts both genres. In fusing the boundaries between first and third persons, discourse and history, Perse also disrupts what Philippe Lejeune calls the autobiographical pact between reader and writer. Autobiographies typically begin by establishing an understanding between author and audience:

> Ecrire un pacte autobiographique (quel qu'en soit le contenu), c'est d'abord poser sa voix, choisir le ton, le registre dans lequel on va parler, définir son lecteur, les relations qu'on entend avoir avec lui: c'est comme la clef, les dièses ou les bémols en tête de la portée: tout le reste du discours en dépend. C'est choisir son rôle.[3]

---

[2] Catherine Mayaux has documented this, most especially, for the letters from China. *Saint-John Perse: Les Lettres d'Asie* (Paris: Gallimard, Cahiers de la *NRF*, 1994).

[3] Philippe Lejeune, *L'Autobiographie en France* (Paris: A. Colin, 1971), 72.

If autobiographers begin by choosing a role, it is characteristic that Perse selected an ambiguous one by adopting the stance of an objective observer. Readers are meant to assume that the life is related by an knowledgeable scholar-narrator, while, in fact, subject and teller merge in an autofictional world on the frontiers between or among genres. The writer is both protagonist and witness, center and circumference of his story. He is Alexander and Xenophon, hero and chronicler of a new *anabasis*. He is also Dante and Virgil, poet and guide. As a guide, Perse is both expert and defective. On the one hand, he has a certain expertise, like the one Montaigne claimed in his own self-portrait "that no man has ever treated a subject he knew and understood better than I do the subject I have undertaken; and that in this I am the most learned man alive."[4] But if Perse is closest to some truths, he is inevitably oblivious to others and understandably possessive of his secrets.

No autobiographer ever fully or accurately knows his past. Nor does he tell all that he knows. In George Moore's phrase, "One reads one's past life like a book out of which some pages have been torn and many mutilated."[5] Some of the pages—the beginning and the end—are unavailable to the writer. In between are gaps, since life is experienced through grids and filters and remembered through a fallible instrument that is both forgetful and selective. Perse himself was aware of the selective nature of memory. In *Exil,* he wrote of the "van de la mémoire" (129), winnowing out some elements while keeping others. In the chronology he appears to usher readers into his private world but, as befits a poet of masks, his words are both revelation and disguise.

Few lives are as colorful as that of the diplomat, poet, traveler, reader, friend, and lover, Alexis Leger/Saint-John Perse. But throughout his life, he maintained a resolutely private posture about his biography. His fictional protagonist was enjoined to describe himself: "Et c'est l'heure, ô Poète, de décliner ton nom, ta naissance, et ta race . . ." (137). But Perse himself was reluctant to accept any such an invitation, despite the financial rewards that could have come from writing memoirs. Unlike Chateaubriand, who wrote his *Mé-*

---

[4] Michel de Montaigne, "Of repentance," *Complete Essays,* tr. D. Frame (Stanford: Stanford UP, 1976), 611.

[5] Wayne Shumaker, *English Autobiography* (Berkeley: U of California Press, 1954), 38.

moires d'Outre Tombe in exchange for income during his lifetime,
Perse declined such arrangements, according to the entry for 1940-
41: "Refusant, pour vivre, les offres de publication de Mémoires qui
lui sont faites en Amérique, il accepte, à Washington [. . .] un poste
de conseiller littéraire [. . .]" (xxiii).

In a letter to Adrienne Monnier, dated 1948, he underscored his
conviction that "La personnalité même du poète n'appartient en
rien au lecteur, qui n'a droit qu'à l'œuvre révolue, détachée comme
un fruit de son arbre" (553). Three years later he used the same
metaphor when writing to Alain Bosquet about his published work
as a "fruit détaché de l'arbre" (1067). Given the poet's repeated determination to reveal the fruit and not the tree, it may seem paradoxical for him to place a tree–notably a genealogical tree–at the
heart of his chronology, and even to compose an autobiography after a lifetime of camouflaging his personal life.

It is not impossible that Perse came to feel the need Victor
Hugo identified in all writers to assess the past, sort out its contradictions and find the hidden patterns in seemingly unconnected
events.[6] But it is more likely that Perse undertook the Pléiade
chronology at least in part to preserve his privacy. By composing
the text himself, he could measure out revelations by teaspoons.
What Renée Ventresque calls the "mise en discours d'une vie"[7] allowed him to create an idealized version of himself. In the literary
constellation, its nearest neighbors might be lives by Plutarch or
Tacitus, as Joëlle Gardes Tamine has noted, saints' lives, as Mireille
Sacotte has suggested, or even myths.[8] For in this text the poet
spins a "mythistoire"[9] about lineage and exemplary events.

While the project of capturing a life's trajectory might appear to
be intensely personal, it often leads autobiographers to borrow
familiar images, actions, and patterns from other stories. Avrom

---

    [6] Victor Hugo, *Littérature et philosophie mêlées* (Paris: Klincksieck, 1976), 1, 3.
    [7] Renée Ventresque, "La *Biographie* de Saint-John Perse dans l'édition de la
Pléiade: d'un masque à l'autre," *Les Mots La Vie*, 9, 1997, 73.
    [8] Joëlle Gardes Tamine, "De la biographie d'Alexis Leger à la Vie de Saint-John
Perse," *Les Mots La Vie* 9, 1996, 82. Mireille Sacotte, *Saint-John Perse* (Paris: Bel-
fond, 1991), 34.
    [9] Georges Gusdorf, *Auto-bio-graphie* (Paris: Odile Jacob, 1991), 482. Serge
Canadas has called the autobiography a "mythologème." "Naissance du mythe poé-
tique," *Saint-John Perse: Les Années de formation,* ed. J. Corzani (Paris: L'Harmattan, 1996), 230. See also Henriette Levillain, "Saint-John Perse et l'Atlantique,"
Souffle de Perse 2, 1992, 33-38.

Fleishman has noted how autobiographers try to make themselves unique by reenacting or revising models that incarnate the core beliefs of a culture: Warrior, Saint, Knight or Scholar.[10] Often these models provide the basic outline for other lives. Augustine, who founded the genre, patterned his autobiography after saints' lives, or, more precisely, after stories about them. Perse's self-portrait is also mediated by stories that constitute scripts, capable of elevating it to a heroic plane.

The poet was conscious of a legendary aura that surrounded him. As early as 1948, he decried efforts to create "la personnalité mythique d'un Saint-John Perse" (552), but in the Pléiade edition, he cultivated this same mythic personality. The very first footnote reproduces a letter to the distinguished American historian Samuel E. Morison in which Perse explains that the modest island of Saint-Leger-les-Feuilles "est loin de mériter la considération qu'on voudrait lui prêter dans ma légende littéraire" (1087). What better way to perpetuate the legend than to evoke it in the pseudo-scholarly apparatus of the volume?

Perse and his contemporary Pléiade readers shared a corpus of familiar legends and models from the classical, biblical, Celtic and chivalric traditions. Strands of each one color the chronology, although the Bible plays only a minor role in this saga whose dominant Ur-texts are medieval epics. From the very first entries, the autobiography ushers us into a heraldic world. In the family tree drawn by the poet, the recurrent designation, *de vieille souche*, designates multiple ancestors of ancient, distinguished, and sometimes even noble lineage. Early entries concentrate on the ancestry of Alexis Leger, while later ones include the literary friends of Saint-John Perse.

By defining himself, from the beginning, as the only son in a family of five children (ix), the poet signals the importance of gender, filiation and birth order in his life as in his work. An early footnote underscores this concern by evoking a family tradition of "plus de deux siècles de vie patriarcale 'aux Iles'" (1088). When kings still reigned and primogeniture ruled society, inheritances passed to first-born sons, while the younger brothers, *puînés* and *cadets*, sought their fortunes elsewhere, sometimes in the clergy, often in

---

[10] Avrom Fleishman, *Figures of Autobiography* (Berkeley: U of California Press, 1983), 47.

the colonies. The poet's father, we are told, descended from one of these younger brothers, who left Burgundy at the end of the seventeenth century (ix).

In summoning or refashioning his origins, Perse returns to earlier, dynastic times when families sought legitimacy and prestige by pushing their origins as far back as possible, ideally to an illustrious, founding ancestor. Aristocratic families of the Middle Ages planted the family tree in their own soil such that genealogy and geography fused; the name of the family became indissociable from its land, its castle, and its status. All three were passed down along a vertical, patriarchal axis. Descriptions of the Saint-Leger Leger and Dormoy ancestors are set against a background of these medieval traditions, as the poet shows the fusion of his name and birthplace. The authenticity of "L'îlet de Saint-Leger-les Feuilles" (ix) is enhanced by its appearance on old English and French maps (ix). According to the poet, the family name is immortalized in other places as well, as in the Burgundian towns of Saint-Léger-sous-Beuvray and Saint-Léger-sur-Dheune (x). A similar eponymity of family and land surrounds his grandmother, Augusta de Caille, whose fifteenth-century ancestors are said to have possessed Provençal baronies called Castellane de Caille et Caille de Castellane (xiv). Three centuries later, Jean-Samuel de Caille, settled on a promontory of Guadeloupe henceforth designated as the "Morne à Caille" (xiv). His patronym is said to have extended to an entire Grenadine island, known as the "île de Caille" (xxxvii).

On the maternal side, the poet posits a similar congruence between family and place names, planting the roots of the Dormoy family in the "village des Ormois" (x), named for D'Ormois le Bourguignon, founder of the lineage. His name evolved first to d'Ormoy and then to Dormoy when, after the French Revolution, an ancestor was said to have renounced his noble status in order to hold political office in Saint-Barthélémy (x). Eliding the crucial particle, he erased the visible sign of nobility that the poet posthumously restores to him two centuries later. Like the linguistic traveler of *Neiges* who traces words back to their etymological origins and to an imaginary home of ancient prefixes (162), Perse traces his family names back to their sources in a magical time and place, real or imaginary, of original spellings and noble particles. Many illustrious branches grow from his family tree. Some are doubly noble, like the de Leyritz branch (xiv) from which descends the poet's great-great-uncle and namesake, Count Alexis de Leyritz (xiv).

Among all the distinguished forebears, one family stands out as the culmination of the entire genealogical journey. This is the house of de Foix, with two larger-than-life inhabitants, both named Gaston (xxi, xxxv). One is the Duc de Nemours, nephew of Louis XII and king of Navarre, an exceptional warrior who was killed in battle at age 23. He is honored by a monument in Italy that Perse describes in the entry for 1965:

> élevée au XVIᵉ à la mémoire de Gaston de Foix, le jeune commandant de l'armée française en Lombardie, au lieu même où il était tombé, les armes à la main après sa victoire de Ravenne. Croit devoir signaler aux autorités italiennes le mauvais entretien de ce monument. (xxxv)

Behind this valiant Gaston, memorialized at Ravenna, lies an earlier, even more famous one. When the poet describes his links to the de Foix family (xxxv) and specifies that his grandmother descended from "les Bonodet de Foix, descendants de Gaston de Foix" (xxi), readers think of this earlier, more famous Gaston, known as Gaston Phebus (1331-1391), the chevalier amply chronicled by Jean Froissart. Calling himself Phebus in honor of the Greek sun god, Gaston aspired to be a Sun King, long before Louis XIV. Known for his prowess during the Hundred Years War, he was also a writer, poet, musician, and patron of the arts. Born in Orthez (a town later associated with Francis Jammes), he moved to the castle of Pau in 1380. Five centuries later, a modern Creole, transplanted from Guadeloupe to Pau, could find retroactive roots in this putative ancestor. Thanks to Gaston, Perse could create, even belatedly, the illusion of a family returning to its place of origin in the realm of an illustrious founding ancestor. And what better ancestor for King Light than this Phebus-Sun King?

Gaston de Foix is the prototype of the cultured, heroic prince, exceptional in battle, in the arts, and even in gallantry. Jean Froissart's overly-flattering portrait describes him as the first French humanist and the exemplar of all talents.[11] Later historians have taken

---

[11] "I must say that although I have seen very many knights, kings, princes and others, I have never seen any so handsome, either in the form of his limbs and shape, or in countenance, which was fair and ruddy, with grey and amorous eyes, that gave delight whenever he chose to express affection. He was so perfectly formed, one could not praise him too much. [. . .] To speak briefly and truly, the

a more nuanced view, but Froissart's idealized picture remains the best known. It is not surprising that Perse should make a point of claiming him as a forebear, for Gaston incarnates chivalric and aristocratic ideals. Through him and through other seemingly precise genealogies and etymologies, the poet thus assimilates Alexis Leger to the grandeur and prestige of a heroic period in French history. He creates an aura of medieval epic or *chanson de geste* and provides the historical context in which Alexis Leger himself can be transformed into an epic poet.

Medieval epics were on the poet's mind during the years he was composing his autobiography, if we judge by his annotated copy of Jean Marx's *Légende arthurienne et le Graal*. Numerous underlinings highlight Perse's continued preoccupation with genealogy, matrimonial alliances, and bastard birth (in this case, of the medieval writer Marie de France). He specifically annotated a long passage enumerating characteristic elements of medieval epics:

> enfances (cachées et secrètes), éducations (comportant l'épreuve qui fait de l'enfant un homme, lui donne un nom et un prestige), quête d'objets merveilleux à travers les périls et les épreuves, cour faite aux filles et aux fées, expéditions, raids, combats dans l'Autre Monde ou avec l'Autre Monde, enlèvements, voyages lointains dans les îles merveilleuses d'où il rapporte des Objets Talismans, signes de souveraineté et sources de prestige, voyages au pays de l'éternel bonheur dans les palais souterrains des Sighe, chasses (dominées par les interdictions et. pleines d'éléments mythologiques [. . .]).[12]

Perse's autobiography is modeled in part on this heroic schema.

The earliest entries outline the education of a youth destined to inhabit King Light's Settlements. Thanks to private tutors, this training spans all of human inquiry: nature and culture, land and sea. When, at age eight, the child receives his first horse, his first boat and his first telescope (xi), the gifts are as symbolically charged

---

count de Foix was perfect in person and in mind; and no contemporary prince could be compared with him for sense, honour, or liberality." Jean Froissart, *Chronicles* II (London: William Smith, 1842), 94-95, 101.

   [12] Jean Marx, *La Légende arthurienne et le Graal* (Paris: Presses Universitaires de France, 1952), 65. I am grateful to May Chehab for indicating this text. Perse also had a much-annotated anthology of texts about the Graal, *Lumière du Graal,* ed. R. Nelli (Paris: Cahiers du Sud, 1959).

as those of the Magi, for they combine earth, sea and sky, lifelong domains of curiosity and passion for the future prince. After the son's precocious beginnings, his family moves back to France, in part because of the father's desire to ensure him a better education (xi).

A veritable passion for learning threads across the autobiography. "Formé très tôt à l'équitation et à la vie sur mer, l'enfant *s'éprend* aussi d'histoire naturelle" (x). During the period 1904-05, he is "*passionné* de droit romain" (xii); while at the same time experiencing his "Premières *passions* musicales" (xiii) along with "L'alpinisme, qui demeurera longtemps sa grande *passion*" (xiii). The leitmotif of intellectual curiosity and the range of disciplines mastered recapitulate for the writer, while foreshadowing for readers, the encyclopedic poetry they will nourish.

Perse claimed to have "une étrange aversion pour les livres" (xi), but this did not prevent him from winning–and enumerating in the very next entry–two baccalaureate degrees "avec mentions" as well as the "Grand prix de discours français en rhétorique, constituant le 'Prix d'honneur' du lycée, et premier prix de composition latine" (xii). In fact, when updating an earlier version of his biography for the Pléiade, one of the few revisions Perse made was to elaborate on these prizes. What he had previously called the "Prix du discours français en rhétorique," he now chose to expand with the additional details. [13] Nor did Perse's supposed aversion to books discourage him from undertaking the studies listed in subsequent entries or devoting his life to reading, writing, collecting and annotating books.

In traditional epics, a hero's education is followed by a ritual set of perilous tasks. Emerging from a long line of adventurous younger sons, seeking fortune and refuge in the Caribbean (xxxvii), Perse portrays himself as a worthy descendant by accomplishing his own exploits. He survives life-or-death situations: "Echappe de peu à une mort solitaire en voulant traverser à la nage un lac de montagne" (xiii) and confronts extreme challenges during solitary sailing journeys around Maine and Canada. To Roger Caillois he describes his sojourn on an isolated island, two hours by boat from everything (959), although the actual setting, in the relative enclo-

---

[13] Jacques Charpier, *Saint-John Perse* (Paris: Gallimard, La Bibliothèque Ideale, 1962), 29.

sure of Penobscot Bay, Maine, is almost swimming distance from a chain of other islands that are linked by ferry to the mainland. After the rigors of the Atlantic, a Mediterranean cruise could appear anticlimatic, were it not for a terrible storm: "déchaînement, près du cap Corse, d'une tempête farouche en pleine lumière méditerranéenne" (xxxvi). Like Odysseus and Aeneas, the poet survives Neptune's furies and credits this perilous combat with reconciling him to southern France.

Epic heroes are often called upon to save others. This part of the ritual is fulfilled by Perse's account of his actions in China. After preparing a defense against the plague (xviii), he comes to the rescue of the ruling family: "S'emploie personnellement au sauvetage de la famille présidentielle" (xviii). Although some of Perse's letters make light of this rather folkloric episode, its presence in the chronology assimilates it to the ritual pattern of helping individuals in danger.

The realm that Perse depicts is predominantly male. Except for a few female relatives, women are mostly absent. When it is time to marry, the protagonist chooses a partner of fitting stature and defines her, as he defined himself, by genealogy: "Epouse, à Washington, Dorothy Russell, née Milburn, famille américaine de vieille souche anglaise" (xxviii). In the manuscript, Mrs. Russell was initially portrayed more simply as an "Américaine d'ascendance anglaise," but Perse elaborated on the phrase to emphasize both the distinguished Milburn family and the long European lineage, including one of his favorite words, *souche,* all of which strengthened the claim that she was a worthy partner for the princely hero.

Beyond biography, Perse's chronology is a rêverie about genealogy, beginning with an island birth, a mythic childhood and a fairytale adolescence amid "tout un monde d'exil et de légende" (xii). An education fit for a Prince prepares him to triumph over trials and dangers and to win an illustrious bride. The traits, tensions and trajectory of the story prefigure, while at the same time summarizing those that unfold in the poems. Across the ritual steps of the autobiography, a protagonist prepares to merge with the fictional heroes of his poetry. He becomes a prince, a King Light, ready to step across the threshold into *Eloges* and take possession of his Settlement.

One of the contradictions inherent in the chronology is the duality of a protagonist who is both an isolated exile and a well-connected insider who is intimate with the influential people of his era. The poet describes himself as an object of curiosity at the Quai d'Orsay, where he arrived for the foreign service examination as an unknown out-of-towner lacking any letters of recommendation (xvii). But this depiction belies many of the writer's conversations, enumerated in the entry for 1911, with leading figures of banking, law, commerce, politics, and government, including Léon Hennique of the Académie Goncourt, Olivier Sainsère, influential advisor to President Poincaré, Judge Alexis Ballot-Beaupré, Arthur Fontaine from the ministry of Labor, and Philippe Berthelot of the Quai d'Orsay, all of whom helped guide him toward a diplomatic career (xv). Nor does this impressive list include the *Who's Who* of literary "friends" (xv) the young poet visited during that same Paris stay. At all stages of his life, the supposedly solitary writer was helped by prestigious advisers and benefactors, from Francis Jammes, whom he met in Pau in 1899, to the donors of his house in Provence some sixty years later. Perse's autobiography chronicles his relations with the rich and famous while, at the same time, depicting himself as a lonely wanderer.

This dialectic between insider and outsider, aloneness and connectedness, is mirrored in the fundamental tension between distance and homeland. The chronology is a story of successive displacements motivated sometimes by outside agency and sometimes by an all-consuming desire to travel. Almost every entry of Perse's adult life chronicles some journey. And yet, this son of the Windward Islands, so enamored of the sea, devotes a significant part of his autobiography to documenting his origins on land, showing that they are both ancient and aristocratic. Perse's life may span continents, but the overriding theme of his autobiography is roots and the family's ties to Burgundy, Normandy and Provence (ix). Perse's self-proclaimed identity as an exile, a Celt (xl), and a citizen of the Atlantic (xl, xli) is counterbalanced by equally strong proclamations of his roots in the "mère patrie" (xli). Even while insisting upon his exile, he proclaims his attachment to a land and a lineage.

Perse's chronology, like his poems, rotates around race, class, caste and color. According to Richard N. Coe, national differences shape childhood, as it is lived and as it is retold. Children raised in the West Indies tend to be acutely aware of color difference, not unlike Perse who evokes it in the earliest entries of the chronology: "Enfance entourée de serviteurs et travailleurs de différentes races,

d'origine caraïbe, africaine ou asiatique (Malabarais, Chinois, Anna-
mites et Japonais)" (ix). [14] Despite an apparent cosmopolitanism in
this multi-cultural entourage, the writer's very description of a
childhood *surrounded* by others reproduces a society where a white
child stands at the center, encircled by others whose role is to serve.
While acknowledging affection for the plantation workers, Perse
betrays a compelling need to affirm and document his own whiteness. In his poetry the words *pur(e)(s), pureté* and *purifications* recur some 75 times. In his autobiography the expression *de vieille
souche* is repeated so often that it takes on the ritual value of a
Homeric epithet. For Perse, lineage and purity are linked and val-
ued, while hybrids or mixtures usually have pejorative connotations. Typical is the homage to Léon-Paul Fargue as a "poète de
pure naissance" (509), praised for being "franc de tout métissage"
(511). The compliment Perse later addresses to Braque's birds is
that they are "jamais hybrides et pourtant millénaires" (424).

Philippe Lejeune has observed that all autobiography is an elab-
oration on the statement: I became myself. [15] Through the elaborate
apparatus of genealogy and etymology, the author of the chronology traces how he became Alexis Leger. But this is only the pre-his-
tory of the poet. A second, more crucial process is how Alexis Leger became Saint-John Perse. The first story is about inheritance,
real or embroidered; the second is about vocation and volition.
Alexis Leger comes at the end of a long lineage; Saint-John Perse is
a beginning. By his family genealogy, Alexis Leger emerges from a
vertical line of filiation. By another, poetic genealogy, Saint-John
Perse generates himself under a new name with myriad connotations. In the family there were examples of individuals assuming
new cognomens when they founded new dynasties. Besides the
D'Ormoy-turned-Dormoy, a certain Leger Saint-Leger is said to
have transposed his name into Saint-Leger Leger when establishing
himself abroad (x). These relatives offer precedents for the poet
whose own re-baptism will be much more radical than theirs.

The entry for 1924 marks a threshold. Before then, the autobiographer refers to himself variously as Saint Leger-Leger, Alexis
Leger, Leger, the young Antillean, the son, and once, in the entry

---

[14] Richard N. Coe, *When the Grass was Taller* (New Haven: Yale UP, 1984),
280. This is a perceptive study of literary depictions of childhood.
[15] Philippe Lejeune, *Le Pacte autobiographique* (Paris: Seuil, 1975), 241.

for 1895, as the poet (xi), in a proleptic description of a then eight-
year-old child. Finally the pen name arrives:

> Il participe, anonymement, à la fondation et à la direction de la
> revue *Commerce* qui publiera, dans son premier numéro (été
> 1924) son poème *Amitié du Prince* [. . .] Apparition enfin d'*Ana-
> base,* sous la signature Saint-John Perse (xix)

A curious lapsus occurs in this passage. Speaking of *Anabase* the
poet mentions an *apparition,* where the word *parution* or publication is appropriate. The true apparition is that of the poet himself,
emerging at last as Saint-John Perse.

Henry James was surprised to discover, half-way through his
own autobiography, that he was really composing "the personal history of an imagination." [16] This may be the nature of all autobiographies, and certainly of Perse's, which, like the overture of a symphony, announces and recapitulates major imaginative loci. If not
entirely reliable as a biography, it is, as J.-F. Guérant has observed,
an excellent preface to the collected works, for it announces the
principal axes of the poet's life and art. [17] While introducing the author and recreating his genealogy back to the Middle Ages, it simultaneously opens onto his poetry, since Perse recreates the past that
will best introduce his *œuvre.*

Perse provides certain guides, which function like the seamarks
of *Amers,* to escort readers into the world of the poems. Some illuminate specific allusions, such as his young sister's death, evoked in
Eloges (xi); others offer a historical context, like the former Taoist
temple where he says he wrote *Anabase* (xviii); or a textual genesis,
as for the "Chanson du présomptif" (xix). Other entries offer more
subtle guideposts by foreshadowing the poems.

The Pléiade series in general and the Saint-John Perse volume
in particular make certain assumptions about their implied readers
and the intellectual and cultural background they bring to a text.
Perse's chronology assumes that readers are familiar with the leading figures of twentieth-century history, politics and the arts, with
world geography, and with Perse's poems. References to individu-

---

[16] Quoted in Roy Pascal, *Design and Truth in Autobiography* (London: Routledge & Kegan Paul, 1960), 182.
[17] J.-F. Guérant, "La Biographie en guise de préface chez Saint-John Perse,"
L'Information littéraire 4, 1990, 3-16.

als, places and events assume a cultivated reader able to situate such names as Pierre Loti (xi), the Dreyfus affair (xv), Fargue, Gallimard, Joseph Conrad, G.K. Chesterton, Hilaire Belloc, the Group of Six (xix), and many others.

The repertory of readings, paintings and concerts that influenced the poet not only illuminates his trajectory but also creates a bond with readers who are expected to understand the allusions and perhaps even to admire the same masterpieces. Perse's chronology is an impressive record of reading and of authors who shaped him. It offers various portraits of the artist as reader and critic, winning a prize for reading at the lycée of Pau, or preparing to be an even better reader: "Il poursuit son étude du grec pour une meilleure lecture d'Empédocle" (xii). His reactions to other writers witness to the centrality of reading in a cultured life. Parallel scenes depict illustrious people reading and praising Perse's poems. The praises of these early, famous admirers create a precedent, scripting the reaction of newer readers who will discover or rediscover Perse's poetry in the Pléiade edition. Like plays-within-a-play, they offer models for ideal, assiduous and appreciative reading. One such early reader is André Gide, who legitimates Perse's poetry both as an admirer and as a publisher (xv). Valery Larbaud, author of the first critical article (xv) was apparently enthusiastic enough to travel to Pau to meet the poet. By the end of 1911, Perse numbered Larbaud, Fargue, Jacques Rivière, Gaston Gallimard, Francis Jammes and Paul Claudel among his literary friends and André Gide, Henri de Régnier and Francis Viélé-Griffin among his hosts.

Some of the embedded acts of reading include these literary friends. Others involve strangers, whose reactions presage those of readers who might not have had the opportunity to meet Perse. In 1922 he returns from China to discover that fans have emerged in his absence. Segments of *Eloges* have been set to music by Louis Durey and Darius Milhaud; the eminent poet Guillaume Apollinaire has cited him in a lecture; Marcel Proust has mentioned him in the *Recherche du temps perdu* (xix). These examples offer a "how-to" guide for future readers and suggest that even those outside the inner circle of friends can appreciate the work and extend its renown through citations, translations or transpositions into other media. Instances of active, enlightened reading continue across the chronology leading to the gift of a house in 1957: "maison offerte par un groupe d'admirateurs et amis littéraires d'Amérique" (xxviii). They culminate with the international acclaim of a Nobel Prize in 1960. Like the young Leger, who corrected maps of the Pyrénées as part of his military service (xiii), the elderly autobiographer also engages in cartography by offering readers both an itinerary through his poetry and an etiquette of reading.

Besides providing a departure point for this collected volume, Perse's chronology continues the poet's lifelong effort to transmute life into language. It draws upon diction, rhythms, imagery and vocabulary characteristic of his poetry. Most of all, this history of a life has its own prior history as a text; it belongs to a lineage of earlier autobiographical texts by the poet himself.

While most writers have only one opportunity to compose their autobiography, Perse had at least three. The Pléiade chronology revises two earlier ones, also composed anonymously and in the third person. One was written for Alain Bosquet's *Saint-John Perse* (Seghers, 1953). For that volume, the poet prepared an eight-page typed biography, which Bosquet adopted almost verbatim, clearly pleased to have been spared an arduous task. When the manuscript was complete, Bosquet sent it along with a reassuring letter: "J'ai traité la question de la biographie comme on traite d'une question secondaire dans un 'appendice'; j'ai d'ailleurs souvent gardé la lettre même du texte que vous m'aviez adressé." [18] This (auto)biography is an important precursor of the Pléiade chronology. It contains many of the elements developed in the later version, although in Bosquet's book Saint-Léger Léger still carries the accents that the poet later jettisoned. Some of the passages of the Bosquet volume are lyrical in a way that would be puzzling if we did not know Perse had composed them. The evocation of his life in Washington, for instance, stands out in an otherwise factual account, calling to mind the *Poème à l'Etrangère* and *Oiseaux:*

> Dans cette capitale de l'abstraction, exempte de toute vie propre, il trouve la commodité d'un "lieu géométrique." De l'immeuble moderne où il vit très simplement, on voit les écorchures de terre rouge et les talus hautement boisés d'une ville encore en voie de terrassement. Le quartier vallonné, coupé d'une gorge profonde, s'étend entre un Parc zoologique, une tranche de Cathédrale en construction et un Observatoire naval de météorologie. La ville

---

[18] Letter from Alain Bosquet, September 22, 1952, Fondation Saint-John Perse.

est survolée le jour par des vautours, le soir par des hérons. Elle entend passer, comme en Asie, les migrations hivernales d'oies sauvages; en été, l'oiseau-mouche la visite.[19]

This description of Washington would have been even more poetic if Bosquet had not excised other passages from Perse's typescript that reached beyond Washington to embrace nation and continent:

Mais ce que Saint-John Perse semble demander surtout à l'Amérique, c'est la réalité de sa vie de nature, à l'échelle planétaire. Il y retrouve au voisinage de l'homme, le désert ou les mers intérieures, la forêt primitive ou la haute montagne, les fleuves puissants et les deltas, îles arctiques ou tropicales, tous les climats et toutes les races.[20]

In another passage which Bosquet excluded, Perse evoked the family ties that linked him to America:

Il y retrouve, de naissance, ses affinités géographiques; des traces aussi d'anciens souvenirs familiaux, car sous la Révolution française, de ses parents des Iles avaient trouvé, pour quelque temps, refuge en Géorgie et en Louisiane.

Although Bosquet omitted both paragraphs, they were not lost forever; almost all the elements of Perse's draft were later assimilated into the more detailed Pléiade chronology.

A decade later, Perse revised his chronology for Jacques Charpier's *Saint-John Perse* (Gallimard, La Bibliothèque Idéale, 1962). This version (updated by a decade to reach 1971) then became the basis for the third and final autobiography in the Pléiade edition. At least two manuscripts of that chronology survive. They serve as preliminary sketches for the careful self-portrait that finally appeared in 1973. More spontaneous and detailed than the printed version, they chronicle the poet's progressive self-portrayal across myriad revisions and deletions and allow us to document his successive forging of an identity.

---

[19] Alain Bosquet, *Saint-John Perse* (Paris: Seghers, 1953), 121-122.
[20] Manuscript of typescript, p. 6. This and subsequent quotations come from manuscripts at the Fondation Saint-John Perse.

Some of the revisions are stylistic, but the most radical ones are personal and political. In the first manuscript of the Pléiade chronology, Perse cites his political clout on behalf of others, including his early mentor: "Obtient en faveur de Claudel, et à sa demande, au delà de la limite d'âge normal, une prolongation de son activité diplomatique pour sa nominat. [sic] à l'Ambassade de Bruxelles." The period 1936-1939 brings other efforts: helping Freud leave Vienna at the request of Marie Bonaparte; arranging French citizenship for Igor Stravinsky. Even in exile, Perse wields influence, writing to President Franklin Roosevelt about American participation in world security. All these gestures are absent from the final version.

The poet also pruned his family tree, after an initial manuscript that included even more ancestors. Typical is the evolution of the grandfather's family that was first identified by its relation to Bernardin de Saint Pierre. In the second version, the eighteenth-century novelist is demoted to a lower rank, below other ancestors the family prefers to claim: "Cette famille [. . .] s'honorait plus, aux Iles, de compter quelques morts en mer et plusieurs foudroyés." Lightning counts more than literature in the family legends. In the final Pléiade version, the survivors of lightning remain but the author of *Paul et Virginie*, whose romanticism might perhaps be embarrassing, is gone.[21]

Another disappearing ancestor, from the Caille branch, was said to have married into the tenth-century Anglo-French family of Charles the Simple. Given this ancestor's evident handicaps, he was eliminated; Charles the Simple was clearly less desirable than Gaston Febus. Also removed were numerous, detailed coats of arms of the Leyritz and Dormoy/Le Dentu branches. In revising his genealogy, the poet removed allusions that might entangle his story, which, as we have seen, is woven with epic strands. For the same reason, apparently, he omitted recent antecedents, uncles, grandfather, great-grandfather Leger, who had been lawyers and public of-

---

[21] Perse was nevertheless conscious of Bernardin de Saint Pierre's place in French letters. When revising the French literature entry for the *World Book Encyclopedia*, he explicitly added his putative ancestor as a "forerunner of exoticism in literature," a not-altogether favorable description, coming from Perse. See André Rousseau, "En Marge d'un article sur la littérature française dans une encyclopédie américaine," *Saint-John Perse: l'obscure naissance du langage*, ed. D. Racine (Paris: Minard, Lettres Modernes, 1987), 97.

ficials in Guadeloupe but did not add to the medieval aura of the biography.[22]

While deleting ancestors, the poet also edited out two exceptional anecdotes. One concerns a great-grandmother du Rozier, whose robust health was so legendary that Napoleon is said to have begged her to become the wetnurse of his son, the Roy de Rome. In the second draft, Napoleon continues every effort to convince the ancestor to nurse his son. All in vain; his persistent desire meets with repeated refusal. It takes a strong-willed person to refuse the Emperor, and for this alone she would be an admirable ancestor.

The anecdote takes an even more intriguing turn when it is juxtaposed with another singular story about wetnursing. While the poet's great-grandmother refused to nurse Napoleon's son, his grandmother, by contrast, "avait donné le sein à son petit fils (Alexis Saint-Leger Leger) pendant les voyages de sa fille." In the second version of the chronology, the poet retells the story of this grandmother "dont il admirait la forte vitalité, qui l'avait nourri, enfant, aux Iles, pendant des absences de sa mère." By the time of the Pléiade version, however, the episode is gone and the poet describes this grandmother as "Anne Dormoy, qui l'avait gardé enfant, aux Iles, pendant les absences de sa mère. (Mère de douze enfants, dont les derniers de l'âge de ceux de sa fille, elle avait, veuve encore jeune, conduit longtemps elle-même la plantation familiale du Bois-Debout.)" The poet's parenthetical explanation, added in the Pléiade edition, could have provided an explanation for his grandmother's prolonged nursing capacity, but ultimately Perse omitted the unusual story. By changing a single word, he transformed his grandmother from the person who nursed him (*nourri*) to the one who watched over him (*gardé*) during his mother's absences. In the final version, all references to maternal milk, both grandmother's and great-grandmother's, are omitted.

It is as if, in the progressive shaping of his genealogy, Perse sought to reinforce the elements of the story that most closely resemble mythic heroes, born directly from the brain or thigh of an all-powerful, archetypal father. Gaston Febus and a panoply of sailors, aventurers and survivors of lightning ultimately eclipse the

---

[22] Claude Thiébaut discusses the Leger lineage in "L'antillanité à tort contestée d'*Histoire du Régent*," *Saint-John Perse: Antillanité et universalité*, ed. H. Levillain and M. Sacotte (Paris: Editions Caribéennes, 1988), 89-115.

more prosaic occupations of law and public administration as well as maternal nurturing, even by an exceptional grandmother.

Also omitted from the final version are several references to celebrities. The cosmopolitan life of Pau in the entry for 1899 was even more exotic in earlier versions. Pau was "un monde romantique d'exil et de haute légende" until the poet removed *romantique* and *haute*. The roster of visitors was even more expansive before the poet excluded a host of painters, philosophers, philanthropists, and aviators. He claimed to have met, in a single month, King Oscar of Sweden, Frédéric Mistral, Buffalo Bill, international virtuosos and elder statesmen, all of whom disappeared in the final edition. As a student in Bordeaux, Perse was "Reçu dans la famille de François Mauriac," according to the manuscript, but this visit was not recorded in the Pléiade edition, nor were later encounters with Anna de Noailles, James Joyce, Adrienne Monnier, Sylvia Beach, and the mathematician Paul Painlevé, who was said to have introduced him to Albert Einstein.

Deletions can have many motivations, but one pattern that emerges in these manuscripts is Perse's silencing of voices that might otherwise reveal too much about his personal life or literary kinships.[23] The importance of the Countess Anna de Noailles in his intimacy undoubtedly made it desirable to exclude the entry for 1911, "invité chez Anna de Noailles." Other passages touched on the poet's indebtedness. The literary milieu of *Shakespeare and Co.*, animated by Adrienne Monnier and Sylvia Beach, where Perse met James Joyce–"Connaissance de Joyce"–disappears, perhaps because of Joyce's early impact on the younger writer.[24] Adrienne Monnier is removed from the chronology, but reappears in the correspondence, as the recipient of a 1948 letter where the poet excoriates Maurice Saillet's articles on "Saint-John Perse: Poète de Gloire" and insists anew that biography is useless for understanding poems.

At first glance, the very act of composing an autobiography might seem to lower the wall between civic and literary identities, but Perse's chronology manages to perpetuate that separation, in

---

[23] Henriette Levillain describes Perse's efforts to "gommer les épanchements, les confidences et les pleurs." "Saint-John Perse, Le poète au masque d'or," *Elseneur* 9, 1994, 53.

[24] Roger Little has pointed out the possible kinship with Joyce's character Persse O'Reilly in *Finnegans Wake*. *Etudes sur Saint-John Perse* (Paris: Klincksieck, 1984), 202.

keeping with his comment to the Argentine writer, Marcos Victoria: "Etre (en littérature) comme ces navires à quai qui offrent seulement leur poupe à la curiosité des passants: un nom, un port d'attache, c'est là tout leur état civil. Le reste est aventure, et n'appartient qu'à eux" (1094). The chronology obeys the poet's sense of what can or should be told. It is an epic story about names, his own and those in his family, and about the ports where their history is anchored. Around these poles, the poet relates the story of a private person who became a public personality and a vocation that led to international acclaim. At the threshold of the volume, Perse's chronology announces the tensions that lie ahead in the poems–between exile and attachment, solitude and alliance, action and creation, fertility and sterility, life and death, time and eternity.

A challenge facing any autobiographer is how to conclude the story of an unfinished life. As Don Quixote learned from the author of *The Life of Gines de Pasamonte*: how can the book be finished, if the life isn't?[25] How can you conclude without knowing the outcome? What kind of chronology can adequately introduce a volume mis-titled *Œuvres complètes*, about a life and a work that are still in progress and necessarily incomplete? Since autobiographers cannot narrate the end of their stories, the only possible closure is some kind of harmony. As Wayne Shumaker observes: "Autobiography characteristically opens with the cry of an infant and closes with the chair tilted against a sunny wall."[26] While Perse's story does not quite end with a tilted chair at les Vigneaux, it does forge structural and thematic reconciliations that give a sense of completion, even as the life continued.

The chronology opens, predictably, under the sign of birth; its first word is *Naissance*. But the next three entries all record deaths –of a grandfather (1888), a grandmother (1890), and a sister (1895). This juxtaposition of life and death offers a sense of proleptic grieving. The poet does not camouflage his regret for a bygone time. In aristocratic families of the Caribbean, the last years of the nineteenth century spelled the end of an era and the decline of Antillean life (xi). Writing about the period 1896-1899 Perse cites the financial crises and ruin of many families (xi). As Claude Thiébaut has

---

[25] Miguel de Cervantes Saavedra, *The Adventures of Don Quixote*, tr. J.M. Cohen (New York: Penguin Classics, 1981), 177.
[26] Wayne Shumaker, *op. cit.*, 130.

documented, this crisis was not only economic, linked to the sugar trade, but also political, foreshadowing the diminishing authority of Europe in the West Indies. In the poet's milieu, the end of the Spanish-American war and subsequent independence of Cuba were causes of concern. The poet turns this worry and nostalgia into mourning: "deuil ressenti aux Iles dans les vieilles familles françaises, alliées à des familles d'Espagne" (xi). The earthquake on Guadeloupe in 1897 and the volcanic eruption on Martinique in 1902 renewed the grieving: "Deuil à Pau chez les Leger en raison de vieilles alliances de famille entre Martinique et Guadeloupe" (xii).

A lyrical account of dying recurs in one of the final entries, dated 1968, where the poet recapitulates human life: "De la naissance à la mort, toute grande demeure antillaise tenait une baie ouverte sur l'Atlantique" (xli). From just such a window, an ancestor had prayed on her deathbed, "pour tous ceux de sa famille qui avaient été, qui étaient, ou qui seraient, un jour, heureux ou malheureux du fait de mer" (xli). Her setting is the closest we get to that chair against a sunny wall, but this forebear's gesture reaches backward and forward to embrace all her lineage, down to the poet himself, as if to bless in advance a foretold death.

A great-grandfather, Augustin de Caille, had already died in Provence, preparing the poet's own end in that same setting. Another proleptic death is that of Alexis de Leyritz, the poet's namesake, born of Hungarian nobility and deceased without leaving an heir (xiv). In an aristocratic world, preoccupied with genealogy, the absence of a male heir condemns a family to extinction. Such is the fictional drama of the "Récitation à l'éloge d'une reine" and "Berceuse" as well as the real-life fate of Alexis Leger, an only son with no children (ix).

In one of the final entries of the chronology, dated 1969, the poet proudly announces the success of his efforts to preserve endangered species of birds:

> Saint-John Perse avait eu enfin la grande satisfaction d'apprendre la discussion, depuis longtemps réclamée, d'une loi pour la protection des derniers grands rapaces de France (loi promulguée seulement en 1972) (xlii)

This effort to perpetuate a threatened lineage is prominently placed at the conclusion of his autobiography, as if to counterbalance the losses of the past and to proclaim survival, despite the poet's place at the end of a lineage. The only remaining entries deal with Perse's poetry and its publication in France and America. The two endeavors are not unrelated, for both the law and the publications are destined to ensure a future, physical or spiritual.

Birds represent a privileged intersection between the two domains, and the Pléiade autobiography is perhaps best understood as a sequel to *Oiseaux*. In the poem, Perse meditates about time and about the power of art to create eternity in the privileged space of a canvas or a page. In the autobiography Perse is both painter and bird, author and subject. By wearing the mask of a biographer, he distances himself from the individual who will die and focuses instead on the writer who will live. If works of art are, as the poet of *Oiseaux* suggests, "graines ailées [qui] ensemencent à long terme nos sites et nos jours" (423), it is fitting that the chronology should end with the announcement of an American publication. Like the Pléiade volume, this bilingual edition will carry the poems into the future.

While ostensibly the most linear of narratives, the autobiography actually has a circular, mythic structure. In a final "set-piece," dated 1968, Perse revisits sites and ideas of the beginning, summarizes longtime preoccupations and achieves a kind of closure. Under a Mediterranean sun, he reaffirms his oft-cited Celtic affinities, partly inherited and partly invented: "d'atavisme ancestral autant que de formation personnelle" (xl). The poet's phrase captures the secret process of the autobiography itself, which is a mixture of ancestral influences and personal creation. Tracing a genealogical circle, he creates the young Alexis Leger, who is, at the same time, his point of origin. Or, as Wordsworth understood, "the Child is father of the Man." [27] In a last, lyrical passage, the poet also embraces the feminine elements of his past, both "France mère" (xli) to which he returns and his women ancestors, "femmes, mères et filles, du littoral" (xli). Prelude and sequel to the poetry, the autobiographical poem recapitulates Perse's concern with genealogy–both ancestors and descendants–and his lifelong effort to find and create his place in a family and a literary lineage.

---

[27] William Wordsworth, "The Rainbow," *The Poetical Works of William Wordsworth*, ed. T. Hutchinson (London: Oxford UP, 1956), 62.

CONCLUSION

Conversation succeeds conversation,
Until there's nothing left to talk about
Except truth, the perennial monologue,
And no talker to dispute it but itself.
Laura Riding, "The Talking World,"
Collected Poems

T HE American poet Stanley Kunitz believed that every writer has a set of abiding images and preoccupations; "So, in a way, all the poems dissolve into one poem, the poem you spend your life writing." [1] Perse spent his life writing about genealogy–about the culture one inherits and the legacy one bequeaths. His work is filled with dramas of birth, race and filiation, with the leaves and branches of a vast family tree on which he sought to consolidate his perch. While he respected tradition (sometimes) and praised the late President John Kennedy for preserving the legacy of his "plus grands Aînés" (639), Perse also challenged, in each poem, the words of others.

This book is the consequence of eavesdropping on Perse's conversations with figures of western culture, from antiquity to the modern period. The colloquies are as diverse as the conversationalists themselves: a panoply of writers (and three artists) with whom the Nobel Prize laureate engaged in an ongoing debate.

From the earliest verses about childhood to the poignant works on old age, Perse and his protagonists glance uneasily over their shoulders at figures who haunt them. Their awareness is a testimony of sorts to the stature and power of predecessors, but if it is

---

[1] Leslie Kelen, "Stanley Kunitz, An Interview," *American Poetry Review,* March/ April 1998, 54.

praise, it is most often paradoxical. While engaging others in conversation, Perse usually contradicts them, renders them anonymous,
and relegates them to the wings. He rewrites or erases their words,
but we can sometimes hear them if we listen carefully enough.

If Perse often sparred (on the page, at least) with other writers,
his disagreement was perhaps most intense with the generation of
French writers that followed him, notably Jean-Paul Sartre. We can
only speculate about the sly pleasure Perse took at updating the
French literature entry for the *World Book Encyclopedia* in 1969.
The original article noted that "Sartre's theory of existentialism has
dominated literary and philosophic thought in France." [2] With a
stroke of the pen, Perse consigned the author of *La Nausée* to the
past, revising the entry in such a way that Sartre dominated French
thought merely "for a time." In that same *World Book*, the poet revised his own entry to characterize the poetry of Saint-John Perse as
"new and highly personal." [3] Both judgments prompt us to recon-
sider the poet's own place on the literary horizon.

In a world attuned to irony and skepticism, his lyric and epic
voices can take us by surprise. In an age of brevity and contrac-
tion, his Whitmanesque scope can be startling. And in an era of
mass media, his cultural references can seem obscure, elitist, and
anachronistic. Yet, despite appearances, Perse is also strikingly
modern.

Uprooted, exiled and stateless, he fashioned his own identity.
Across a life of continual self-invention, he embraced multiple personae, even beyond the ones thrust upon him by world events.
When Perse won the Nobel Prize for Literature in 1960, a Swedish
journalist laconically noted that "The man with the two names and
the five personalities got into a big black car and disappeared." [4]
The observation is perceptive, but the arithmetic is far too modest.
Perse used upward of a dozen names, with others continually
emerging as new correspondence comes to light. And how to count
the personalities? Perse himself mused, in his homage to Léon-Paul
Fargue, about the successive masks that poets don and that time

---

[2] Fondation Saint-John Perse, ms. 78.
[3] *Ibid.*
[4] *Dagens Nyheter*, December 8, 1960, cited by Marie-Noëlle Little, *Saint-John Perse: Correspondance avec Dag Hammarskjöld*, 64. In response to journalist's question about his dual identities as Alexis Leger and Saint-John Perse, the Nobel Prize
winner quipped that everyone has at least five personalities.

gradually strips away (512). Time and many critics have sought to uncover Perse's masks, only to discover yet more faces.

This is a doubly fortunate era for readers. Not only can we ask new questions of familiar poems, as each generation necessarily does, but we can also examine new texts: letters, manuscripts, notes and notebooks. Love letters to Lilita Abreu and Mina Curtiss offer both revelations and new layers of mystery, as do the friendships with Archibald MacLeish, Francis and Katherine Biddle.[5] Beyond them lies the tantalizing possibility of undiscovered documents. If the Gestapo did indeed seize manuscripts of poems and plays from the diplomat's apartment in 1940, then we can always dream of unearthing them some day, like a buried treasure, in a Russian archive.

Perse's library helps us understand the poems as products of *bricolage*, vast collages juxtaposing canonical texts with fragments from newspapers, magazines, travel brochures, postcards and even advertisements. In an assemblage of disparate elements, Perse combined high and low cultures; he also cultivated a syncretism that blurs the distinctions among eras and civilizations. Fascinated by scientific discoveries, he straddled the divide between C.P. Snow's two cultures, praising in science as in art the primordial role of intuition.

In recent decades, the issues Perse most cared about–meaning, happiness and permanence–have not been particularly timely. But the intellectual climate of a new century, more reflective about spirituality and ethics, may be better attuned to Perse's fundamental preoccupations.

One sign of a changing climate is philosophers' return, after a long hiatus, to the study of aesthetics and the previously taboo subject of beauty. For Alexander Nehamas beauty "makes life and art continuous."[6] It leads to what Elaine Scarry calls a "more capacious regard for the world."[7] Perse's poems act in a similar way, enhancing ways of seeing and confronting us with fundamental questions about life and happiness.

The bankruptcy of Marxism generated an understandable skepticism about big claims and master narratives. But seasons change

---

[5] See *Courrier d'exil: Saint-John Perse et ses amis américains,* ed. C. Rigolot (Paris: Gallimard, 2001).

[6] Alexander Nehamas, Tanner Lectures, Yale University, April 2001.

[7] Elaine Scarry, *On Beauty and Being Just* (Princeton: Princeton UP, 1999), 81, 48.

and with more perspective on twentieth-century débacles, many have resumed the search for some kind of meaning and plenitude at the intersection of matter and spirit. In Perse's poetry they find human beings at such a crossroad: "l'argile humaine où perce la face inachevée du dieu" (288).

In modern French letters, one of Perse's closest kin is the preeminent poet Yves Bonnefoy. Disagreeing with those who proclaim the so-called Death of the Author, Bonnefoy reaffirms the value of specific voices speaking about everyday realities, "dans l'urgence des jours." [8] A similar sense of urgency pervades Perse's poetry, both about the present and about the future.

Dante, claimed Perse, is a "suzerain de naissance, et qui n'a point à se forger une légitimité" (456). But Perse himself engaged in a lifelong effort to forge his own legitimacy through colloquy with ancestors, peers and posterity. Two phrases he underlined in his reading reveal this concern:

> La qualité d'une œuvre tient à la force, à la multiplicité des échos qu'elle éveille [. . .]
> Les œuvres ont autant de visages que leur en découvrent les générations successives: elles ne survivraient pas sans cela. [9]

One of the signs of Perse's own survival is the multiplicity of echoes that his work awakens in younger writers. Today some of the most creative and committed reading is taking place in the Caribbean where writers are reevaluating an ambiguous forefather, born in Guadeloupe to a white family, a *béké* deeply anchored in his Creole childhood. Derek Walcott of Trinidad devoted a long section of his 1992 Nobel Prize speech to Perse, examining that ambiguity:

> To celebrate Perse, we might be told, is to celebrate the old plantation system, to celebrate the beque or plantation rider, verandahs and mulatto servants, a white French language in a white pith helmet, to celebrate a rhetoric of patronage and hauteur; and even if Perse denied his origins, great writers often have this folly of trying to smother their source, we cannot deny

---

[8] Yves Bonnefoy, *Leçon inaugurale*, Collège de France, 4 décembre 1981.
[9] Bernard Pingaud, undated review of Jean-Pierre Richard's *L'Univers imaginaire de Mallarmé*, Doc. Poésie, n. 61, Fondation Saint-John Perse.

him any more than we can the African Aimé Césaire. This is not accommodation, this is the ironic republic that is poetry, since, when I see cabbage palms moving their fronds at sunrise, I think they are reciting Perse.[10]

Edouard Glissant and Maryse Condé began by rejecting their Guadeloupean predecessor, only to discover, much later, some unexpected affinities. Glissant's poem, Les Indes, is a response to this white ancestor. Even as it echoes rhythms and themes of Eloges, La Gloire des Rois and Anabase, it portrays the neglected protagonists of New World exploration: native Indians and African slaves. Maryse Condé traveled a similar path from hostility to respect, culminating in an assimilation of a whole passage of Eloges into her novel, La Vie scélérate.[11]

Younger Guadeloupean authors in search of Creole roots have undertaken their own conversations–and debates–with Perse, revising his portrait of Caribbean society to recount an African Antillean experience.[12] Patrick Chamoiseau's Texaco converses with both Eloges and Anabase, while Raphaël Confiant's Ravines du devant-jour ends with Perse's question: "Sinon l'enfance qu'y a-t-il qu'il n'y a plus?"[13] Adopting the verse without attribution, Confiant and others reverse the tables on Perse and engage in precisely the kind of exchange we have witnessed all through this book: honoring a predecessor while at the same time rendering him anonymous. But for these writers, Eloges, no less than Aimé Césaire's Cahier d'un retour au pays natal, is a "référence obligatoire."[14] Jean Bérubé, Patrick

---

[10] Derek Walcott, "The Antilles: Fragments of Epic Memory," Nobel Prize Lecture, 1992. www.nobel.se.

[11] In La Vie scélérate (Paris: Seghers, 1987), 221, Maryse Condé rewrites Eloges IV (26) to read: "Velma était négresse et sentait la ganja; toujours j'ai vu sous le grand foulard tricolore qui enserrait sa lourde chevelure des perles brillantes de sueur à l'entour de ses yeux noirs de nuit et sa bouche [. . .] avait le goût des fruits du goyavier sauvage cueillis avant midi." See Mireille Sacotte, Saint-John Perse (Paris: Belfond, 1991), 61.

[12] Writers include Patrick Chamoiseau, Rafaël Confiant, Daniel Radford, Daniel Maximin and Bertène Juminer. Mary Gallagher discusses their work in La Créolité de Saint-John Perse, Cahiers Saint-John Perse 14, 1998, 37-39, 412-429.

[13] Raphaël Confiant, Ravines du devant-jour (Paris: Gallimard, 1993), 208. In another instance of appropriation, Daniel Maximin's L'Ile et une nuit reproduces a letter supposedly written by Perse but actually drawn from the poet's interviews with Pierre Guerre. For other examples, see Mary Gallagher, op. cit., 423.

[14] Mary Gallagher, op. cit., 38.

Chamoiseau and Raphaël Confiant affirm Perse's role when they refer in *Eloges de la Créolité* to "la reconnaissance maintenant unanime, dans nos pays, du poète Saint-John Perse comme l'un des fils les plus prestigieux de la Guadeloupe [. . .]." [15]

The narrator of *Vents* watched shadows projected upon walls by "des feuilles en tous lieux" and concluded: "nous les avions déjà tracés" (237). In a parallel effort, I have sought in this book to trace shadows projected on Perse's poetry by a family tree of letters, but, unlike that protagonist of *Vents,* I do not claim to have traced them all. As in *Chronique*, "la chose est dite et n'est point dite" (397). This book about conversations ends with an invitation for others to add what I have not been able to hear or say. Future eavesdroppers will, I hope, overhear other conversations–with Napoleon and Nietzsche, Goethe and Ralph Waldo Emerson. They will also listen to Perse's dialogue with popular culture–advertisements, brochures, cowboy films (which he loved), newspaper clippings, how-to books, horoscopes and dictionaries–to see how these, too, nourished his poems. Much remains to report, for Saint-John Perse's poems, like his five–or twenty-five–personalities, are manifestations of a vast creative energy forever forging itself anew in the crucible of words: "au feu des forges votre éclat" (250).

---

[15] Jean Bérubé et al., *Eloge de la Créolité* (Paris: Gallimard, Presses Universitaires Créoles, 1989), 29.

BIBLIOGRAPHY

WORKS BY SAINT-JOHN PERSE

Œuvres complètes. Paris: Gallimard, Pléiade, 1982.
Collected Poems. Princeton: Princeton UP, Bollingen, 1971.
L'Animale. Ed. Albert Henry. *Cahiers Saint-John Perse* 4, 1981, 11-26.
Amitié du Prince. Ed. Albert Henry. Paris: Gallimard, Publications de la Fondation Saint-John Perse, 1979.
Anabasis. Tr. T.S. Eliot. New York: Harbinger, 1949.
Anabase. Ed. Albert Henry. Paris: Gallimard, Publications de la Fondation Saint-John Perse, 1983.
Exil. Ed. Roger Little. London: Athlone, 1995.
Nocturne. Ed. Albert Henry. Paris: Gallimard, Publications de la Fondation Saint-John Perse, 1985.
Croisière aux Iles Eoliennes. Cahiers Saint-John Perse 8-9, 1987.

CORRESPONDENCE

Letters. Ed. and tr. Arthur J. Knodel. Princeton: Princeton UP, Bollingen, 1979.
Lettres à l'Etrangère. Ed. Mauricette Berne. Paris: Gallimard, 1987.
Roger Caillois - Saint-John Perse Correspondance 1942-1975. Ed. Joëlle Gardes Tamine. *Cahiers Saint-John Perse* 13, 1996.
Lettres d'Alexis Leger à Gabriel Frizeau. Ed. Albert Henry. Bruxelles: Académie Royale de Belgique, 1993.
"Saint-John Perse à Yvan Goll: Huit lettres inédites." Ed. Roger Little. *Cahiers Saint-John Perse* 2, 1979, 105-126.
Saint-John Perse: Correspondance avec Dag Hammarskjöld. Ed. Marie-Noëlle Little. *Cahiers Saint-John Perse* 11, 1993.
Correspondance Saint-John Perse - Jean Paulhan. Ed. Joëlle Gardes Tamine. *Cahiers Saint-John Perse* 10, 1991.

EXHIBITION CATALOGUES

Les Oiseaux dans l'Œuvre de Saint-John Perse, Pierre Guerre, Jean-Louis Lalanne. Aix-en-Provence: Fondation Saint-John Perse, 1976.

Saint-John Perse: Documentary Exhibition and Works on the Poem Amers. Washington, D.C.: Anderson House Museum, 1984-85.

La Jeunesse de Saint-John Perse/Alexis Leger. Yves-Alain Favre, René Rouyère. Pau: Hôtel de Ville, 1987.

Saint-John Perse et ses Illustrateurs: un compagnonnage. Paris: Maison de la Poésie, Forum des Halles, 1987.

Regards sur l'Asie. Aix-en-Provence: Fondation Saint-John Perse; Pointe-à-Pitre: Musée Saint-John Perse, 1989.

Pour fêter une enfance: Saint-John Perse et les Antilles. Aix-en-Provence: Fondation Saint-John Perse; Pointe à Pitre: Musée Saint-John Perse, 1990.

Saint-John Perse et le Sud. Aix-en-Provence: Fondation Saint-John Perse, 1993.

COLLECTIVE VOLUMES ABOUT SAINT-JOHN PERSE

Cahiers du XXe siècle 7: Lectures de Saint-John Perse. Ed. Jean Burgos, Roger Little, 1976.

Cahiers Saint-John Perse. Ed. Jean-Louis Lalanne. Paris: Gallimard, 1978 ff.

Europe 799-800, novembre-décembre 1995 (numéro spécial).

Hommage à Saint-John Perse. Paris: NRF 278, février 1976.

Honneur à Saint-John Perse. Paris: Gallimard, 1965.

La Nostalgie: Analyses et reflexions sur Saint-John Perse: Eloges. Ouvrage collectif. Paris: Editions Marketing, 1986.

Portulans pour Saint-John Perse. Actes du Colloque de Pau. Ed. Yves-Alain Favre. Pau: J&D Editions, 1989.

Pour Saint-John Perse: Etudes et essais pour le centenaire de Saint-John Perse (1887-1987). Ed. Pierre Pinalie. Schœlcher: Presses Universitaires Créoles; L'Harmattan, 1988.

Revue d'Histoire littéraire de la France 3, mai-juin 1978 (numéro spécial).

Saint-John Perse: Les années de formation. Ed. Jack Corzani. Paris: C.E.L.F.A./ L'Harmattan, 1996.

Saint-John Perse: L'obscure naissance du langage. Ed. Daniel Racine. Paris: Minard, 1987.

Saint-John Perse 2: Saint-John Perse et les arts. Ed. Daniel Racine. Paris: Minard, 1989.

Saint-John Perse: Antillais universel. Ed. Daniel Racine. Actes du Colloque de Pointe-à-Pitre, 1987. Paris, Minard, 1991.

Saint-John Perse: Antillanité et universalité. Ed. Mireille Sacotte, Henriette Levillain. Actes du colloque de 1987. Paris: Editions Caribéennes, 1988.

Saint-John Perse et les Etats-Unis. Actes du colloque 1980. Aix-en-Provence: Université de Provence, 1981.

Saint-John Perse: Eloges. Ed. N. Blandin. Grenoble: Fondation Hébert d'Uckermann, 1987.

Souffle de Perse, Revue de l'Association des Amis de Saint-John Perse. Aix-en-Provence: Fondation Saint-John Perse, 1991 ff.

SELECTED CRITICAL WORKS ABOUT SAINT-JOHN PERSE

Aigrisse, Gilberte. *Saint-John Perse et ses Mythologies*. Paris: Imago, 1992.

Antoine, Régis. *Les Ecrivains français et les Antilles*. Paris: Maisonneuve et Larose, 1978.

————. "Une Echappée magnifiante sur la Guadeloupe." *Saint-John Perse: Antillanité et Universalité*. Ed. Henriette Levillain, Mireille Sacotte. Paris: Editions Caribéennes, 1988.

Aquien, Michèle. *Saint-John Perse. L'être et le nom*. Seyssel: Champ Vallon, 1985.

Aranjo, Daniel. *Saint-John Perse et la musique*. Pau: J&D Editions, 1988.

————. "Deux lettres inédites de Saint-John Perse." *Arts, Sciences, Techniques 3*, mai 1992.

Bosquet, Alain. *Saint-John Perse*. Paris: Seghers, Poètes d'aujourd'hui, 1971 (first edition 1953).

————. *La Mémoire ou l'oubli*. Paris: Grasset, 1990.

Brincourt, André. *Messagers de la nuit. Roger Martin du Gard, Saint-John Perse, André Malraux*. Paris: Grasset, 1995.

Caduc, Eveline. *Saint-John Perse: Connaissance et création*. Paris: Corti, 1977.

————. *Index de l'œuvre poétique de Saint-John Perse*. Paris: Champion, 1993.

Caillois, Roger. *Poétique de Saint-John Perse*. Paris: Gallimard, 1954.

Camelin, Colette. *Eclat des contraires: La poétique de Saint-John Perse*. Paris: CNRS Editions, 1998.

————. "Le peintre et le poète assembleurs de saisons: Saint-John Perse et la peinture de Georges Braque." *Souffle de Perse 3*, janvier 1993, 43-58.

————. "L'orage d'Orthez." *Souffle de Perse 4*, janvier 1994, 92-102.

————. "Saint-John Perse lecteur de Pindare." *Revue d'Histoire littéraire de la France* 91:4-5, juillet-octobre 1991, 591-611.

Canadas, Serge. "Passage de l'équinoxe: Introduction à la notion et à l'expérience de *Sécheresse*." *Cahiers Saint-John Perse 2*, 1979, 17-34.

Castin, Nicholas. "La Stratégie de la négation: *Sécheresse*." *Souffle de Perse 3*, janvier 1993, 82-91.

Céry, Loïc. "La dure vie de l'oiseau Annaô." *Souffle de Perse 9*, janvier 2000, 52-68.

Charpier, Jacques. *Saint-John Perse*. Paris: Gallimard, Bibliothèque Idéale, 1962.

Chehab, May. "Le Thème de la mer chez Claudel et Saint-John Perse." *Souffle de Perse 5-6*, juin 1995, 65-78.

————. *Saint-John Perse et la Grèce*, thèse de doctorat de l'Université de Provence - Aix-Marseille I, 1999.

Cluse, Jean-Louis, and Desazars de Montgailhard, Sylvia. *Entre Amériques et Castilles, Lilita Abreu, l'étrangère de Saint-John Perse*. Aix-en-Provence: Fondation Saint-John Perse, 1987.

Condé, Maryse. "Eloge de Saint-John Perse." *Europe* 799-800, novembre-décembre 1995, 20-25.

Corzani, Jack. *La Littérature des Antilles-Guyane françaises*, t. 2. Fort de France: Desormeaux, 1978.

Coss-Humbert, Elisabeth. *Saint-John Perse. Poésie, science de l'être*. Nancy: Presses Universitaires, 1993.

Crouy-Chanel, Etienne de. *Alexis Leger ou l'autre visage de Saint-John Perse*. Paris: Jean Picollec, 1989.

Dolamore, Charles. "A propos de *Sécheresse*." *Cahiers du 20e siècle* 7, 1976, 115-127.

Dorst, Jean. "*Oiseaux* vus par un ornithologue." *Espaces de Saint-John Perse* 1-2, Université de Provence, 1979, 327-334.

Doumet, Christian. *Les Thèmes aériens dans l'œuvre de Saint-John Perse.* Paris: Minard, 1976.

Elbaz, Schlomo. *Lectures d'*Anabase *de Saint-John Perse.* Genève: L'Age d'homme, 1977.

Favre, Yves-Alain. *Saint-John Perse: le langage et le sacré.* Paris: Corti, 1977.

Frédéric, Madeleine. *La Répétition et ses structures dans l'œuvre de Saint-John Perse.* Paris: Gallimard, 1984.

Galand, René. *Saint-John Perse.* New York: Twayne, 1972.

————. *Canevas: Etudes sur la poésie française.* Paris: Corti, 1986.

Gallagher, Mary. "La Création comme médiation: la réflexivité des Hommages persiens," *Souffle de Perse* 5-6, juin 1995, 202-210.

————. *La Créolité de Saint-John Perse.* Paris: Gallimard, Cahiers Saint-John Perse 14, 1998.

Gardes Tamine, Joëlle. *Saint-John Perse ou la stratégie de la seiche.* Aix-en-Provence: Presses de l'Université de Provence, 1996.

Girard, Alain. "Le Mallarmé de Saint-John Perse." *Souffle de Perse* 5-6, juin 1997, 79-95.

Guérant, J.-F. "La Biographie en guise de préface chez Saint-John Perse." *L'Information littéraire* 4, 1990, 3-16.

Guerre, Pierre. *Portrait de Saint-John Perse.* Ed. Roger Little. Marseille: Sud, 1989.

Henry, Albert. Amers *de Saint-John Perse: une poésie du mouvement.* Neuchâtel: Baconnière, 1963.

Holger, Christian Holst. "Une correspondance perdue: Karen Bramson/Alexis Leger, 1916-1918." *Souffle de Perse* 9, janvier 2000, 28-46.

————. "Quelques parallèles et contrastes dans l'œuvre de Saint-John Perse, Conrad et Loti." *Souffle de Perse* 5-6, juin 1995, 29-40.

Hommage à Dorothy Leger. Ed. Henri Colliot, André Rousseau. Aix-en-Provence: Fondation Saint-John Perse, 1985.

Kemp, Friedhelm. "Annotations de Saint-John Perse." *Cahiers Saint-John Perse* 6, 1993, 39-131.

Knodel, Arthur J. "*Eloges:* . . . Lesquels?" *La Nostalgie: Analyses et reflexions sur Saint-John Perse,* Eloges. Ouvrage collectif. Paris: Editions Marketing, 1986.

————. "Marcel Proust et Saint-John Perse: le fossé infranchissable," *Revue de Paris* 76, décembre 1976, 80-92.

————. *Saint-John Perse: A Study of His Poetry.* Edinburgh: U of Edinburgh P, 1966.

————. "Towards an Understanding of *Anabase.*" *PMLA* LXXIX, June 1964, 329-343.

————. "'V Street': Une première version de *Poème à l'Etrangère,*" *Cahiers Saint-John Perse* 3, 1980, 47-70.

Kopenhagen-Urian, Judith. "La Condition de la femme biblique dans la poésie de Saint-John Perse." *Souffle de Perse* 4, janvier 1994, 55-66.

Le Guen, Jean-Michel. *L'Ordre exploratoire: l'*Anabase. Paris: SEDES, 1985.

Léoni, Anne, and Antoine Raybaud, "La Référence absente: une lecture de *Récitation à l'éloge d'une reine.*" *Espaces de Saint-John Perse* 1-2. Aix-en-Provence: Université de Provence, 1979.

Levillain, Henriette. *Le Rituel poétique de Saint-John Perse.* Paris: Gallimard, 1977.

————. "Saint-John Perse, le poète au masque d'or." *Elseneur* 9, 1994, 51-57.

————. *Sur deux versants, la création chez Saint-John Perse d'après les versions anglaises et son œuvre poétique.* Paris: Corti, 1987.

Little, Marie-Noëlle. "L'Aile, motif et réseaux des poèmes d'Amérique." *Espaces de Saint-John Perse* 3. Université de Provence, 1980, 285-311.

Little, Roger. *Word Index of the Complete Poetry and Prose of Saint-John Perse.* Southampton: the author, 1967. *Supplement A,* 1967.

———. *Saint-John Perse: A Bibliography for Students of his Poetry.* London: Grant and Cutler, 1971. Supplements 1 (1976) and 2 (1982).

———. *Saint-John Perse.* London: Athlone, 1973.

———. *Etudes sur Saint-John Perse.* Paris: Klincksieck, 1984.

———. "Saint-John Perse et les arts visuels." *Revue d'Histoire littéraire de la France* 86:2, mars-avril 1986, 220-234.

Mayaux, Catherine. "Les Illustres prédécesseurs de Michaux en Chine: Claudel, Segalen et Saint-John Perse." *Henri Michaux: un barbare en Asie.* Ouvrage collectif. Paris: Editions Marketing, 1992.

———. *Les Lettres d'Asie de Saint-John Perse: Les récits d'un poète.* Paris: Gallimard, *Cahiers Saint-John Perse* 12, 1994.

———. "Saint-John Perse, lecteur de Claudel," *Claudel Studies* XXIV, 1-2, 1997, 110-116.

Nairac, Diane. "Valeur des réminiscences bibliques dans l'œuvre de Saint-John Perse." *Cahiers Saint-John Perse* 7, 1984, 63-88.

Nasta, D.I. *Saint-John Perse et la découverte de l'être.* Paris: Presses Universitaires de France, 1980.

Neumeister, Sébastien. "Saint-John Perse et le mythe de Robinson." *Cahiers Saint-John Perse* 2, 1979, 61-76.

Noulet, Emilie. *Le Ton poétique.* Paris: Corti, 1971.

Oster Soussouev, Pierre. *Saint-John Perse. Alexis et Dorothée Leger.* Mazamet: Babel, 1992.

Parent, Monique. *Saint-John Perse et quelques devanciers: études sur le poème en prose.* Paris: Klincksieck, 1960.

Paulhan, Jean. *Enigmes de Perse.* Mazamet: Babel, 1992 (first edition 1969).

Philippon, Michel. "Discours de la rééducation volontaire: la lettre à Frizeau de mars 1907." *Saint-John Perse: Les Années de formation.* Ed. Jack Corzani. Paris: L'Harmattan, 1996, 205-215.

Picard, Jacqueline. "Les *Images à Crusoé* comme variation textuelle et picturale." *Souffle de Perse* 7, mai 1997, 102-120; 8, 1998, 65-66.

Poulet, Georges. *Etudes sur le Temps Humain,* t. III, *Le Point de Départ.* Paris: Plon, 1964.

Raybaud, Antoine. "Eloge du non-savoir?" *Espaces de Saint-John Perse* 1-2, 1979, 347-358.

———. "*Exil* palimpseste," *Cahiers Saint-John Perse* 5, 1982, 79-107.

Richard, Jean-Pierre. *Onze études sur la poésie moderne.* Paris: Seuil, 1964.

———. "Petite remontée dans un nom-titre (Saint-John Perse)." *Microlectures.* Paris: Seuil, 1979.

———. "Figures avec paysages." *Microlectures II.* Paris: Seuil, 1984.

Rieuneau, Maurice. "Sur Saint-John Perse et les oiseaux d'Audubon." *Espaces de Saint-John Perse* 1-2, Université de Provence, 1979, 335-345.

Robichez, Jacques. *Sur Saint-John Perse.* Paris: Société de l'Enseignement Supérieur, 1982.

Rousseau, André. "Conversation à la Fondation Saint-John Perse." *Saint-John Perse: Eloges.* Ed. N. Blandin. Grenoble: Fondation Hébert d'Uckermann, 1987.

Rouyère, René. *La jeunesse d'Alexis Leger/Saint-John Perse.* Bordeaux: Presses Universitaires de Bordeaux, 1989.

Sacotte, Mireille. "Comment peut-on être un enfant?" *Saint-John Perse: Les années de formation.* Ed. J. Corzani. Paris: C.E.L.F.A./L'Harmattan, 1996.

————. *Parcours de Saint-John Perse.* Paris-Genève: Champion-Slatkine, 1987.

————. "Le Rire de Saint-John Perse." *Europe* 799-800, novembre-décembre 1995, 135-142.

————. *Saint-John Perse.* Paris: Belfond, 1991.

Thiébaut, Claude. "Alexis Leger / Saint-John Perse dans l'œil du cyclone." *Trois poètes face à la crise de l'histoire.* Ed. Paule Plouvier, Renée Ventresque, Jean-Claude Blachère. Paris: L'Harmattan, 1997, 79-99.

————. "'Ecrit sur la porte' de Saint-John Perse à l'épreuve de la traduction en créole." *Pour Saint-John Perse.* Ed. Pierre Pinalie. Paris: L'Harmattan, 1988, 73-96.

————. *Guadeloupe 1899. L'année de tous les dangers.* Paris: L'Harmattan, 1989.

————. "Modeste proposition . . . (au sujet du pseudonyme 'Saint-John Perse')." *Souffle de Perse* 2, janvier 1992, 27-31.

————. "Rôle et influence de Francis Jammes sur Alexis Leger/Saint-John Perse." *Souffle de Perse* 5-6, juin 1995, 106-137.

van Rutten, Pierre. *Le Langage poétique de Saint-John Perse.* La Haye, Paris: Mouton, 1975.

Ventresque, Renée. "Alexis Leger et Gauguin: un allié substantiel occulté." *Les Mots La Vie* 8, Paris: L'Harmattan, 1994.

————. *Les Antilles de Saint-John Perse: itinéraire intellectuel d'un poète.* Paris: L'Harmattan, 1993.

————. "La *Biographie* de Saint-John Perse dans l'édition de la Pléiade: d'un masque à l'autre." *Les Mots La Vie* 9, 1997, 71-80.

————. "Décidément *Cohorte* n'a pas été écrit en 1907." *Souffle de Perse* 9, janvier 2000, 47-51.

————. "Saint-John Perse, un grand poète du XIXe siècle: l'héritage symboliste de Mallarmé." *Souffle de Perse* 5-6, juin 1995, 96-105.

————. "Saint-John Perse face à la crise de l'histoire: le sens de ce très grand désordre." *Trois poètes face à la crise de l'histoire.* Ed. Paule Plouvier, Renée Ventresque, Jean-Claude Blachère. Paris: L'Harmattan, 1997, 101-115.

————. *Le Songe antillais de Saint-John Perse.* Paris: L'Harmattan, 1995.

Winspur, Steven. "Le Signe pur." *Cahiers Saint-John Perse* 4, 1981, 45-63.

————. "*Exil* signifiant: le signifiant en exil." *Espaces de Saint-John Perse* 3, 1981, 29-51.

————. "*Vents* et la rhétorique retournée de Saint-John Perse." *Saint-John Perse: l'obscure naissance du langage.* Ed. Daniel Racine. Paris: Minard, 1987, 23-40.

————. *Saint-John Perse and the Imaginary Reader.* Genève: Droz, 1988.

Yoyo, Emile. *Saint-John Perse ou le Conteur.* Paris: Bordas, 1971.

PRINCIPAL WORKS CONSULTED

Aristotle, *Rhetoric.* New York: Modern Library, 1954.

Audubon, John James. *Audubon's Birds of America.* Ed. Roger Tory Peterson, Virginia Marie Peterson. New York: Abbeville Press, Audubon Society Baby Elephant Folio, 1981.

————. *Bird Biographies.* Ed. Alice Ford. New York: Macmillan, 1957.

Bachelard, Gaston. *L'Eau et les rêves.* Paris: Corti, 1942.

————. *Poétique de l'espace.* Paris: Presses Universitaires de France, 1957.

Baudelaire, Charles. *Œuvres complètes.* Ed. Marcel Ruff. Paris: Seuil, 1968.

Beaujour, Michel. *Poetics of the Literary Self-Portrait.* Trans. Y. Milos. New York: New York UP, 1991.

Bérubé, Jean, Patrick Chamoiseau and Rafaël Confiant. *Eloge de la Créolité.* Paris: Gallimard, Presses Universitaires Créoles, 1989.

Bloch, R. Howard. *Etymologies and Genealogies.* Chicago: U of Chicago P, 1983.

Bloom, Harold. *The Anxiety of Influence.* New York: Oxford UP, 1975.

——. *The Poetics of Influence.* New Haven: H.R. Schwab, 1988.

Bonnefoy, Yves. *Baudelaire parlant à Mallarmé: Entretiens sur la poésie.* Neuchâtel: La Baconnière, 1981.

Borges, Jorge Luis, *Other Inquisitions 1937-1952.* Ed. J. Irby. Tr. R. Simms. Austin: U of Texas P, 1988.

Calin, William. *A Muse for Heroes: Nine Centuries of the Epic in France.* Toronto: U of Toronto P, 1983.

Cendrars, Blaise. *Œuvres complètes.* 8 vols. Paris: Denoël, 1960-65.

Chateaubriand, François-René de. *Mémoires d'Outre-Tombe.* Ed. Maurice Levaillant. Paris: Flammarion, 1949.

——. *Œuvres romanesques et voyages.* Paris: Gallimard, Pléiade, 1969.

——. *Génie du Christianisme, Œuvres complètes,* t. 3. Paris: Krabbe, 1854.

Claudel, Paul. "Un Poème de Saint-John Perse," *Revue de Paris* 56, novembre 1949, 3-15.

——. *Théâtre* I, II. Paris: Gallimard, Pléiade, 1956.

——. *Œuvre poétique.* Paris: Gallimard, Pléiade, 1957.

——. "Introduction à un poème sur Dante." *Positions et Propositions I. Œuvres complètes,* t. 15. Paris: Gallimard, 1959.

——. *Œuvres en prose.* Ed. J. Petit. Paris: Gallimard, Pléiade, 1965.

——. *Journal.* Paris: Gallimard, Pléiade, 1968.

——. *Correspondance Paul Claudel-Darius Milhaud 1912-1953. Cahiers Paul Claudel 3.* Paris: Gallimard, 1961.

Coe, Richard N. *When the Grass was Taller.* New Haven: Yale UP, 1984.

Crèvecœur, Hector St. John de. *Letters from an American Farmer.* Ed. W.B. Blake. New York: Dutton, 1951 (reprinted from 1912).

Curtius, Ernst Robert. *European Literature and the Latin Middle Ages.* Tr. W.R. Trask. New York: Pantheon, Bollingen, 1953.

Eliot, T.S. *Selected Essays 1917-1932.* New York: Harcourt, Brace, 1932.

Emerson, Ralph Waldo. *Selected Writings of Emerson.* Ed. Donald McQuade. New York: Modern Library, 1981.

Entrikin, J. Nicholas. *The Betweenness of Place: Towards a Geography of Modernity.* London: Macmillan, 1991.

Erkkila, Betsy. *Walt Whitman among the French.* Princeton: Princeton UP, 1980.

Fleishman, Avrom. *Figures of Autobiography.* Berkeley: U of California P, 1983.

Ford, Alice, ed. *Audubon, by Himself.* Garden City: Natural History Press, 1969.

Froissart, Jean. *Les Chroniques, t. II.* Ed. J.A.C. Buchon. Paris: Desrez, 1811.

Fumaroli, Marc. *L'Age de l'éloquence.* Genève: Droz, 1980.

Genette, Gérard. *Palimpsestes.* Paris: Seuil, 1982.

——. *Seuils.* Paris: Seuil, 1987.

Gide, André. *Prétextes.* Paris: Mercure de France, 1903.

Glissant, Edouard. *Le Discours antillais.* Paris: Seuil, 1995.

Greene, Thomas M. *The Light of Troy.* New Haven: Yale UP, 1982.

Gusdorf, Georges. *Auto-bio-graphie.* Paris: Odile Jacob, 1991.

Heraclitus, *Fragments.* Tr. T.M. Robinson. Toronto: U of Toronto P, 1987.

Homer, *The Iliad.* Tr. Robert Fagles. New York: Penguin Classics, 1990.

——. *The Odyssey.* Tr. Robert Fitzgerald. New York: Random House, Vintage, 1990.

Hugo, Victor. *William Shakespeare*. *Œuvres complètes*, v. 12. Ed. Jean Massin. Paris: Club Français du Livre, 1969.

——. *La Légende des siècles*. Ed. Jacques Truchet. Paris: Gallimard, Pléiade, 1950.

——. *Poésies, I, II*. Paris: Hachette, 1950.

——. *Littérature et philosophie mêlées*. Paris: Klincksieck, 1976.

Jammes, Francis. *Œuvre poétique complète*. Ed. M. Haurie. Pau: J&D Editions, 1995.

Kristeva, Julia. "Narration et transformation." *Semiotica* 1:4, 1969.

La Bruyère, Jean de. *Œuvres complètes*. Ed. Julien Benda. Paris: Gallimard, Pléiade, 1941.

Larbaud, Valery. *Œuvres*. Ed. G. Jean-Aubry, Robert Mallet. Paris: Gallimard, Pléiade, 1957.

Lejeune, Philippe. *L'Autobiographie en France*. Paris: A. Colin, 1971.

——. *Le Pacte Autobiographique*. Paris: Seuil, 1975.

Lindsay, Jack. *Helen of Troy*. Totowa: Rowman and Littlefield, 1974.

Li-Po, *Li-Po The Chinese Poet*. Tr. S. Obata. New York: Dutton, 1928.

Loti, Pierre, *Le Mariage de Loti–Rarahu*. Paris: Calmann Lévy, 1886.

——. *Les Derniers jours de Pékin*. Paris: Balland, 1985.

MacLeish, Archibald. *Letters of Archibald MacLeish 1907-1982*. Ed. R. H. Winnick. New York: Houghton Mifflin, 1983.

Mallarmé, Stéphane. *Œuvres*. Ed. Yves-Alain Favre. Paris: Garnier, 1985.

Marchal, Bertrand. *Lecture de Mallarmé*. Paris: Corti, 1985.

May, Georges. *Autobiographie*. Paris: Presses Universitaires de France, 1979.

Monnier, Adrienne. *Les Gazettes d'Adrienne Monnier 1925-1945*. Paris: Julliard, 1953.

Montaigne, Michel de. *Complete Essays*. Trans. D. Frame. Stanford: Stanford UP, 1976.

Moura, Jean Marc. *Lire l'exotisme*. Paris: Dunod, 1992.

Nietzsche, Friedrich. *The Wanderer and his Shadow, Complete Works* v. 7. Ed. O. Levy. Trans. P. Cohn. New York: Russell, 1964.

Olney, James, ed. *Autobiography: Essays Theoretical and Critical*. Princeton: Princeton UP, 1980.

Pascal, Roy. *Design and Truth in Autobiography*. London: Routledge & Kegan Paul, 1960.

Plato, *Republic*. Tr. G.M.A. Grube. Indianapolis: Hackett, 1974.

——. *Œuvres complètes*. 2 vols. Tr. L. Robin. Paris: Gallimard, Pléiade, 1950.

Poe, Edgar Allan. *The Complete Tales and Poems of Edgar Allan Poe*. New York: Modern Library, 1938.

——. *Œuvres*. Tr. Charles Baudelaire. Genève: Edito Service, n.d.

Poggioli, Renato. *The Spirit of the Letter*. Cambridge: Harvard UP, 1965.

Polo, Marco. *Le Livre de Marco Polo*. Trans. A. T'Serstevens. Paris: Albin Michel, 1955.

Proust, Marcel. *A la Recherche du temps perdu*. Paris: Gallimard, Pléiade, 1954.

Richard, Claude, ed. *Edgar Allan Poe*. Paris: L'Herne, 1974.

Riffaterre, Michael. *Fictional Truth*. Baltimore: Johns Hopkins P, 1990.

——. "L'Illusion référentielle," *Littérature et réalité*. Ed. Roland Barthes et al. Paris: Seuil, 1982.

——. *Sémiotique de la Poésie*. Paris: Seuil, 1983.

Rimbaud, Arthur. *Œuvres*. Paris: Garnier, 1970.

Said, Edward W. *Beginnings*. New York: Basic Books, 1975.

——. *Orientalism*. New York: Vintage, 1979.

Schliemann, Heinrich. *Troy and its Remains.* Ed. and tr. P. Smith. London: John Murray, 1975.

Segalen, Victor. *Lettres de Chine.* Paris: Plon, 1967.

——. *Œuvres complètes.* Ed. Henri Bouillier. Paris: Laffont, 1995.

Shakespeare, William. *The Dramatic Works of William Shakespeare.* 35 vols. Ed. T. Campbell. Paris: Galignani, 1941 (reprint of 1838 edition).

——. *(Plays).* 20 vols. Tr. Victor Hugo. Paris: Alphonc Lcmcrre, n.d.

Shumaker, Wayne. *English Autobiography.* Berkeley: U of California P, 1954.

Soulié de Morant, Georges. *Essai sur la littérature chinoise.* Paris: Mercure de France, 1912.

——, tr. *Florilège des poèmes Song.* Paris: Plon, 1923.

Tocqueville, Alexis de. *Œuvres complètes,* t. V. Ed. J.-P. Mayer. Paris: Gallimard, 1957.

Valéry, Paul. *Œuvres I, II.* Ed. Jean Hytier. Paris: Gallimard, Pléiade, 1957.

Verne, Jules. *Les Grands navigateurs du XVIIIe siècle.* Paris: Ramsay, 1977.

——. *Michel Strogoff.* Paris: Hachette, 1978.

——. *Les Tribulations d'un Chinois en Chine.* Paris: Hachette, Grandes Œuvres, 1979.

——. *Twenty Thousand Leagues Under the Sea.* Tr. W. Butcher. New York: Oxford UP, 1998.

Villon, François. *Œuvres poétiques.* Ed. A. Mary, D. Poirion. Paris: Flammarion, 1965.

Virgil, *The Aeneid.* Tr. A. Mandelbaum. New York: Bantam, 1981.

Whitman, Walt. *Feuilles d'herbe.* Tr. Léon Bazalgette. Paris: Mercure de France, 1909.

——. *Poèmes et proses.* Tr. André Gide et al. Intro. Valery Larbaud. Paris: Gallimard, 1930.

——. *Complete Poetry and Selected Prose.* Ed. J. Miller, Jr. Boston: Houghton Mifflin, 1959.

Wordsworth, William. *The Poetical Works of William Wordsworth.* Ed. T. Hutchinson. London: Oxford UP, 1956.

Xenophon, *Anabasis.* Tr. W.H.D. Rouse. Ann Arbor: U of Michigan P, 1964.

——. *Cyropaedia.* Ed. J. Tatum. Tr. W. Barker. New York: Garland, 1987.

INDEX

NORTH CAROLINA STUDIES IN THE ROMANCE LANGUAGES AND LITERATURES

I.S.B.N. Prefix 0-8078-

Recent Titles

When ordering please cite the *ISBN Prefix* plus the last four digits for each title.

Send orders to: University of North Carolina Press
                   P.O. Box 2288
                   CB# 6215
                   Chapel Hill, NC 27515-2288
                   U.S.A.